HOTEL MANAGEMENT : HEALTH CARE

HOTEL MANAGEMENT : HEALTH CARE

C.S. Jain

CYBER TECH PUBLICATIONS
4264/3, Ansari Road, Daryaganj, New Delhi-110002 (India)
Ph.: 011-23244078, 011-43559448 Fax: 011-23280028
E-Mail: cyberpublicationsdelhi@yahoo.com
Website: www.cybertechpublications.com

HOTEL MANAGEMENT : HEALTH CARE

C.S. Jain

First Edition 2010

Published by :

G.S. Rawat for **Cyber Tech Publications**
4264/3, Ansari Road, Daryaganj, New Delhi-110002 (India)
Ph.: 011-23244078, 011-43559448 Fax: 011-23280028
E-Mail: cyberpublicationsdelhi@yahoo.com
Website: www.cybertechpublications.com

Printed at: Asian Offset Printers, Delhi-53

Preface

In the simple language we can say that this book describes the industry in relation to social trends and cultural patterns. It will help you develop the leadership skills that are so important in this dynamic industry. Perhaps the most striking contemporary trend affecting the hospitality industry is "globalization." Nations no longer exist in quiet independence but in growing, mutual dependence. As a result, Western countries and cultures have begun to recognize the strength, vitality, and complexity of other nations and cultures. This book has been prepared with a deep appreciation of other traditions and cultures. But it is not an "international" book in the sense that all cultural and historical forms of hospitality are represented. The authors acknowledge that their own cultural heritages and industry experiences are limited.

One historical aspect of hospitality is the obligation to treat strangers with dignity, to feed them and provide them drink, and to protect their safety. As the world becomes increasingly "smaller" and aware of its vast diversity, this "spirit of hospitality" seems especially important. This book invites you to share in this spirit.

—*Author*

Preface

CONTENTS

1

Introduction

A litany of wrongs plague the health care delivery system: medication errors, missed diagnoses of cancer, amputation of the wrong leg, neurologically impaired infants, abused elderly patients, denial of care, kidnapped newborns, violence in the emergency room, malfunctioning medical devices, removal of the wrong organ, sponges left in the surgical field, nosocomial infections. These plagues result in lawsuits, allegations, settlements, trials, verdicts, discipline, premium increases, and lawsuits again!

BASIC QUESTIONS NEED ANSWERS: WHY? HOW? WHERE? WHEN? WHO? WHAT?

Simply put, risk management for health care institutions involves the protection of the assets of the organizations, agencies, and individual providers.

Informed risk managers can do a great deal to achieve that financial well-being by eliminating, mitigating, preventing, and defending against errors. These risk management activities result in cost savings for all types of institutions and organizations. Investigations indicate that almost 1 percent of people admitted to hospitals incur an injury resulting from negligence while in the institution. Accordingly, risk managers must initiate a directed effort to reduce these medically adverse occurrences, because medical malpractice has a severe impact on the institutions as well as on the practitioner.

An effective risk management program for health care institutions ensures a high quality of care and reduces or limits potential liability. Operative risk management activities include risk identification; preparation for emergencies and disasters; proper discharge and appropriate patient transfer; attainment of informed patient consents; optimal medical staff monitoring and peer review; claims investigation and claims management; and specific disease policies such as infection control. Administrative control areas critical to risk management activities include elements such as administration, operations, environmental concerns, patient care, medical ancillary departments, legal and ethical issues, and financing for these activities.

Cost containment is the dominant moving force in the health care industry today and will continue to be so in the future. At present, risk management administrators in hospitals and other health care facilities are faced with rapidly spiraling costs associated with varied liability risks; malpractice suits; federal, state, and local legislation and regulations; financing and insuring risk; risk prevention transfer techniques; and patients' rights. Specific risks include accidental falls, property damage, reduction in cash flow, employee benefit risks, and a lowering of community image. The integration of risk management with quality assessment and utilization review adds to the burgeoning cost overload.

As the ideals and culture of corporate America have seeped into the health care industry, the organizational emphasis has switched to concepts of a managed care delivery system to reduce expenditures. In response to the continuing emphasis on cost containment and the growth of managed care schemes to provide health care for all Americans, health care providers, trustees, and administrators must examine their activities and programs. To expedite this evaluation, strategic health planning experts suggest seeking the answers to three basic questions: 4

Where are we now?

Where do we wish to go?

How will we get there?

Although these questions appear simplistic, their complexity grows as health care managers try to respond. Difficulties arise because many organizations have not really adjusted the status quo since they were established, or even reconsidered their goals and objectives as time has progressed. Noted industrial management consultant Peter Drucker translated the main question of a strategic approach formulation into a straightforward interrogatory: "What is the business of this business?"5 Such organizational soul searching is crucial for the development of a strategic approach to a risk management program. Deliberations could focus upon questions such as:

Do the trustees want to eliminate the obstetrical service or any other service that increases the risk of a malpractice suit?

Should the organization's marketing efforts aim to attract a population that may be less litigious?

To reduce workers' compensation, should care be provided through the company's managed care entity?

Should funds be allocated for in-house risk management staff or should this function be contracted out?

Critics of the business approach to health care declare that this is just another way of saying: "Pay attention to the bottom line in this business." Despite the critics who argue that health care should not be a business, it is obvious that if cash outflow exceeds cash intake, the health care provider cannot stay in business very long. No matter how the situation is phrased, there are strategic planning methods and techniques to master.6 Considering the numerous and ever-growing areas involved in risk management for health care institutions, it is imperative that health care providers have a strategic approach for the program. Ten hospital case studies illuminate the basic steps in a strategic approach to risk management:

1. Identification of the organization's current position, including present mission, long term objectives, strategies, and policies.
2. Analysis of the environment.
3. Organizational audit.

4. Identification of the various alternative strategies based on the relevant data.
5. Selection of the best alternative.
6. Gaining acceptance of the chosen strategy.
7. Preparation of long range and short range plans to carry out the strategy.
8. Implementation of the plan and conducting an ongoing evaluation.

To survive and prosper, "many experts advise risk managers to concentrate on managing uncertainty instead of managing exposures."8 Specifically, risk managers should focus on pooling and contingency planning in risk financing; on risk avoidance and mitigation in risk control; and on scenario analysis9 in risk assessment. Furthermore, risk managers need to (1) engender an organizational milieu in which everyone participates to help control risks, (2) create new tools to measure how one risk affects another, (3) determine how public opinion affects the hospital's risks, and (4) develop long term risk financing partnership agreements with insurers. Basically, risk managers must become strategic thinkers.

Our book offers governing boards, chief executive officers, administrators, and health profession students the opportunity to organize and devise a successful risk management program. Section 1 is an introduction to risk management and covers five areas of generic concern: (1) operation dynamics, (2) regulations, (3) workplace risks, (4) patient communications, and (5) financing. In Section 2, there are three chapters, on strategic approaches to evaluation, ethics, and safety and security. Section 3 deals with specific strategies for seven specific risk areas: (1) malpractice, (2) liability, (3) psychiatry, (4) long term and home health care, (5) high risk hospital departments, (6) managed care, and (7) integrated health care delivery systems.

To emphasize real situations, real case studies are presented in highlighted boxes throughout the book, and practical guidelines for risk managers are provided. Some relevant material is repeated, briefly, in more than one chapter. Other information is not repeated, and the index will guide readers to the desired data.

2

Risk Management Dynamics

Risk management for health care institutions is not a new socially and/or legally ordained program. About four thousand years ago, the Babylonian Code of Hammurabi ordained severe punishment for physicians who caused death or harm through their own malpractice:

> If a physician operates on a man for a severe wound with a bronze lancet and causes a man's death, or opens an abscess in the eye of a man with a bronze lancet and destroys the man's eye, they shall cut off his fingers.

In the 1970s, an upsurge in malpractice suits created a crisis situation for health care providers. Faced with the threat of lawsuits involving huge dollar amounts, the health care institutions and agencies employed risk management personnel and initiated activities designed to prevent adverse patient outcomes (APOs) and potentially compensable events (PCEs).2 In this prevention mode, focusing on the organization's bottom line, a governmental risk manager earned a place on the 1994 Business Insurance Risk Management Honor Roll for effecting programs that attacked losses on several fronts.

RISK MANAGEMENT DEFINED

Risk management for health care entities can be defined as an organized effort to identify, assess, and reduce, where appropriate, risks to patients, visitors, staff, and organizational assets. Another definition is: a program designed to reduce the incidence of preventable accidents and injuries to minimize the financial loss to the institution should an injury or accident occur.

From a managed care viewpoint, the risk management definition can be expanded to encompass a comprehensive rationale:

Risk management is the process of assuring that covered persons (members) receive all of the health care services they need, to which they are entitled under the contract, no more and no less at the most cost-effective level possible by reducing or eliminating untoward incidents (occurrences) that might lead to injury or illness of patients, visitors or employees.

Untoward or adverse outcomes tend to yield a broad spectrum of possible explanations. A research scientist argued that there was no such thing as a medical accident. As a caveat for the doctors, he quoted from Shakespeare's Julius Caesar: "The fault... is not in our stars, but in ourselves." He concluded that more precise medical terminology would help physicians reduce harm. "Accident conveys a sense that bad outcomes are to be explained in terms of fate and bad luck rather than a set of understandable, and possibly changeable, antecedents."

PROGRESSIVE STEPS IN THE RISK MANAGEMENT PROCESS

In straightforward terms, risk management is the protection of assets. Risk management personnel usually accomplish this goal by following four steps in progression or combination: risk identification, risk analysis, risk control/treatment, and risk financing. In slightly different wording, the risk management process can move from (1) identifying exposures to accidental loss which may interfere with an organization's objectives to (2) examining feasible alternative risk management techniques for dealing with these exposures to (3) selecting the best risk management techniques to (4) implementing the chosen risk management techniques to (5) monitoring the results of the chosen techniques to determine effectiveness. Arguing that this risk management process needs refinement to reflect reality,

Burlando opts for the 5i system, a measured application of five descriptors:

Investigate: observe or study by close examination and systematic inquiry.

Inform: present in material form.

Influence: affect or alter by indirect or intangible means.

Interpret: explain or tell the meaning of; present in understandable terms.

Integrate: form or blend into a whole; unite with something else.

Furthermore, Burlando declares that the mission of risk management "is to select, coordinate and efficiently apply interdisciplinary skills to harmful uncertainties which may diminish the future value of public, private or personal resources."

A physician/lawyer operating a risk management firm advises clients to adhere to the "Big A" strategy. "Big A" means to "anticipate" what can go wrong and to be prepared to handle that possibility. Even if a patient specifies no allergy to penicillin, prudent risk managers find it appropriate to be ready if an unanticipated reaction occurs.

Risk Identification

Risk identification involves the collection of information about current and past patient care occurrences and other events that present potential loss to the institution. In alphabetical order, such risks can be identified as antitrust violations, breach of contract, casualty exposure, defamation, embezzlement, environmental damage, fraud and abuse, general liability, hazardous substance exposure, professional malpractice, securities violations, transportation liability, and workers' compensation. It is vital to realize that risk identification is not a one-time static analysis. The continuous identification of possible liability risks, such as unexpected treatment outcomes, patient complaints about care, and adverse events that did, or could, cause harm, must be an ongoing process.

Early warning data can occur in security reports, quality assessment studies, accreditation and/or licensure surveys, and patient complaints. Risk managers should receive a steady stream of information from specific departments, such as when attorneys seek chart information from medical records in preparation for a suit; billing offices, following up on delinquent statements, hear aggravated complaints; volunteers hear complaints because patients don't regard them as employees; and quality assessment activities yield data connected with their screening and review procedures. Furthermore, statistical data from insurers can identify the high risk individuals and services involved in the payment of claims.

Risk Analysis

Risk analysis entails the evaluation of past experience and current exposure to eliminate or limit substantially the impact of risk on cash flow, community image, and employee and medical staff morale. Seriousness of the risk must be considered in terms of the probable severity to the individual and to the organization, the number of people possibly harmed, and the likelihood and/or frequency of occurrence. Closed claims data are most helpful in gaining an insight into the evaluation of current risks. A priority of high risk activities for the risk manager logically develops from risk analysis information.

Risk Control/Treatment

Risk control and/or treatment is the organization's response to significant risk areas as well as its rejoinder to limit the liability associated with incidents that have occurred. This is the most common function associated with risk management programs. Loss control activities within an institution should not be viewed as a single formal program, because of the varied interrelated and overlapping elements. Often, loss control activity is equated with safety management, since the basic objectives are similar. At times, the quality assessment functions also cloud the specifics of loss control. It is not unusual for a loss/risk control program to be a collaborative effort involving risk management, quality assessment, and safety management. Ideally, a risk control/loss management program should categorize the potential liability problems into four areas: bodily injury, liability losses, property loss, and consequential losses. Exhibit 1-1 illustrates some elements of risk exposure. Note that the health care organization's governing board and the chief executive officer (CEO) are responsible for the overall risk control system. In the second circle surrounding the board and the CEO are the administrative personnel who implement the programs. Specific elements in the third and fourth circles illustrate bodily injury, liability losses, property loss, and consequential losses.

There are a variety of methods and a combination of techniques for controlling the risks: risk acceptance, exposure avoidance, loss prevention, loss reduction, exposure segregation, and contractual transfer.

Risk Acceptance

Essentially, risk acceptance means that the facility decides not to purchase insurance against specific adverse events because the risk cannot be avoided, reduced, or transferred. In addition, the probability of loss is not great and the potential fiscal consequences are within the institution's capabilities to resolve.

Exposure Avoidance

After he investigated a hospital's major liability losses, a consultant advised: "Eliminate the emergency room!" In theory, exposure avoidance aims to rid the institution of the service, personnel, or equipment that may cause the loss, or never to be involved in providing the service or program at all.

Loss Prevention

Using early detection and investigation, risk managers examine the medical records, incident reports, patient complaints, and patient billing to pinpoint loss prevention areas. Some losses in specific services can be prevented by the involvement of medical and ancillary staff in educational programs and preventive maintenance. Some even advise keeping the patient fully informed of all mishaps, thereby relying on the satisfied patient not to sue the institution.

Loss Reduction

Although there may be loss prevention activities, loss reduction usually involves the management of claims and ensures that all records are preserved and that all personnel are prepared in the event of a loss. Settlements and releases conclude loss reduction efforts. Without abandoning high risk services, loss reduction or minimization aims to control adverse events by focusing on activities such as staff education, revisions of policy, and procedures.

Exposure Segregation

Administrators can decide to separate out or to duplicate the specific offending services, personnel, or activities identified as exposure risks to the institution. Risk managers can suggest intensive control actions; for example, to reduce medication errors in a hospital, all pharmaceuticals can be disbursed from a central location. If the problem appears to be the distance between medication source and delivery, satellite pharmacies can be established on selected floors.

Contractual Transfer

A facility can transfer or shift the risk to the organization that provides the service through insurance or contract. This allows the institution to provide a high risk service while avoiding liability loss. If a contracted company operates the emergency room of a hospital, the facility avoids risk by ensuring that the contract includes the assumption of all risk by the contractor. Although private insurance premiums can handle contractual liability coverage, the facility may still be responsible for selecting a qualified contractor.

Risk Financing

Appropriate indemnification of risk requires a comprehensive prospective and retrospective organizational analysis of the direct expenditures associated with quantifying and funding losses and risk management activities. Financing choices are self-insurance, commercial insurance coverage, insurance premiums, and funding for any related risk management activities and liability payouts. While risk financing may be the responsibility of the institution's or agency's financial office, risk managers can make a valuable contribution to the deliberations by communicating effectively with the finance department, using terminology that finance personnel can understand.

Risk Management Activities

An examination of the eight minimal components of a risk management program, as defined by the American Society of Healthcare Risk Management (ASHRM), engenders a fuller understanding of a risk management program:

1. There must be a designated, trained, and experienced risk manager who must obtain at least eight hours of continuing risk management education annually.
2. Risk managers must have access to all necessary credentialing, management, and medical data.
3. Institutions must commit the necessary resources to risk management through a written policy statement that is adopted by the governing body, medical staff, and administration.
4. Facilities must have a system in place for the identification, review, and analysis of unanticipated adverse outcomes.
5. Organizations must have the means to centralize risk management data and to share and integrate data collection and analysis with other clinical and administrative departments.
6. Periodically, at least annually, risk managers must provide the organization's governing body a report that reviews and evaluates risk management program activity.
7. Risk managers must ensure that medical staff and new employee educational programs on minimizing patients' risks and addressing high-risk clinical areas are provided.

8. Risk managers must forward information on individual practitioners, such as malpractice claim history, knowledge of adverse outcomes and incident reporting data, to the committees that evaluate the competency of medical staff.

Strictly from a business-oriented approach, risk management aims to accomplish three major functions:

- Reducing the organization's risk of a malpractice suit by maintaining or improving the quality of care.
- Reducing the probability of a claim being filed after a potentially compensable event (PCE) has occurred.
- Preserving the institution's assets once a claim has been filed.

Without doubt, risk management includes quality assessment and related activities, such as medical staff credentialing, occurrence screening, incident reporting, and peer review. In addition, risk management seeks to promote effective communication and a positive attitude between patients and staff and to make patients less likely to sue for malpractice.

Physicians agree on three ideal attributes for a professional risk manager: the ability to present facts rather than feelings, the ability to be concise in writing or stating the situation; and the wherewithal to understand the facts and to respond to critical questions. In contrast, nurses identify three common qualities of a good risk manager: a demonstrated willingness to listen, an understanding of the other person's responsibilities and problems, and a team approach to problem solving that involves asking input from others in forming solutions. These responses lead to the conclusion that a risk manager's basic skills must include the art of persuasion, the expertise to be a keen listener, and knowledge about team building.

Importantly, risk managers must realize that the board of directors or governing body is part of the team, even though that directorate is not the immediate supervisor. Communicating effectively with the board requires the use of these basic risk management skills. Risk events, PCEs, and APOs are quite diverse, as revealed in a survey of more than two thousand corporate executives, who identified the fifteen most important risk management areas.

Legislative and regulatory mandates also guide risk management activities to focus on preventive maintenance of equipment and devices, on patient safety measures, and on enhancing the safety of employees and visitors. Examples of such measures include ensuring that equipment is clean, properly calibrated and in good repair, that a nurse call system is functional, and that security personnel patrol well-lighted parking lots and hallways.

CLASSIFICATION OF RISK LIABILITIES

Risk events include a multitude of sins: untoward incidents occurring to patients (clients), employees, or visitors; use of inadequate equipment or procedures to perform a task; use of improperly trained or qualified individuals to perform a task; improper manufacture of a product; and contamination and/or pollution of the environment. Failure to perform a service may prevent the achievement of a desired outcome or lead to an undesired outcome, may cause harm or injury, and may result from an error of omission or commission. Some specific examples of risk events, classified by type, are:

- Property risks: structural damage; vehicular accidents; technological obsolescence; theft; sabotage; production breakdown; and consequential losses.
- Casualty/liability risks: professional negligence (PCEs and APOs); workers' compensation; directors and officers liability; environmental liability; and product liability.
- Employee benefit risks: cost of benefit plans; disability claims; and Employee Retirement and Income Security Act (ERISA) violations.
- Risks can be identified through the use of records and files, flowcharts, personal inspections, expert consultations, surveys, questionnaires, and financial statements. Risk analysis considers the frequency and severity of the loss as related

to profit, stable earnings, growth, continuous operation, legal requirements, and humanitarian concerns. A comparative assessment combines cost-benefit analyses with frequency of risk events and with populations affected to yield a weighted risk analysis. Interestingly, people may accept new technology with perceived injury risks or reject the technology because of a minimal risk of injury. Using a mortality standard, researchers identified comparative risk data.

From an expenditure viewpoint, the median cost of a life saved by childhood immunizations or prenatal care is negligibleless than zero. Other interventions can be calculated in terms of the cost of a life saved: flu shots ($600); heart disease ($14,000); breast cancer screening ($17,000); kidney dialysis ($46,000); and heart transplant ($104,000). Medical care generally saves lives at less cost than workplace safety or environmental measures do.18 Substantial resources may be devoted to problems that are relatively minor. Since the viability of the institution is at stake, efforts must be made to evaluate and weigh the risk to preserve assets and to restrict the loss.

Comparative Risk of Death per Million People per Year 17

Twenty-one cigarettes in a lifetime	10
Airline crash in ten trips	10
Appendectomy operation	200
Auto accident	210
At least one pack of cigarettes per day	3,000
All risks, age 4554	5,840

Risk Red Flags

One or more "red flags" in connection with a patient's care should alert health care providers to take actions to remedy the situation. Appropriate care and treatment should be provided, and patient records should reflect that care. In addition, the risk management department should be notified. Some specific red flags are:

- Treatment conditions: poor treatment results; repetition of the problem; lack of follow-up care; and equipment malfunction.
- Patient relations: dissatisfied patient; antagonistic patient or family members; complaining relatives; patient discharged against medical advice; intimidated patient; poor physician/patient relationship; and poor staff/patient relationship.
- Practice management: poorly maintained medical records; lack of critical policies and procedures; and excessive volume of patients.

Conduct of staff: acting outside the scope of training; lack of qualified supervision; performance of a procedure for the first time without supervision; outspoken or rude behavior; personality conflict; and poor physician/staff relationship.

Risk Management Tools

Prompt identification of injuries and accidents to patients, visitors, and staff members has been a primary concern of risk management programs since they were first used in hospitals. In this manner, institutions address potential problems and correct their causes before they can occur again. In addition, administrators can take immediate action to avoid or lessen the cost of a lawsuit. Three systems are used to accomplish prompt identification: incident reporting, occurrence reporting, and occurrence screening.

Incident Reporting

Incident reporting systems were developed in the late 1940s and early 1950s to identify events that were not consistent with the routine operation of the hospital or the routine care of particular patients or visitors, such as malfunctioning equipment or medication errors.

Incident reporting systems have incorporated computer technology. Calgary General Hospital (Alberta, Canada) devised a computer program that identifies five major incident categories: falls, medication errors, treatment/procedure errors, assaults, and computer errors. Another computer system focuses on the early identification of patterns and trends in the "how" and "why" of untoward events. Coded vulnerability indicators include the following specific options: system failure (22 choices); diagnostic tests (12 choices); consultation (28 choices); documentation (37 choices); patient rapport (7 choices); clinical conduct (50 choices); human factors (14 choices); and a miscellaneous narrative section. Analysis of the adverse events yields an awareness and a basis for improved clinical practice and professional risk avoidance.

Reporting systems rely on facility personnel to recognize and report an incident to a risk manager, a quality assurance coordinator, or a member of the management team. Reports tend to focus on treatment procedures, medication, intravenous and blood errors, infections, birth injuries, falls, burns, and equipment problems that could result in claims against the organization. By themselves, the reports do not produce a complete picture of the number of incidents that occur in a facility. According to some estimates, incident reports identify about 5 to 30 percent of adverse patient occurrences at a hospital. Staff may not report incidents for several reasons: lack of understanding of what a reportable incident is, fear of punitive action, concern that incident reporting exposes them to personal liability, reluctance to report incidents involving physicians, lack of time for paperwork, and lack of knowledge about the results that an effective incident reporting system can achieve.

Only the person who witnessed the incident, or first discovered it, should file and sign an incident report. Anybody else with firsthand knowledge should file a separate report. Critically, anybody filling out an incident report should keep in mind that the written report will be available to lawyers, and any admissions or accusations could be damaging to the reporting individual as well as to the employer. There are several do's and don'ts regarding the filing of an incident report:

- Do record the details in objective terms, describing exactly what was seen and heard and nothing else: Jones writes that she found Mrs. Smith on the floor beside the bed, not that she fell.

- Do describe what actions were taken at the scene: helping patient back into bed; assessment findings; any instructions to patient.
- Do document the time of the incident, the name of the doctor notified, the time notified, and have the supervisor review the report.
- Don't include names and addresses of witnesses, even if the form requests such information. Such data make it easier for attorneys to sue the institution. Check with the supervisor on supplying this information.
- Don't file the incident report with the patient's chart. Send the incident report to the person designated by the organization to collect and review such matters.
- Don't admit liability or blame or identify others as responsible. Obviously, this incrimination could be harmful to the agency if a lawsuit ensues.

Occurrence Reporting

Some states and insurers require or encourage institutions to develop lists of specific adverse patient occurrences (APOs) that must be reported by staff, physicians, or boththat is, occurrence reporting. APOs could include maternal or infant death, a surgical patient's unplanned return to the unit, or an allergic reaction to medication. Although the lists vary at the discretion of the organization, the insurers, or the states, specifying the reportable events increases the APO identification process by 40 to 60 percent. Because the system depends on individuals for reporting, however, many incidents still may not be written up. To promote better reporting, some states grant immunity from legal action to persons who provide or evaluate risk management information. There are also efforts to protect against the possibility that documents generated by the risk management program will become public information.

Occurrence Screening

Occurrence screening systems identify deviations from normal procedures or expected treatment outcomes and may be used in both risk management and quality assessment. An occurrence screening system uses criteria to identify APOs but does not rely on staff members to report the adverse events. Typical examples of APOs that can be identified using such a system include transfer from a general care unit to a special care unit, nosocomial infection, or unplanned return to an operating room.

Medical record analysts or trained data screeners systematically review patient records using the prespecified criteria to discover APOs. Peer reviewers then determine if a deviation from acceptable standards of care occurred. This screening can be conducted during or after the patient care or at both times. An estimated 80 to 85 percent of APOs can be identified by occurrence screeninga much higher percentage than obtained through incident reporting systems. Furthermore, a risk management program that combines occurrence screening with other data sources, such as incident reporting, infection surveillance, antibiotics use review, and medical staff peer review, can identify 90 to 95 percent of APOsa greater proportion than any individual method can identify.

RISK AND QUALITY OF CARE

Any risk management process may sound harsh and lead to the conclusion that the health care industry is adopting a businesslike, bottom-line approach without consideration for the humane aspects of providing care to people in need. This perception is not accurate, although even charitable and well-meaning organizations must maintain financial viability to continue their worthwhile endeavors.

Significantly, governmental and voluntary non-profit health care agencies must compete with proprietary health care providers in an open marketplace. That fact is a major stimulus in moving all health care providers to reduce their losses and to attract patients to the services being offered. For this reason, risk management by health care institutions becomes an integral tool of sound management. Effective risk management strategy "should be judged not just in terms of whether it saves the provider money, although that certainly is a legitimate and important goal, but also should be judged against the fundamental objective of contributing to the quality of services." 22 It is possible, however, that some patients covered by different insurance programs receive differential care. A study of problems in the quality of care among Medicare and Medicaid patients came to a startling and disturbing conclusion:

Of great concern is the fact that premature death directly resulted from confirmed quality problems in 53 (7.4%) of 706 Medicare and in 42 (27.2%) of 154 Medicaid patients. These deaths were avoidable and were directly due to departures from accepted standards of medical care. Also of concern is the fact that readmission occurred in 60 Medicare and 18 Medicaid patients, resulting from confirmed quality of care problems during the previous admission.

These connections are affirmed by the accreditation standards of the Joint Commission on Accreditation of Healthcare Organizations (JCAHO). Effective January 1, 1989, every applicable institution that seeks JCAHO accreditation must show substantial compliance with several standards that apply only to the quality of care and patient safety aspects of risk management:

- A hospital's governing body must provide resources and support systems for the quality assurance and risk management functions related to patient care and safety.
- A hospital's chief executive officer, through the management and administrative staff, must assure appropriate medical staff involvement in and support for the identification of areas of potential risk in patient care and safety the development of criteria for identifying cases with potential risk re patient care and safety and the evaluation of these cases.
- The correction of problems in patient care and safety identified by risk management activities.

- The design of programs to reduce risk in patient care and safety.
- A hospital's management must establish and maintain operational linkages between risk management functions related to patient care and safety, and quality assurance functions.
- A hospital's management must ensure that existing information relative to the quality of patient care is readily accessible to both the quality assurance and the risk management functions.

RISK MANAGEMENT/QUALITY ASSURANCE FUNCTIONS AND ACTIVITIES

In 1980 the American Hospital Association (AHA) formed the Interdisciplinary Task Force on Quality Assurance and Risk Management to define the relationship of hospital risk management (RM) to quality assurance (QA). There is a causal connection between risk management, the quality of care, and quality assurance programs. A quality-risk continuum exists, and quality assurance and risk management programs must work together to achieve their own goals. Four dicta emerge from the quality-risk spectrum:

- Quality control is the process of assuring that standards are met. The objective is 100% met, or zero defects.
- Risk control assures that losses due to property, casualty, or employee benefit risks are prevented, reduced in frequency and/or severity, or transferred.
- Quality control is doing what you want to do: meeting standards.
- Risk control is not doing what you don't want to do: preventing errors.

RM and QA Comparisons

The AHA task force established in 1980 concluded that risk management and quality assurance are two activities whose functions sometimes overlap. When that overlap occurs, their purposes and methods are almost indistinguishable. During their deliberations, the task force identified the functions of RM and QA, as well as the major differences between them. An examination of the comparison between RM and QA leads to the relevant conclusion that a close working arrangement between the two activities is unavoidable. The AHA task force concluded that integrating RM and QA, where feasible, could achieve the following results:

- Maximization of the use of limited resources.
- Elimination of duplication because data sources for both activities are the same.
- Creation of a means for developing new solutions to problems.
- Facilitation of the development of training programs.
- Improvement of the budget process by identifying and consolidating budget requirements for both activities.

A requirement of the JCAHO mandates that hospitals seeking approval have programs that link risk management with quality assurance. 24 The question is whether this linking of quality assurance and risk management increases the proclivity of physicians to order an excessive number of diagnostic tests and/or procedures. A review by the U.S. Congress Office of Technology Assessment (OTA) concluded that the QA-RM link "may promote quality-enhancing rather than wasteful defensive medicine."

ADMINISTRATION OF RISK MANAGEMENT PROGRAMS

Goals and Prime Objectives

A risk management system aims to identify, evaluate, and reduce risks to patients, visitors, employees, and professional staff involved in the provision of health care services. There should be a written description of the program, periodic revisions and review, and amendments when changes are made. All federal, state, and local legislation and regulations should be complied with and documented. Incidents such as fires, equipment malfunction, poisoning, strikes, disasters, and termination of vital services should be reported to the proper authorities. With the help of a Risk Management Committee responsible to the Board of Directors, Mt. Sinai Hospital (Toronto, Canada) identified three objectives for its risk management program:

1. To reduce the frequency of preventable adverse occurrences that lead to liability claims.
2. To reduce the probability of a claim's being filed after an adverse event has occurred.
3. To help control the costs of claims that do emerge.

Initiatives integrated into this risk management program included acting on the risks identified in the recommendations of a coroner's jury, in departmental reports, in incident analysis, in occurrence reporting, and in a claims summary database.

Responsibilities of a Risk Management Committee and/ or Coordinator

Because a risk manager's activities involve the entire institution and all its programs and services, the responsibilities can evolve into a long, overwhelming list of tasks. 28 Many tasks overlap with other units and are cooperative in nature. Grouping the responsibilities delineates the descriptive scope of a risk manager's job.

- Purpose, Accountability, and Authority Functions:
- Coordinate and carry out risk management activities in line with the program objectives.
- Secure written statements affirming the support of the governing body, the administration, and the medical staff for the risk management program.
- Describe the organizational reporting lines and the relationships between the risk manager and the rest of the institution.
- Prepare a written statement detailing the involvement of every department and service and their responsibilities in risk management activities.

- Provide for the flow of information among quality assurance, credentialing, peer review, and any risk management committee.
- Monitor all incidents related to patient care.
- Define the responsibility to recommend and implement corrective actions.
- Prepare a statement assuring the confidentiality of all data collected for the risk management program.

Specific Functions:

- Review the potentially compensable events (PCEs).
- Investigate the PCEs.
- Analyze and pinpoint trends in PCEs.
- Report appropriate PCEs to the insurance carrier.
- Assist in the resolution of conflicts among patients, physicians, and institution to avoid claims.
- Settle claims, obtaining liability releases, at the authority level approved by management. Adjust or write off bills as necessary within authority approved by management.
- Maintain files of all lawsuits.
- Assure protection of records and other evidence.
- Prepare the necessary material and people for a legal defense under the guidance of the insurance company and defense counsel.
- Represent the institution in legal proceedings within defined parameters.
- Assist and monitor the activities and charges of defense counsel.
- Provide risk management support/input to appropriate medical staff and institutional committees.
- Act as the institution's resource for risk management topics.
- Prepare reports to the board, the health care system, management, and other entities as directed.

- Comply with applicable regulatory codes and professional standards.
- Provide risk management education for institutional personnel, medical staff, and residents.
- Maintain professional competence through participation in seminars, conferences, and so on, and through membership in appropriate professional societies.

QUALITY ASSURANCE

- Protects the institution's financial assets.
- Protects human and intangible resources.
- Prevents injury to patients, visitors, and property.
- Reduces loss by focusing on individual loss or on single accidents.
- Prevents incidents by improving the quality of care through continuing and ongoing monitoring of agency activities.
- Reviews each incident and the pattern of incidents through the application of the risk management process: risk identification; risk analysis; risk control; and risk financing.
- Reflects the institution's caring philosophy.
- Improves the performance of all professionals and protects patients.
- Focuses on the quality of care delivered by the organization.
- Sets the quality of care rendered according to standards and measurable criteria.
- Prevents future losses or patient injuries by continuous monitoring of problem resolution areas.
- Searches for patterns of nonconformance with goals and standards using the following quality assurance processes: problem identification; problem assessment; corrective action; follow-up; and report of findings.

Differences

- Concerned with acceptable levels of care from a legal standpoint.
- Directed toward all persons, events, and environs in the health care setting.
- Focused on legal, insurance, and risk financing activities.
- Concerned with optimal level of care.
- Directed toward patient care.
- Focused on improving care.
- Develop the annual risk management budget.
- Determine general, short-term, and long-term objectives.
- Evaluate the program regularly and update it as necessary.

Functional Relationships:

- Biomedical engineering re new products, equipment involved in PCE, record keeping, and risk management alerts.
- Quality assurance re PCE, professional staff, and incidents.
- Safety/fire/disaster committees.
- Employee health services.

RISK MANAGEMENT COMMITTEE

Programs should include a risk management committee to assist in prioritization of risk reduction activities and to act as a liaison to the various professional staffs in the hospital. A typical risk management committee has a physician chairman, as well as representation from the major medical and surgical services, the nursing department, the technical staff (biomedical engineering, radiology, respiratory services, clinical laboratory), the quality assessment department, and the risk manager. One or more members of the governing body and hospital counsel may be members.

A risk management committee reviews key risk exposure information: all claims; all state-reported incidents; internal incidents of concern because of either the extent of injury or the potential for injury; emerging trends in delivery of care that present new avenues of exposure; and any other issues or events that may occur, or be averted, that may have the actuality or potential of heavy loss of financial resources or good reputation. A mix of clinical and technical personnel on the committee provides for multifaceted examination of loss potential and risk exposure of any situation. This committee reports to the medical staff, governing body, and administration and frequently serves as the primary source of ongoing education on loss prevention in a facility.

The goals of the risk managers and the administration in working within this committee are to facilitate information flow among various departments and services and to provide a central focus for collaborative loss control and risk reduction actions.

Responsibility of the Governing Body

A commitment, including accountability, to an institutionwide risk management program must be adopted in a written governing board policy. Governing body bylaws should include mechanisms for the approval of medical staff bylaws, including the appointment and reappointment of physicians. A mechanism must be established for reporting risk management activities to the board. If possible, a governing body member should be appointed to any risk management advisory group or committee.

Under the guidance of the governing board, one risk manager suggested that "chaos theory" offers an opportunity to enhance risk management. Chaos theory is "based on the simple principle that order can be found in disorder." This theory concentrates on events that do not adhere to established principles, are unpredictable, do not result in a rational aftermath, and appear to disregard a lucid explanation. At a minimum, chaos theory provides a few buzzwords for risk managers. At most, chaos theory presents a unique prototype that has direct application to the risk management process. Five chaos theory concepts forge links to risk management practices:

1. Predictable patterns exist in apparent random events, since the nature of risk is universal; only the scale changes. Risk managers need to change their perspectives to study the

larger universe, need to examine parallel systems, and need to avoid the isolation of increasing specialization.

2. There is a sensitive dependence on initial conditions. Small initial events need to be studied and related.to larger outcomes. Could the minuscule wind from a butterfly's wings cause severe weather changes elsewhere in the world?
3. Risk managers usually deal with apparently discrete or chance events. Over time, specific patterns begin to materialize as the random repetitive behavior produces information. Risk managers need to know where to look for this information and extract the data to apply in their activities.
4. Risk managers must comprehend the intricate interconnected network of forces and external influences that determine the variety of eventual outcomes. Predictably, these forces include the institutional values, goals, and rules, such as a smoke-free workplace, a policy of hiring the handicapped, or a mandate to recycle waste products.
5. To move from the conspicuous and make connections to the improbable, risk managers must adopt new ways of looking for risks using a combination of intelligence and perspicacity.

SPECIFIC RISK MANAGEMENT FUNCTIONS

Incident Identification, Reporting, and Tracking

An identification and reporting process must exist to identify any circumstance or occurrence that may be injurious to a patient or that may result in an adverse outcome to a patient. Mortality, morbidity, infections, complications, errors in diagnosis, transfusions, results of treatments, and unimproved cases other than those related to the natural course of disease or illness should be reviewed.

Each institution must define and list what constitutes a reportable incident and transmit that information to all employees and all regulatory bodies. A management system should include these elements:

- A time frame within which incidents must be reported.
- Designation of the individual to receive incident reports.
- Requirement that any employee or medical staff appointee who is aware of an incident must report it to the appropriate person.
- The sharing of information, at a minimum, between quality assurance and risk management.

Utilizing general purpose computer software, a multihospital group developed an automated quality assessment incident tracking system. 30 This computer program provided an efficient and effective mechanism to control and organize multiple staff assignments, to track tasks through due dates and participants, and to manage multiple objectives over the resolution cycle associated with hospital incident reporting. An individualized record of the incident's progress helped to identify useful and dysfunctional patterns in the resolution of the incident. Importantly, the system used existing computer hardware and software (WordPerfect and Lotus Agenda) while avoiding expensive resources and staff increases.

A successful program depends on the risk management staff's skill in obtaining relevant information. In any risk management program, the keystone to information gathering is the incident report. Originally designed by the insurance industry, the incident report is a tool that is the mainstay for risk assessment in all risk management programs in all industries.

Incident report forms are usually custom designed for a health care facility by the risk management department, taking into consideration the type of information and the amount of detail for any event that needs to be collected for adequate computer tracking. To foster use, most risk managers prefer to sacrifice detail in favor of quick notification of an incident. Incident report forms should be devised so that they are unlike any other forms in use in the facility, and they should be easy to complete. User-friendly forms have frequently occurring incidents listed in alphabetical order, with a checkoff box, allowing space for a brief description of any detail the reporter thinks may be relevant to the situation. Some facilities include a space for physician's comment if the event required medical intervention. On prompt notification of a serious event or situation, risk management staff can conduct their own investigation immediately and institute any needed loss control measures simultaneously.

Routing of the incident report must be clearly defined. In some facilities the incident report is sent immediately to the risk management office. In most hospitals, if a report is completed by nursing staff, it is routed through nursing administration before being transmitted to the risk manager. An industry standard for transmitting the incident report is no later than twenty-four hours, with telephone notification to the risk manager as soon as possible after any serious injury or other significant event. A combination of user-friendly forms, staff education, and feedback through risk management trend reports will encourage information flow that meets or exceeds the standard of 4.5 incident reports per licensed bed per year.

Incident reports can be categorized by type of event and severity of situation for computer tracking. A severity index or scale might be based on the type of injury and/or the type of breach of procedure. On a scale of 0, 1, 2, or 3, the 0 represents "no injury" and 3 may be an injury requiring significant "therapeutic intervention," or significant "breach of procedure," such as giving medication to the wrong patient. This information can easily be developed into a graphic report to accompany the risk manager's analysis and recommendations of loss exposures and risk activities as reported in monthly, quarterly, and annual reports to the safety committee, the quality assessment committee, and the CEO and finance officer.

State Mandated Incident Reporting

Some states have recognized the utility of risk management programs for the identification of major areas of patient vulnerability within the health care system and mandate the reporting of "incidents" to a state regulatory agency, but details vary considerably from state to state. New York State mandates reporting of hospital staff strikes; disasters or emergency situations affecting hospital operations; termination of any vital services in the hospital, such as telephone, laundry services, and pest control; and poisoning occurring within a hospital.

When the peer review process finds that the standard of care was not met and a patient death or impairment of bodily function unrelated to the normal disease process occurred, the incident must also be reported to the state Health Department. In addition, events requiring police or other legal notification are reportable. In contrast, Massachusetts mandates quarterly and annual reporting of adverse patient events to the Board of Registration in Medicine. Events that are reportable in Massachusetts are defined as incidents of patient harm or death as an outcome of medical intervention. Meeting the standard of care is implied but not explicit in the regulations, leaving facilities to make their own interpretations as to whether or not an incident is reportable. Both states reserve the right to conduct an on-site review of any incident, including examination of the credentials of any personnel involved in an event.

At least ten states (Arkansas, Colorado, Florida, Kansas, Maryland, Massachusetts, New York, North Carolina, Rhode Island, and Washington) have legislative mandates for risk management programs. These state regulations relate to the administration of a risk management program, investigation and analysis of identified risks, education programs, patient grievance procedures, and confidentiality of risk management data. Obviously, it is incumbent on risk managers to be aware of specific legislation in their own states. Risk managers and quality assessment professionals can use statewide statistical data to compare the type and severity of events by region and/or type of health care facility to "improve" modalities of care.

Incident Review and Evaluation

- There must be an incident review and evaluation process that provides for:
- Investigation of all incidents, even if no injury resulted.

- Identification of trends among incidents.
- Referral of incidents and trend summaries to be evaluated to determine if further action is necessary.
- Referral of incidents requiring further action to the appropriate institutional individuals, departments, services, and committees.

Actions to Prevent Recurrence of Incidents

- Any actions taken by quality assessment, peer review, or medical staff committees regarding referred identified problems must be documented in a written record. These actions can be classified by the acronym, PACED: preventive, administrative, corrective, educational, and documentary.
- Preventive activities could include a patient relations program; an employee newsletter; a formal safety and security program; a community input effort; and ongoing planning, coordination, and review functions.
- Administrative actions relate to an active process, involvement of department heads, and a formal philosophy regarding administration.
- Corrective activities focus on the encouragement of problem identification, the monitoring of problem situations, the existence of internal audit functions, and the expeditious resolution of problems.
- Educational programs concentrate on creating an interdepartmental educational services unit, upgrading medical and technical skills, having a patient education program, and maintaining records of educational activities.
- Documentary activities include attention to personnel files, financial records, medical charts, regulatory requirements, and written policies and procedures.

Examples identify a host of work area concerns that could be involved in risk management actions. Examples include:

- Hazards at work

- Fire safety
- Disaster plans
- Electrical safety
- Central services safety
- Employee/patient safety
- Nursing safety
- Malpractice/legal liability
- Medical staff
- Anesthesia personnel
- Surgery personnel
- Surgical suite hazards
- Surgery and anesthesia
- Nursing treatment
- Dietary safety
- Housekeeping safety
- Pathology safety
- Respiratory safety
- Radiology/laser safety
- Nursing/pharmacy errors
- Nursing and law
- Internal Documentation

Institutions must maintain complete files of all risk management documentation along with malpractice liability coverage documentation, individual malpractice case files involving the institution, and records of all expenses involved in safety programs to reduce or eliminate patient injuries. Documentation should be contained in the recorded minutes of appropriate bodies, as well as in reviews of credentials and personnel files of sta i.

Credentialing and Privileging

Professional staff credentialing aims to ensure that institutions **are staffed** only by qualified individuals and that their **performance** is maintained at an acceptable level. Credentialing activities consist of a complete review of the licenses, education, and training of all applicants seeking appointment or employment. In addition, physicians must regularly have their privileges updated. This process of recredentialing involves an evaluation by the institution of the physician's clinical experience, competence, ability, judgment, and demonstrated performance in specified functions, such as open heart surgery, before any reappointment. Specifically, a profile of each physician and dentist must be compiled from at least the following data sources:

- Morbidity and mortality review
- Blood utilization review
- Safety committee review
- Peer review organization data
- Medical care evaluations
- Incident report review
- Liability claims data
- Continuing education programs and training
- Utilization review
- Infection control review
- Surgical case review
- Tissue review
- Medical record review
- Complaints
- Prescription review
- Medical case review

In addition, hospitals are mandated to make inquiries to the National Practitioner Data Bank under the Health Care Quality Improvement Act of 1986 concerning each physician, dentist, and others. Inquiry of the Federation of State Medical Boards, individual state medical boards and societies, and the insured's malpractice insurance carrier provide additional information on adverse professional actions, discipline, and sanctions. This legislation also mandates reports to the National Practitioner Data Bank of disciplinary actions or dismissals of medical staff from hospitals and institutions based on peer review activities and adverse situations.

In terms of risk management, credentialing and privileging is critical because it is the primary mechanism available to hospitals, agencies, managed care organizations, and other institutions to help ensure that only competent personnel are employed and that they perform only those clinical duties and procedures for which they are deemed clinically competent. This evaluation process, in turn, reduces the likelihood of the occurrence of any negligent acts that could result in a claim against the organization. A facility or agency with a nonexistent or ineffective credentialing or privileging process could find itself in a nondefensible position if a malpractice claim were filed, since the absence of such a process might indicate that the institution was negligent in ensuring that it employed only competent health care providers.

Patient Complaint Program

A copy of the patients' "Bill of Rights" should be given to each patient on admission and be available in the patient's own language. These rights should be posted in conspicuous areas throughout the institution or agency. There must be a formal written program for addressing patient complaints, as well as documentation of any action taken to resolve grievances. All complaints must be investigated promptly and thoroughly. Patients must be provided with the name and phone number of the representative designated to respond to such complaints. Representatives must treat complaining patients with dignity, courtesy, and due regard for their privacy while providing information about the following:

- Whom the patient may contact regarding the complaint.
- Whom the patient may contact if dissatisfied with the resolution.
- Procedures for investigating the complaint.

- When the patient can expect a verbal or written response or resolution to the complaint.
- Tracking patients' complaints and identifying trends in those complaints should be routine and reported to the risk management and other committees as necessary.

Risk Management Education

Risk management education should be included in orientation and annual in-service training programs for all institutional employees and professional staff in the following areas:

- Organization and goals of the risk management program.
- Patients' "Bill of Rights."
- Patient relations and complaint program.
- Incident-reporting program.
- Reporting responsibilities for alleged professional misconduct.
- Safety program and department-specific safety practices.

On the basis of the theory that "happy patients do not sue," a California insurance company initiated a mandatory loss prevention seminar for physicians in June 1984. By 1993, almost ten thousand physicians had attended the 472 seminars and received three hours of continuing medical education credits. Core educational units fall into four categories. Opening with the perceived reasons for the malpractice problem, the seminar covers the public patient, plaintiff attorneys, laws, the standard of care, and the role of physicians in iatrogenic injuries and defensive medicine. Second, the seminar focuses on loss prevention strategies, including rapport between physician and patient, communications, satisfaction, informed consent, office staff strategies, relationships between physician and hospital, and medical record documentation. Third, the seminar highlights litigation awareness, emphasizing the do's and don'ts if physicians are sued. Finally, arbitration details the alternate dispute resolution forum, the binding legal resolution, and the advantages and disadvantages of each method. In theory, these seminars may prevent claims, conserve the institution's financial resources, prevent patient injury, and improve the quality of patient care delivered. About 95 percent of the participating physicians stated that they would change their behavior based on the information presented at the seminar.

INSURANCE COMPANIES AND RISK MANAGEMENT

Insurance companies offer their insured institutions a variety of risk management services, including consultation, educational programs, publications, closed-claim studies, and computer software packages. Consultations between insurance company representatives and institutional risk management personnel aim to help the organization minimize the risk of malpractice claims. Services may include claims auditing, chart review, policy review, and evaluation of specific clinical areas. Individual insurance company personnel may spend time in loss prevention and loss control activities. In this role, these individuals keep up to date with changes in laws and standards of practice having implications for facility liability, including lessons learned from cases involving actual losses and case law decisions. Sometimes, the problem is a misunderstanding of the insurance policy.

Educational services seek to help organizations minimize the frequency and severity of malpractice claims. Programs can be provided in several formats, including national, regional, local, and institutional seminars and individualized focused training workshops. Seminars allow representatives of all the insured organizations to meet and discuss clinical, administrative, and legal risk management issues. Focused workshops give individual risk managers a more in-depth examination of issues that directly affect their specific facility. Companies may offer formal certificate programs for risk managers in areas such as an overview of risk management, risk exposure identification and evaluation, or functions of risk management. Each course may consist of self-study, specified readings, study questions, and projects. At the end of each course, participants may be tested and evaluated by qualified faculty.

Publications are designed to aid the insured institution to manage and reduce their liability risks. Material can vary from pamphlets on a single issue to workshop proceedings to multivolume books to a combination of mass media approaches. Often, insurance companies publish and distribute regular newsletters, case alerts, and bulletins. Available videotapes, audiotapes, films, and slide presentations may deal with topics such as malpractice in the emergency department, medication errors, and minimizing risks in surgery.

Claims are studied continuously by the insurance companies. A database of open and closed claims filed against their insured organizations and individuals is routinely analyzed to identify lessons learned, so that future claims can be avoided. Professional liability representatives periodically analyze claims to identify factors that may have caused their submission.

These factors are evaluated jointly by insurance company representatives and institution officials in an effort to correct situations that led to the claims. This process is facilitated by computer reports that pinpoint the frequency and severity of malpractice claims.

While none of the insurance companies require a prescribed risk management program, the surveys of the agency or institutional program and the data analysis may reflect on the adequacy of the program and variation in the premium. Continuing professional liability coverage may be conditional on implementing corrective action based on recommendations for improvement in the program or in specific situations which can cause liability.

Computer software packages may be provided by the insurance companies to enable their insured to analyze physician performance in areas such as adverse patient occurrences, infection rates, and pharmaceutical complications. New analysis software emerges from the claims studies to track the identified risk factors as they are discovered. This is a dynamic service, and risk managers will be exposed to creative and innovative software applications from insurance companies and others to limit liability.

DO'S AND DON'TS OF RISK MANAGEMENT: A CLAIMS PERSPECTIVE

Small things that hospital employees, departmental supervisors, and medical staff members doand don't docan have a significant impact on the frequency and severity of claims made against a hospital. Risk management experts urge hospitals to enforce do's and don'ts relative to documentation, product malfunction, contracts, confidentiality, and conflicts.

DO'S AND DON'TS OF RISK MANAGEMENT

DOCUMENTATION :

- Do follow all policies and procedures pertaining to documentation.
- Do document any changes in patient's status, attempts to contact patient's physicians or family members, and other activities relevant to patient's care. The absence of such documentation makes defending a medical malpractice action against the hospital difficult. In the words of one plaintiff attorney: "If it's not in the chart, it never happened."
- Do complete documentation entries contemporaneously. If changes or updates are necessary, they should be documented in a timely manner, with the date, reason for the change or update, and the initials of the person making the change included.
- Don't alter records out of fear of litigation or disciplinary action. Altered records discovered by a plaintiff attorney can make a case practically indefensible.
- Don't make changes to documentation days after an event occurs. Outline in memo form the situation surrounding the need for a change and discuss it with the hospital risk manager.

PRODUCT MALFUNCTION

- Do contact risk management whenever a product malfunctions, regardless of the perceived consequences at the time of the malfunction.

- Do notify the manufacturer of the malfunctioning product as soon as possible.
- Don't return the malfunctioning product to the manufacturer after it has caused an injury.
- Don't discard the malfunctioning equipment, product, or disposable accessories. Store it in a secure location until the hospital's professional liability company can be notified. Without the product as evidence, securing a contribution from a manufacturer would be very difficult if the incident ultimately warranted settlement, and the hospital could be solely liable.
- Don't attempt to recreate the malfunction to discover what or how something happened. A report from an independent third-party investigation will be less credible if the product has been altered in any way.

CONTRACTS

Do review all vendor contracts to ensure that the hospital is not exposed to additional risks.

Do have all contracts reviewed annually by the hospital attorney.

Don't sign a contract without reading it and understanding it first.

CONFLICTS

Do keep conflicts involving physicians and hospital out of the public area.

Do familiarize all hospital personnel with hospital policies and procedures that affect their daily jobs. Lack of knowledge of hospital policies is not a viable defense.

Don't allow or engage in open criticism of health professionals' treatment of a patient. Any documented conflicts over patient care would not only make a case very difficult to defend, but could also raise the ultimate value of the judgment. Don't enact policies or procedures that are unrealistic. The hospital will be held to its stated policies and procedures as standards of care.

CONFIDENTIALITY

Do hold professional discussions about patients in hospital settings, not in public areas.

Don't discuss patients' problems outside of the hospital.

Computer Use in Risk Management

Next to an involved risk management committee, the most valuable asset for any risk management program is a one-gigabyte computer and all the software the risk management department can afford.

Although smaller agencies and facilities (with fewer than two hundred beds) can manage data for trend analysis manually, the need for long term trend analysis of incidents, claims, equipment problems, internal disasters (for example, floods occurring from broken pipes only on weekends), cannot be overemphasized. While there are many software packages available that provide for central entry of data and specialized modules for RM, QA, or utilization review, the purchase decision should be based on a thorough analysis of the risk management data needs. Standard database software can be selected and customized to a particular program's needs at a significant savings over the special risk management packages available. In selecting software, the type of information the risk manager will be analyzing and the type of reports that will be generated from the analysis are the key factors in making the purchase decision.

Data that risk management most frequently analyzes for trends are events with patient injury, with financial loss to the institution (floods, fires, theft), malpractice suits naming the facility, dates and allegations of malpractice suits filed against medical staff members (obtained on appointment and reappointment), and "indicators" specific events with potential for patient injury or financial loss, such as a missing surgical consent, antibiotic given to the wrong patient, a patient chart missing, or narcotic cabinet keys missing from the pharmacy. It is common to track hospital incidents and events by date, time, and location. Malpractice claims are usually tracked by date, allegation, person(s) involved, and damages requested, and are followed through the entire defense process, listing information collected and individuals deposed for the defense, to judgment, settlement, or dismissal of the case. The amount of the judgment or settlement is tracked, as are the expenses incurred. Any one of the many risk management packages currently on the market or one of the database software packages would handle this type of information readily.

Whether or not a facility is self-insured, consideration should also be given to purchase of a spreadsheet package, for analysis of claims payments and costs of defense. For a facility that traditionally has purchased insurance coverage, a four-year cost analysis, if readily available, may point the way to cost savings by self-insurance. This is rapidly becoming an industry trend; the risk manager should prepare for the possibility that this move will occur as a natural outcome of the shifts in delivery of and payment for health care.

Toward the Future

Usually, risk managers aim to reduce preventable adverse events and to minimize financial loss to their organizations should such events occur. In a rapidly changing business environment, risk managers must be able to accurately determine where their health care organization is headed and effectively plan methods and techniques to mitigate the risks to their institutions. Within these goals, risk managers, along with everybody else, from top management to the lowest level employee, appear to be involved in almost every aspect of the health care delivery system. Health care organizations that survive the constant turmoil in the industry will be abetted by an effective, strategic risk management program.

3

Regulatory Environment: Standards and Risk Management

Health care is one of the most regulated industries in the United States. A regulatory environment is generated by the establishment of standards by legislative acts, by regulations administered by official executive agencies, and by standards of professional organizations. Violations of the law and/or regulations or standards could considerably interrupt revenue stream and even result in jail time for high level management personnel. An understanding of the regulations is vital for individuals and institutions engaged in health care risk management.

A Standards Primer

In a health care milieu, standards are statements concerning proper procedures and/or actions to be taken in given clinical or administrative situations. Using juxtaposed terms, standards can be created within the following boundary dimensions:

- Explicit or implicit
- National or local
- Validated or consensual
- Used or ignored
- Periodically updated or static

Explicit standards are written guidelines to ensure that everyone follows the same specific procedures in given clinical or administrative situations. Implicit standards, on the other hand, are usual and customary or based on collective experience but are unwritten, understood, assumed, or implied. Standards that are documented by scientific testing are verifiable and replicable; thus, their validity can be authenticated. Consensual standards develop by mutual agreement among involved parties.

Government jurisdictions, professional associations, or voluntary organizations at national, state, or local levels may develop and promulgate standards that may be incorporated into codes of ethics or separate guidelines, or be embedded in legislation and regulations. Excellent standards may be in force when the precepts are first established, but without a dynamic process of periodic review and updating, standards can fall into disuse and be ignored.

Promulgation and Implementation of Standards

Standards may be promulgated in four classifications: legal, regulatory, reimbursement, and practice guidelines. To compound matters further, there may be crossovers between the classifications.

Three particularly troubling areas for health care institutions illustrate the conflicting legislative interplay: Occupational Safety and Health Administration (OSHA) standards provoke conflicts with the Americans with

Disabilities Act (ADA) relative to preemployment medical examinations. Health insurance guidelines evoke interplay between the Employee Retirement and Income Security Act (ERISA) and ADA regarding health insurance plans that exclude or limit benefits for disabling conditions. State workers' compensation laws may conflict with the ADA by using examinations of the back to screen out injury-prone job applicants.6

Legai Standards

Legislatively, standards have been required relative to a broad spectrum of health care issues, such as public health rules, disease reporting requirements, utilization of immunizations, workers' compensation, health insurance, and licensing of institutions, agencies, and professionals. Usually, legislation is followed by regulations issued by the appropriate executive department.

A judicial system provides the primary legal initiative for implementing standards. If disagreements arise, the parties involved meet in a courtroom to decide the issue before a judge and/or a jury. Subsequently, the decision of the court yields a basis in law for future actions. Statutes and court orders constitute the framework for the legal implementation of standards. These legal renderings provide the foundation for health care institutional policies relative to alternative directives, living wills, informed consent, access to medical records, and information about practitioners.

Federal Mandates

Mandatory regulations cover a multitude of activities in the health care industry. A health care institution must meet the Conditions of Participation (COP) established by the federal Health Care Financing Agency (HCFA) before they can be reimbursed for treating people covered by the Medicare health insurance program. Like members of any other industry, health care providers must meet the mandates of federal regulations such as those required by OSHA. One official at a large hospital summed up the effect of federal regulations on the health care industry as follows:

Although workplace regulations are serious, time-consuming and expensive, in the scheme of things, federal workplace regulation is not the worst thing.

The sections that follow look at some examples of federal regulation of the health care industry.

Occupational Safety and Health

Legislative mandates that apply to the workplace illustrate the complex spectrum of conceivable risk management activities in health care institutions. Exhibit 2-1 lists the legislative chronology of almost thirty federal acts from the 1920s into the 1990s. Most of the statutes and the one executive order that form the framework of federal workplace regulations were put in place during three periods. 1931 to 1940; 1963 to 1974; and 1986 to 1993. Although seven statutes had been enacted by 1940, only eight major statutes were in place as of 1960. Congress initiated a second wave of legislation during the 1960s that addressed civil rights issues and regulated new areas, such as employee pensions. Finally, during the mid-1980s Congress passed a series of labor standard statutes focusing on narrower workplace issues. Exhibit 2-2 lists examples of regulatory statutes, giving details about each law and enumerating the civil and criminal, monetary and nonmonetary, enforcement sanctions and remedies available under the statute. However, enforcement agencies commonly negotiate settlements with employers even when not required by the regulation.

Focusing on the workplace, an examination of just one piece of legislation can demonstrate the probability, complexity, and cost of risk management for health care institutions and offices. Joseph A. Dear, the OSHA Administrator, estimated that 350 to 400 hospitals would be inspected by OSHA in 1995.8 A survey by the American Dental Association indicated that dental practices spend an estimated $23,713 annually to comply with OSHA regulations.9 This amount translates into a less than 1 percent risk of being inspected but a sizable financial investment to avoid violations. On a federal level, the Occupational Safety and Health Act of 1970 requires employers to furnish each employee with work and a workplace free from recognized hazards that can cause death or serious physical harm. By itself, this law contains a myriad of regulations required of health care facilities that apply to accidents, blood-borne pathogens, drug testing for employees, ergonomics, hazard communication, infection control, inspections by OSHA, lasers, maintenance and sterilization of medical equipment, medical wastes, medication safety, radiation, record keeping, reproductive hazards, safety and health committees, self-audits, staff training, and violence in the workplace.10 Furthermore, new rules can be adopted as the federal government emphasizes the enforcement of standards in the health care workplace. As of February 9, 1994, new OSHA rules require facilities that use nonsolid prescription drugs, such as aerosols, liquids, and powders, to maintain material safety data sheets (MSDSs) for these drugs and to use the MSDSs in training. In late 1993, new guidelines for controlling the spread of tuberculosis (TB) were mandated, with particular attention to the high risk of TB exposure in health care facilities and nursing homes. Federal Centers for Disease Control and Prevention (CDCP) recommendations called for the use of improved masks, the use of ultraviolet light to kill airborne TB germs, ventilation standards, and tightened record keeping.

A 1992 OSHA blood-borne pathogen standard dealt with the handling of blood, blood products, contaminated instruments, and contaminated sharps. Pathogens of greatest concern include human immunodeficiency virus type 1 (HIV) and hepatitis B virus (HBV). OSHA concluded that hazards could be minimized in several ways: engineering and work practice controls, personal protective equipment, HBV vaccination, training and education, and appropriate use of signs and labels. In 1993, OSHA reported 2,064 violations of the blood-borne pathogen regulations by health care industry organizations. This regulation was the most frequently violated standard in the industry that year. Specific blood-borne pathogen standards that were violated fell into five deficiency areas: exposure control plan (28%), methods of compliance (24%), communication of exposure to employees (23%), hepatitis B vaccination and postexposure evaluations and follow-up (19%), and record keeping (6%). Violations of the OSHA regulations can result in civil and/or criminal penalties, but as one hospital official put it:

> The sheer volume and nitty-gritty of regulations make compliance difficult.

Difficulties in complying with OSHA regulations are so pervasive that the American Management Association has dozens of seminars detailing how to meet the OSHA-mandated training requirements, and how to maintain employee and patient safety. Furthermore, a computer software program can be used to satisfy OSHA requirements for injury and illness record keeping. A potent risk analysis package simplifies the maintenance of accurate data.

ENFORCEMENT, COMPLIANCE, AND PENALTIES

OSHA attempts to control or shape the behavior of a regulated community through the enforcement of certain rules or commands monitored by compliance inspections, administrative adjudication, or the courts. In 1993, federal health care inspections took place in the following broadly inclusive seven classifications of health care providers: general medical and surgical hospitals (36%); offices and clinics of dentists (16%); skilled nursing care facilities (15%); offices and clinics of physicians (13%); other nursing and personal care facilities (7%); other health care facilities, including health and allied services, psychiatric hospitals, specialty outpatient clinics, and dental laboratories (7%); and specialty hospitals (7%).

Obviously, employer compliance is influenced by the employer's awareness of the regulatory requirements. A randomly selected mail survey of almost two thousand employers found that more than 50 percent reported little or no awareness of OSHA's Hazard Communication Standard (HCS) or were not knowledgeable about its key requirements.

Significantly, the effectiveness of command and control regulation is influenced by the level of available regulatory resources and the sanctions for noncompliance. There are only about two thousand compliance officers to enforce standards in more than 6.5 million workplaces. Historically, OSHA penalties have been inconsequential: the average penalty for a serious violation was $750 in fiscal year 1993; criminal sanctions are infrequent, and a conviction is rare. In comparison, the allowable legislative sanctions are quite severe. Maximum civil monetary penalties under OSHA are substantial (see Box 2-2, for example): from thousands of dollars to a half million, plus imprisonment in more severe cases.

In addition to setting standards for the workplace, federal legislation affects individual health care providers. Seeking to improve the quality of health care, legislators have created some potentially high liability risks for institutions that employ or contract with licensed health care practitioners.

EMERGENCY MEDICAL TREATMENT AND LABOR ACT OF 1986

This law bars hospitals and physicians from ordering transfers of emergency patients or women in active labor until they are stabilized. "Dumping patients" through inappropriate transfers (see Box 2-3), such as diverting patients via radio messages to ambulances or denying services to psychiatric patients, could incur fines of up to $50,000 per violation. Repeat offenders could be terminated from the Medicare program.

Six hospitals have been terminated since the law went into effect, but four of those have been recertified. A report from the Public Citizen's Health Research Group claimed that enforcement of the dumping law lagged behind the increased complaints about the practice.21 Extending the regulation, several courts ruled that this law applies not only to patient dumping but also to the more general allegations of inadequate care of insured patients.

MAMMOGRAPHY QUALITY STANDARDS ACT OF 1992

Public Law 102-539 requires national uniform quality standards for mammography facilities, whether in a hospital, physician's office, mobile van, military base, or any other public or private enterprise. By October 1, 1994, all mammography facilities had to be certified by the Food and Drug Administration (FDA) or alternatively by the American College of Radiology. Facilities must apply for accreditation annually and submit to several procedures: a periodic review of clinical images; an annual survey by a medical physicist; and compliance with quality standards for equipment, personnel qualifications, quality assessment programs, record keeping, and reporting.

Safe Medical Devices Act of 1990

A report from the National Committee for Quality Health Care (NCQHC), a coalition of providers and manufacturers, urges mandatory federal FDA-like premarket review of emerging technology involving modified tests and treatments. From the viewpoint of its vested interest, the NCQHC seeks to curb inappropriate use of medical technology.26 This group recommended that medical and surgical procedures be required to demonstrate their clinical efficacy before being adopted outside the research setting. Currently, new drugs and devices must undergo rigorous FDA premarket review. However, no such requirements exist for emerging medical tests and treatments that do not involve a new product. Critics of such requirements believe that a formal regulatory system could impede providers and delay access to promising new technology and procedures.

Manufacturers of medical devices aver that liability concerns threaten their implant research activities. Since "there are no inert materials," the climate of litigation in the United States may "ultimately push device manufac turers to introduce their new devices in countries less prone to litigation." Furthermore, in light of cost containment restraints, health care organizations are considering the reuse of disposable medical devices. However, the FDA says that "providers that reuse disposable devices are liable for the products' safety and effectiveness."

Risk managers must contemplate possible causes of injury relative to medical devices: design defects, manufacturing defects, random component failure, packaging errors, user errors, idiosyncratic patient reaction, sabotage, faulty repair, or maintenance or calibration errors. Estimates attribute 50 to 80 percent of medical-device accidents directly to user error, on the part of patient, technician, physician, nurse, or other professional.

Corporate giants in American medical device production have been involved in regulatory sanctions invoked by the FDA. In February 1994, for example, Siemens Medical Systems, Inc., signed a consent decree stating that it had improperly manufactured certain devices, such as hearing aids, pacemakers, patient monitors, and ultrasound monitors. Siemens was granted time to correct the violations, and by November 1994, Siemens had received approval from the FDA to resume marketing of its devices. Box 2-4 gives other examples. Medical devices continue to raise the specter of huge liability risks, as evidenced by lawsuits regarding breast implants, foreign-made kidney dialysis units, and lymphedema pumps.

Medical Waste Tracking Act (MWTA) of 1988

This legislation was a political response to the highly publicized hysteria over hypodermic needles that washed up onto the beaches of three states. Although the MWTA was a federal law, the mandates were limited to two years and for only three states: Connecticut,

BOX 2-4

Pfizer Inc. and Shiley, Inc., agreed to pay $10.75 million to settle claims and to monitor patients who had received a heart valve device.

Federal marshals impounded more than two thousand sphygmomanometers from the Surgical Instrument Company of America because these devices allegedly had defective pressure gauges and leaking and torn inflator bladders.

Wire leads on twenty-two thousand pacemakers manufactured by Telectronics Pacing Systems, Inc. (Englewood, CA) were declared a potential lethal risk for patients with cardiac problems because of possible fractures in the wire leads, causing severe heart injury or death.

New Jersey, and New York. Participation was voluntary for any other state. The MWTA requires tracking of seven types of waste: cultures and stocks, pathological wastes, human blood and blood products, sharps, animal waste, isolation waste, and unused sharps. By 1991, when the MWTA expired, the problem had evaporated. A review of the scientific literature on medical waste concluded: "Medical waste is no more dangerous than non-medical waste."

MEDWatch

In June 1993, the FDA announced a new program, MEDWatch: The FDA Medical Products Reporting Program. Because many health professionals do not routinely report adverse events, MEDWatch was designed to encourage the voluntary reporting, by professionals and consumers, of serious adverse events caused not only by medical devices but also by biologics, dietary supplements, and drugs. Problems such as defective devices, inaccurate or unreadable product labeling, packing or product mix-up, contaminations or stability problems, and particulate matter in injectable products should be reported promptly.

Eight months after MEDWatch was launched, 4,625 adverse events had been reported; 2,270 were drug reactions (64%), 856 were device problems (20%). Pharmacists were the overwhelming source of reporting (2,531, or 55%) distantly followed by physicians (683, or 16%). Importantly, many hospitals and physicians still do not report malfunctions of medical equipment as the law requires.

Of concern to risk management, up to 10 percent of hospital admissions in the United States are due to adverse reactions. If an adverse event occurs in the hospital, approximately two additional inpatient days, costing about $1,000 per day, are needed. Critically, up to 75 percent of adverse drug reactions are preventable. On a less positive note, a medical marketing trade journal alerted its readers to the hidden negative aspects of MedWatch relative to their business concerns.

Environmental Protection Agency (EPA)

Although individual hospital incinerators are relatively small, an EPA report stated that collectively, medical waste incineration by hospitals may be the largest source of airborne dioxin emissions in the United States.46 Such emissions constitute a risk because the EPA has concluded that dioxin causes cancer in animals and is a probable human carcinogen. Hospitals use many disposable medical products typically made of chlorinated plastics. These waste materials, high in chlorine, are burned, freeing the element during combustion to form dioxin. Often, medical waste incinerators lack technologies to reduce, control, and monitor toxic emissions into the air. Opponents of this method of waste disposal vehemently assert that medical waste should not be incinerated under any circumstances.47 As of 1996, new EPA regulations require hospitals using medical waste incinerators to eliminate toxic emissions and to monitor compliance. As a result, hospitals have changed the way they handle medical waste. In Florida, high-volume regional incinerators have replaced smaller on-site units. Since 1989, about ninety small hospital incinerators, 75 percent of Florida's total, have shut down. In 1994, the Mayo Clinic in Rochester, Minnesota, opened a $10.6-million state-of-the-art incinerator ten miles north of the clinic. Advanced incineration technology is combined with an aggressive recycling program to reduce the volume of waste burned. This incinerator also accepts waste from other area hospitals.

Regulatory Implementation Mandates

Legislation allows governmental agencies to audit and survey health care facilities to determine if the institution is abiding by regulatory standards. These audits and surveys can be accomplished through personal visits, written questionnaires, or telephone inquiries. They may be by appointment or random, without notice to the agency, such as by the state health department. Inspectors have the power to review the physical plant and the operations of facilities, and to examine documentation. Serious violations can result in a loss of a license to operate, as well as monetary fines. Risk managers must ensure that the organization is prepared at all times for an unannounced or expected audit or survey.

State Legislation and Regulations

Historically, general health regulation has been a matter of local concern. Health care facilities such as hospitals, skilled nursing facilities, intermediate nursing facilities, and managed care entities require a license before they can become operational. Individual professionals such as physicians, dentists, registered nurses, physical therapists, and psychol ogists must have a state license or state registration before they can render care to their clients. Reacting to "oppressive health care regulations," in 1994 New York's governor revised sixteen edicts, including those mandating on-site inspections, hospital social work departments, the education and experience requirements for emergency room staffs, the explanation to all patients of their rights, and the indicators for reporting adverse events. A New York Times editorial labeled the plan "a modest easing of hospital regulations." This action by a state governor follows the example set at the federal level of reducing the government's involvement in the regulation of industry. New Jersey legislators also considered reforming twenty-five years of a tight rein over health care facilities and services, but not before flexing regulatory power again (see Box 2-5). The sections that follow look at some examples of state regulation of the health care industry.

Licensure and Registration of Professional Institutions

State governments have always had the responsibility of licensing health care professionals and defining the parameters of their practices. All the states license professionals such as physicians, dentists, and registered nurses. However, not all the states license or register providers such as physical and occupational therapists. Licensing or registration remains a state prerogative and is subject to change. In addition, legislation concerned with professional malpractice is embedded in state tort law that deals with civil and criminal injury and harm. Box 2-6 raises a malpractice question and answers with a real example.

BOX 2-5

Blue Cross/Blue Shield of New Jersey was fined $106,000 for setting up a string of family health centers without prior approval from the state health department. These centers were part of a $13-million network of ten centers to serve 200,000 managed care policyholders.

Smoke-Free Workplace

More than forty states have enacted legislation to restrict smoking in public places, including health care facilities, and eleven states regulate smoking in the workplace. Civil court judges in California,

Georgia, and Ohio have found that "battery," which usually entails touching people against their will, can apply to secondhand cigarette, cigar, or pipe smoke (see Box 2-7).

Although many states and cities have adopted laws restricting smoking in public places, when it come to enforcement, such laws are usually regarded as self-policing. Efforts to eliminate the risk of secondhand cigarette smoke were stimulated by a five-hundred-page 1992 report from the Environmental Protection Agency that estimated three thousand deaths per year from such exposure. Even small amounts of smoke can endanger nonsmokers and may double or triple their risk of heart disease.56 Indoor air quality regulations are evolving to protect workers from various outdoor contaminants and to control microbial contaminants by routine inspection.

BOX 2-6

Should an insurer deny malpractice coverage to a nurse who rendered a service that, under statute, is defined as "medical" practice? Nurse Valerie Tomlinson was suspended from the Royal Cornwall Hospital for operating on a patient.

BOX 2-7

Bank receptionist Bonnie Richardson claimed that a colleague maliciously directed pipe smoke at her. She went to the hospital twice for severe headaches, nausea, and weight loss. She sued and won. A judge for the Georgia State Appeals Court declared: "Pipe smoke is visible. It is detectable through the senses and may be ingested or inhaled. It is capable of touching or making contact with one's person in a number of ways."

Violence Prevention

California passed a law requiring all hospitals to provide training and education in security measures. All hospitals were required to initiate violence prevention programs by July 1995. This legislation was prompted by statistics revealing that almost 60 percent of the hospitals in the five largest cities in the state had reported attacks on staff, patients, and visitors. Beefing up security was particularly critical for emergency rooms. A survey by the journal Topics in Emergency Medicine reported˙ that 43 percent of hospitals experienced at least one physical attack per month on a medical staff member.

State Mandated Risk Management Legislation

Several states have passed legislation or promulgated regulations requiring hospitals to implement risk management programs. A federal government study7 compared the major characteristics of ten state programs: Alaska, Colorado, Florida, Kansas, Maryland, Massachusetts, New York, North Carolina, Rhode Island, and Washington.

Legislative and regulatory requirements of Maryland and New York that apply to health care are relatively comprehensive. Maryland is unique because it is the only state where the requirements represent a consensus of the hospital industry, legal interests, and the state government. New York mandates reveal detailed requirements for a combined risk management and quality assessment program supported by an extensive survey process to monitor compliance.

In most of these states, risk management requirements are specifically designed to interrelate with other quality assessment initiatives in the hospital environment. Significantly, the requirements are made a condition for the hospital's licensure by the state. Generally, the mandates focus on preventing and controlling risk to patients, rather than on risks such as fire prevention, equipment maintenance, safety, and security. A ten-state comparison illustrates the considerable variabilities among the mandated risk management regulations.

Not every state mandates every risk management characteristic. Nevertheless, a framework emerges for implementing a basic risk management program in all instances. These nine main legislative and regulatory attributes are compared in Exhibit 2-3 and examined further in the sections that follow.

Risk Management Responsibility

Depending on the state, hospitals must assign risk management responsibility to a single risk management coordinator or to a committee or in some instances, states can choose between the two. Two states (Arkansas and Rhode Island) do not assign such responsibility.

Governing Body Involvement

When state regulations require governing body involvement, emphasis ranges from ensuring that governing bodies provide an adequate level of resources and support systems to a minimal requirement that the governing bodies formally approve a risk management plan. States can require that the governing board or hospital administrator receive reports on the risk management program. Reporting varies from a general statement to specific language calling for quarterly reports. A few states mandate that a member of the governing body also be a member of the risk management and/or quality assessment committee.

Risk Identification

Most states require systems to identify risks to patients. Legislative wording can be general, without establishing procedures, or it can be specific. Sometimes the legislation specifies the types of incidents to be reported by hospital staff, the patient grievance data required, and the additional quality assessment information demanded. Colorado commands its hospitals to submit for state approval a general description of the types of cases, problems, or risks to be reviewed, and the criteria to be used for identifying potential risks. Massachusetts' detailed requirements call for three risk identification methods: incident reporting, occurrence reporting, and occurrence screening. Exhibit 2-4 compares seven state mandated requirements for risk identification systems.

Risk Analysis

Legislative mandates for risk analysis can range from a general obligation to specifics such as what to include in such analysis (for example, frequency and causes of injuries, time, place, persons involved). Exhibit 2-5 indicates the scope of analysis of identified risks by state.

Risk Management Education

State legislation can specify topics to include in risk management activities, can compel annual risk management education for designated staff, or can merely call for educational programs without giving a time frame. Examples of relevant subject matter include injury prevention, patient safety, principles and techniques of infection control, incident reporting or staff responsibility to report professional misconduct, legal aspects of care, causes of malpractice claims, patients' rights, improved communications, and topics related to employees' job responsibilities. Staff education can be for all staff, for appropriate staff, or for staff engaged in patient care activities. One state excludes physicians from the education requirement.

Sharing of Information

Colorado obliges hospitals to coordinate all pertinent case, problem, or risk review information with other applicable institutional quality assessment or risk management activities. Maryland requires "a flow of information" among quality assessment, credentialing, peer review, and any risk management committees. North Carolina dictates "operational linkages" between risk management and other functions relating to patient care, safety, and staff performance. New York orders hospitals to review extensive information, including quality assessment data, complaints, incident reports, and utilization review data to identify problems in patient care. Massachusetts indicates that credentialing, quality assessment, risk management, and peer review functions should be strongly and thoroughly integrated. Maryland, New York, and Washington have legislative requirements on credentialing information. New York, Washington, Maryland, and Kansas specifically require that a quality assessment or peer review committee be responsible for acting to correct identified problems.

Patient Grievance Procedures

Most states regard patient grievance data as an important element in their risk management requirements. Maryland detailed its mandates for a patient complaint program with four specifics:

Risk management programs must include a formal written program for addressing patient complaints.

Patients must be given information about the program, including the name and phone number or address of a hospital representative whom the patient may contact to register a complaint.

A hospital representative must treat the complaining patient with dignity, courtesy, and due regard for privacy and must provide the patient with certain information about the complaint-handling process.

A hospital representative must document the complaint and any action taken as a result of it.

Massachusetts requires that all patients receive written notice of their rights within twenty-four hours of admission and be informed as to how to file complaints. Alaska's general requirement orders the hospital to have a procedure to investigate, analyze, and respond to patient grievances related to patient care.

Immunity and Confidentiality for Providers of Risk Management Information

Seven states grant immunity from liability to those who provide information on incidents; six provide for confidentiality. Immunity and confidentiality provisions have two goals: to shield those who report or evaluate risk management information; and to protect privileged risk management records from subpoena, discovery, or other public disclosure.

Risk Management Follow-up Procedures

Legislation and/or regulations may require a follow-up or review of a hospital's specific risk management actions and can include a summary report of risk management actions to the governing body.

New York and Colorado oblige hospitals to institute a method for evaluating the effectiveness of actions taken to address risks or problems. Maryland mandates that hospitals establish an internal committee structure to conduct reviews and evaluations of risk management activities. Massachusetts obligates hospitals to create a system to ensure compliance with incident reporting requirements.

Local City and County Legislation Controls

Regulations and rules that affect risk management may be created at city and county levels. Although city and county legislative bodies often adopt and/or adapt federal and state requirements, there may be local variants. A city health department may enact its own regulations, such as procedures for the reporting of tuberculosis or communicable diseases of a sensitive nature (for example, positive lab results for sexually transmitted diseases), guidelines for sanitation and disposal of hazardous waste, restrictions on the transport of radioactive and/or nuclear materials through city streets, and the functions of patient advocates. A county water department may set thresholds for purification chemicals added to drinking water or to be found in waste water. Building codes, fire safety regulations, and occupancy permits are generally a function of local government. A risk manager should be aware of the major laws and regulations at all levels of government.

Reimbursement Requirements

Third-party insurers set their own standards for reimbursement to providers and to the insured parties. Usually, the insurers establish an indemnification system wherein the providers agree to reimbursement standards such as accepting whatever fee schedule the insurer establishes as the total payment, accepting predefined amounts for specific services but billing the patient for any differential from their regular fee, or agreeing to a discount off their usual and customary fee. Some variations on these standards involve a patient out-of-pocket copayment or co-insurance, and private insurance companies set their own standards for the types of services for which they will pay and for when the services are appropriate. A major controversy of recent years has concerned insurance reimbursement for so-called experimental therapies, such as bone marrow transplant therapy for patients with cancer.

Managed care organizations negotiate their reimbursement fees with individual practitioners, with clinical groups, and with hospitals. Significantly, these reimbursement guidelines can include financial incentives or disincentives. If practitioners reduce their referrals and hospitalizations, they may receive a bonus from any surplus funds. On the other hand, if practitioners use too many resources in rendering care, the potential bonus could be reduced. However, such financial awards or punishments are within the standards for quality of care that the managed care entity establishes. Despite their critics, health maintenance organizations (HMOs) and preferred provider organizations (PPOs) maintain that their subscribers receive whatever medical care is appropriate; no medically necessary care is denied. There are serious arguments about the financial incentives in health care, and the money/care relationship raises liability issues for risk management.

Reimbursement by public entities requires adhering to their respective standards as well. Medicare is an insurance program; Medicaid is a type of welfare. Since Medicare is a federal program, the standards are uniform for the entire nation. Fees are calculated based on federal determinations. Medicaid, on the other hand, is a combined federal/state/local financing program with fifty different standards as established by each of the states. Each state also makes its own determination of reimbursement policies.

In 1994, the federal government spent $158 billion for Medicare and $146 billion for Medicaid services, about one-third of the national expenditure for health care: about $1 trillion. It is obvious that any agency with that amount of financial clout can create its own standards for reimbursement for services rendered by providers. Through a prospective payment systems using a payment mechanism of diagnosis-related groups (DRGs), the federal Health Care Financing Administration (HCFA) requires that every patient be classified into one of the approximately five hundred DRGs in order for the institution to receive payment for services rendered. Furthermore, the HCFA sets a length of stay for each DRG, and providers must explain why patients are remaining in the facility if the outside limit of the length of stay is exceeded.

A resources-based relative value scale (RBRVS) is another reimbursement mechanism for services rendered by providers. An RBRVS aims to set fees for ambulatory care provided by physicians. Generally, the reimbursement relies on a written calculation of the relative value of specific procedures as compared to an initial base service. In essence, a price is set by agreement with the insurers, and standards are implemented to follow the rules. Violations could disqualify the facility and/or the individuals from providing care to people covered by that insurer.

In reimbursement, "bundling" and "un-bundling" refer to the manner in which services are billed. When care is rendered as a package with all the resources included in the billed amount, the services are said to be bundled together. Nursing care, for example, is usually included in the predetermined amount reimbursed by the insurer. Unbundled services are itemized and billed for separately. Regulations need to be checked to determine if revenue flow can be increased by unbundling individual items of care. Whereas inpatient care services may be bundled together in a set fee for each DRG, outpatient care may not be reimbursed in a similar fashion. To enable un-bundling, facilities could convert selected inpatient services to outpatient services, assuming that such conversion were feasible and posed no harm to patients.

Practice Guidelines

Voluntary regulatory programs, such as the Joint Commission on Accreditation of Health-care Organizations (JCAHO), the National Committee for Quality Assurance (NCQA), and board certification by professional specialty societies, have a decided impact on risk management considerations. Health care institutions may be denied reimbursement by government programs and third-party insurers if they are not accredited by the JCAHO. With the increased competition in the health care field, voluntary accreditation can be used in marketing and advertising activities, since the public views such accreditation as evidence of high quality care.

JCAHO's nationwide prominence in promoting high quality health care has influenced most state regulatory agencies to accept its findings when considering accreditation and/or licensure applications. Third-party insurers rely on JCAHO decisions in reimbursement matters. On the federal level, the Department of Health and Human Services (HHS) accepts the JCAHO accreditation as evidence that the institution meets the Medicare conditions of participation.

That recognition allows the provider to bill for services rendered to individuals having Medicare coverage. Disturbingly, a 1992 validation sample by the federal HCFA of hospitals accredited by the JCAHO revealed that one of three failed to meet Medicare/ Medicaid standards.

The October 1994 Health Letter of the Public Citizen's Health Research Group reported that 57 (34%) of 167 hospitals failed to meet one or more of the federal conditions of participation. Profound questions can be raised about the safety and quality of care rendered. This validation suggests that between a thousand and nineteen hundred hospitals may have placed millions of patients at risk without timely intervention by the JCAHO, raising serious questions as to whether government regulators should continue to rely on the JCAHO for hospital accreditation.

Acreditation programs for seven different types of health care are sponsored by the JCAHO: ambulatory health care, home care, hospice care, long term care, psychiatric facilities, hospital care, and managed care. Each of these accreditation programs develops standards and uses a peer-based consultative and educational survey process to stimulate the provision of high quality patient care. In addition, each accreditation program encompasses a variety of organizations and providers: Ambulatory care: clinics, surgery centers, college or university health services, community health centers, emergency care centers, group practices, primary care centers, and urgent care centers.

Home care and hospice care: independent programs, home health care agencies, hospital-based programs, long term care organizations, and psychiatric agencies. Areas covered include home visits by health care professionals, setting up equipment, education of family members providing care, homemaker services, drug administration in the home, personal services such as shopping, and support services such as lawn mowing.

Long term care: hospital-based care, free-standing care, nursing homes, rehabilitation centers, and custodial facilities.

Psychiatric facilities: community mental health services, programs for the developmentally disabled, forensic psychiatric services, substance abuse programs, and psychiatric services.

Hospital care: about 75 percent of the general and specialty hospitals in the United States accredited by the JCAHO.

Managed care: a variety of developing managed care entities, such as HMOs, PPOs, and Individual Practice Associations (IPAs).

Standards may be implemented within an institution, and apply only in that facility, through utilization management, quality assessment, and peer review. Utilization management tends to focus on the efficacy and effective use of resources. Quality assessment aims to ensure that the procedures followed abide by the internal standards and guidelines.

Peer review occurs in tissue committees, mortality conferences, infection control committees, and quality improvement committees. In addition to these activities that implement standards, organizations usually have their own mandates regarding admissions, readmissions within a brief time period for the same condition, appropriate laboratory and diagnostic tests, repeated surgery for the same problem, length of stay, the process of care, and discharge planning. Risk managers must be alert to any violations of internal standards, since there is a direct relationship to outside regulatory requirements. Most of these internal guidelines could have an impact on reimbursement from third-party insurers.

To complicate the situation, internal requirements may be duplicated by outside organizations. Notable examples include the JCAHO, the Medicare and Medicaid programs, the Institute of Medicine, the Agency for Health Care Policy and Research, the National Committee for Quality Assurance, and a variety of specialty professional societies.

A directory of practice parameters, titles, sources, and updates delineates about sixteen hundred practice guidelines developed by seventy organizations. 66 Risk management programs can use the outside standards as a minimum to establish their internal guidelines. If internal standards are better than the outside guides, violations and penalties are less likely.

What if Practice Guidelines are Not Met?

Failure to fulfill the legal obligation to provide a quality of care that meets professional standards constitutes a breach of standards. Although medical malpractice awards may occupy the mass-media headlines, however, the majority of Americans do not sue their health care providers. Legislation noted in Box 2-8 attempted to raise the mandated level of physician competence. Falls are the most common adverse event reported by health care institutions. An elderly patient may fall from a bed because its railings are missing, an employee or a visitor may slip on a wet floor when a warning sign is absent, and a nurse may be stuck by a needle if syringes are not disposed of correctly. All of these incidents are covered in the practice guidelines and training of health care workers. All are preventable.

Potential damages from these breaches of standards could result in physical, emotional, social, and/or environmental harm. An individual could receive merely bumps and bruises or could be permanently disabled or even die. Embarrassment, humiliation, and mental distress are typical allegations included under "pain and suffering." Breakage and structural damages may also be involved. Damages appear to be limited only by the creativity of the people suing the health care facility. A broad range of possible damage outcomes includes censure, personnel action, monetary loss from fines, loss of individual practitioner privileges, facility closures and/or reductions, loss of licensure, loss of accreditation, a professional or criminal negligence lawsuit, imprisonment, loss of confidence in the facility, revenue stream disruption, mergers, bankruptcy, and corporate dissolution.

Ignorance of the Law is No Excuse

Numerous complicated laws, regulations, and standards seriously affect the management of risks in health care institutions. Violations of the mandates can result in fines and penalties that could damage the health care facility's financial well-being. Risk management personnel help prepare for regulatory or voluntary inspections, maintain documentation relative to administrative and clinical issues mandated by good operations, and establish appropriate oversight of the medical care provided by the agency or hospital. To carry out these functions effectively, risk managers must initiate mechanisms to learn about all the laws, regulations, and standards, on federal, state, and local levels, and to implement risk prevention and control activities.

A dentist was granted provisional hospital staff membership and placed under observation of designated proctors. Unfavorable reports claimed that the dentist spent too much time on certain procedures, that blood loss in some patients was excessive, and that too many patients needed follow-up and repeat procedures. A hospital decision denied the oral and maxillofacial surgeon privileges beyond tooth extraction.

Antonio Benedi, a special assistant to ex-President George Bush, habitually drank wine with his dinner. To combat the flu, he took Tylenol for several days. There was no warning on the box or bottle about the danger of mixing alcohol with the drug. Benedi lapsed into a coma and was hospitalized. Later, he had a kidney transplant and expects to start kidney dialysis. Benedi claimed that his liver had been "sensitized" to react to Tylenol. A jury awarded him $7.855 million for compensatory damages and $1 million for punitive damages.

Infusaid Inc. of Norwood, Massachusetts, paid a $290,000 fine for marketing an unapproved implantable drug infusion pump and for failing to manufacture the device under good manufacturing practice regulations. This was the first fine imposed by the FDA under the Safe Medical Devices Act of 1990.

4

Identifying and Controlling Risks in the Workplace

Health care institutions and other employers have many workplace legal risks in common, including potential employment law liabilities. A risk manager who is not familiar with the legal rights of employers and employees will encounter numerous unforeseen difficulties. Potential liability can arise in a variety of areas: wrongful discharge, racial or religious discrimination, sexual harassment, age discrimination, disability law, AIDS, workers' compensation, accidents and injuries, and even the provision of treatment.

Wrongful Dismissal or Discharge

A new and rapidly growing area of employer liability centers around the allegations of wrongful dismissal or discharge. Approximately 65 to 70 percent of the workforce are considered employees-at-will, meaning that "an employer may dismiss an employee hired for an indefinite period of time for any reason or no reason at all without incurring liability to the employee."1 However, an employer may not discharge an employee for an unlawful reason, such as racial discrimination. Historically, employers had broad powers to dismiss employees. In recent years, courts and state legislatures have whittled away at this unrestricted doctrine. Exceptions to the employment-at-will rule have been expanding based on a variety of legal concepts, including claims in contract, torts (civil wrongs), and the fact that a particular termination violates public policy.

A number of courts have found an implicit contract assurance of job security in employer communications such as employer policies, handbooks, oral assurances, industry customs, employer conduct, and the duration of employment. Most commonly, the claim is based on a personnel manual or handbook.

Although courts do not always find that these documents establish contracts between an employer and its employees, employment contracts have been inferred from them in some instances, and the more detailed the document's descriptions of disciplinary procedure, the more likely it will be found to be an implied contract. Furthermore, courts have used the legal concept of an implied covenant of good faith and fair dealing to find an existing contractual relationship restricting an employer's decisions to dismiss an employee.

Intentional infliction of mental distress can be used as the basis for a wrongful discharge claim. However, this type of claim has been confined to employer conduct that is outrageous or extreme. To qualify as intentional infliction of mental distress, employer conduct must result in behavior that no reasonable person could be expected to endure, or in embarrassment, fright, or intense humiliation. The positions of both employer and employee illustrate the complexity of a wrongful dismissal situation.

Terminations of employment may embroil an employer in claims of defamation. Defamation occurs where, purposely or carelessly, an employer disseminates incorrect or derogatory information about an employee. An employee alleging defamation must show that the information concerned the employee, that it was published or disclosed to others, that it is false, that it damages the employee's reputation, and that the employer either acted negligently or had malicious intent.

Daniel Tripodi, a former vice president for a Johnson & Johnson subsidiary, won a $434,000 jury award when he sued the company for dismissing him in violation of a written company credo. On appeal, a U.S. judge overturned the verdict and ruled that a company credo is not a legally binding contract. A dental assistant alleged wrongful dismissal and claimed to have been humiliated because she was terminated while she was in the hospital with pregnancy difficulties.

An employee claim that discharge violates a public policy and may be wrongful has gained some acceptance. To prove this claim, employees must show clear and convincing evidence that they carried out an act encouraged by public policy or refused to act in a way discouraged by public policy, and that employer retaliation for this act was the factor motivating the discharge. To qualify as a discharge in violation of public policy, the issue at stake must affect the public at large, not only the individual employee. Moreover, the public policy relied on must be unambiguous, and in some jurisdictions, must be based on a statute. Elsewhere, it is considered sufficient that the policy be clear from a statutory scheme. Generally, the employee must have acted in good faith; the employee need not report correct information to invoke this legal protection. An employee may be found to have been discharged in violation of public policy if the discharge resulted from the employee's refusal to commit illegal or unethical acts, or from the employee's filing of a workers' compensation claim.

ARBITRATION IN WRONGFUL DISMISSAL

Arbitration may be an effective remedy to decide wrongful dismissal cases without litigation and within the legal framework. Utilization of existing organizational and/or union contract procedures should precede arbitration, and state legislation determines if arbitration is allowable. Investigators conducted a comprehensive review of state laws, developed a model employment termination act, selected court decisions covering both sides of the issue, and concluded that trying wrongful dismissal arbitration was a proper approach for health care organizations. In a variation of arbitration, a risk management director suggests an alternative dispute resolution method, such as employment dispute resolution, as a way to reduce employment-related litigation risks.

Due Process in Wrongful Dismissal

Wrongful discharge law is diverse and changing rapidly. Any alteration in the traditional employment-at-will principle may drastically increase an employer's liability for terminations. Risk managers should make their employers aware that discharging employees for exercising certain rights is best avoided. However, problems that appropriately point to potential discharge include absenteeism, tardiness, carelessness, negligence, inappropriate dress or grooming, insubordination, theft, falsification of records, substance abuse on the job, or any deviation from practice standards. As a litigation prevention measure, there should be progressive discipline protocols that include verbal warnings and written reprimands before a termination. These protocols should be characterized by due process that is consistent and predictable. Courts have been favorable in cases where the employer followed progressive disciplinary procedures bolstered with due process for the employee. When due process is not followed and an employee is fired, however, the court can rule for the employee. If termination is necessary, employers should consider safeguarding against sabotage initiated by a disgruntled employee.

A nurse's aide helped a patient to a commode and left him there. A half hour later another employee discovered the patient in a pool of blood on the floor, and the patient died two days later. After being fired for gross negligence, the aide sued for wrongful discharge. A lower court returned a $56,456 verdict for the aide for lost wages, mental suffering, and humiliation. Reversing the verdict, the West Virginia Supreme Court held that the evidence did not support a wrongful discharge finding; the patient's injury and death were the primary reason for the aide's termination.

Keys, computer codes, and access to vital information should be secured as soon as the employee is discharged.

Discrimination Law

Most of the law against employment discrimination is about thirty years old. Although the law is based on a variety of sources, the primary federal statute is Title VII of the Civil Rights Act of 1964 (Title VII). Title VII prohibits discrimination on the basis of race, color, sex, religion, pregnancy, and national origin affecting the terms and conditions of employment. This statute was modified in important ways by the Civil Rights Act of 1991 (Public Law 102-166). A significant change was the provision for jury trials in cases pursuant to Title VII. For the first time, the 1991 act allowed punitive damages for Title VII violations, with monetary recoveries capped on the basis of the size of the employer: a $50,000 ceiling for employers having fifteen to a hundred employees, and a $300,000 ceiling for employers with three hundred or more employees. Because of these changes, the potential verdicts in Title VII lawsuits can be much higher than those of the past.

An anesthesiologist was fired by a prestigious hospital for malpractice based on false information, and the jury awarded him $5.1 million for defamation.

Based on past experience, risk managers should be particularly wary of jury trials. A majority of jury trials of employment discrimination claims are decided in favor of the plaintiff. Juries tend to favor the "little guy" against any adversary and may award large sums. 16 The potentially devastating outcomes of jury trials motivate many employers to consider out-of-court settlements and other means to reduce their potential costs when discrimination complaints are filed.

Sources of employment discrimination law, in addition to Title VII, include state laws, local ordinances, the federal civil rights legislation of 1866 and 1871, the Equal Pay Act, the Americans with Disabilities Act, and the Age Discrimination in Employment Act.

Risk managers should be sufficiently aware of discrimination law to assist their organization in preventing lawsuits and to be able to participate when a suit does occur. In today's diverse workforce, many employment decisions create the potential for a discrimination claim; these have to be recognized and evaluated. Risk managers can take proactive steps to minimize liability. Potential legal issues can be identified for employers, and the involvement of the organization's counsel can be suggested when necessary. An informational program about the extent of discrimination prohibitions can make supervisors and managers aware of actions that may involve legal issues.

Ferdinand Maiorino, sixty-four years old, had rejected two earlier retirement offers when he was fired by Schering-Plough Corporation for poor job performance after thirty-five years of satisfactory work. Claiming he couldn't afford to retire, he sued for age discrimination. A jury awarded Maiorino $450,000 in compensatory damages and $8 million in punitive damages.

Discrimination law covers more than a lawsuit brought on the basis of a particular promotion or dismissal. Claims of discrimination can include problems arising on the job, such as religious bias. While the scope of unlawful discrimination varies from state to state, state laws frequently prohibit more forms of discrimination than do federal laws. In addition to the familiar prohibitions against discrimination based on race, religion, sex, and national origin, many states ban discrimination based on pregnancy, age, handicap, or disability. Several states prohibit discrimination based on sexual orientation, which is not prohibited by the major federal antidiscrimination statutes. Other prohibitions include discrimination based on family responsibility or obligations, association with protected groups, personal appearance, height, weight, arrest or conviction records, and status with regard to public assistance.

Since there is such diversity among state antidiscrimination laws, risk managers must become familiar with state and local mandates and know which groups are protected, to allow for an analysis of whether an employer's position is precarious in a specific situation.

A nurse asks for every Saturday off because that is her sabbath. Her colleagues usually have only two weekends off per month. This request raises the issue of religious accommodation.

Employees refuse to shave facial hair for religious reasons, despite requirements instituted to protect them from tuberculosis.

Specifically, facial hair may result in an inaccurate reading of a test to determine if masks used when working with tuberculosis patients fit well enough to protect the employee.

Three Primary Discrimination Theories

Different theories underlie the three primary types of employment discrimination lawsuits: the individual disparate treatment case, the disparate impact case, and the disparate treatment pattern and practice case.

Individual Disparate Treatment

These cases require the plaintiff to prove that the employer's actions resulted from a discriminatory motive. An employer's motive can be proved directlyfor example, through statements by the employeror indirectly. Most often, the means of indirect proof is evidence that similarly situated persons who are not in the protected class have received better treatment than members of the protected group. When a plaintiff presents evidence of a discriminatory motive, the defendant must respond that the challenged action was the result not of discrimination but of a legitimate, nondiscriminatory motive. The plaintiff's task is to show that the employer's stated reason is only a pretext, a cover-up for a discriminatory motive.

Disparate Impact

A disparate impact case, in contrast, does not require proof of intent. An employment practice that is neutral on its face but has an adverse effect on a protected group is unlawful.

A black plaintiff claims he was overlooked for promotion because of his race. Responding, the employer says that the plaintiff was not the best candidate for the job. The plaintiff tries to discredit this nondiscriminatory explanation by attacking the employer's evaluation of the qualifications of the applicant pool. He points out ways in which his qualifications are better than those of the person promoted. Employers must defend the practice by showing a business necessity for it.

Disparate Treatment Pattern or Practice

In these cases, the plaintiff is required to show that discrimination was the employer's standard operating procedure. Usually, plaintiffs use statistical evidence to make this showing. Defendants have two basic arguments to make in response; either or both may be advanced. The defendant may try to show that the statistical evidence is flawed and/or that the challenged employment practice is a business necessity.

Burden of Proof

A notable amount of litigation and legislation has focused on the key legal concept of burden of proof in Title VII cases. Litigants having the burden of proof are required to prove that their position is more correct than that of their adversaries. Where both sides have equally credible positions, the party who has the burden of proof is said not to have established his or her case. A variety of standards are used to measure the burden of proof. "Beyond a reasonable doubt," the standard placed on the prosecution in a criminal case, is the most familiar. In civil litigation, the burden of proof generally is on the plaintiff, who must show by a "preponderance of the evidence" that his or her position is more convincing. A preponderance of the evidence is a majority, or more than half. However, this decision is not made mechanically by weighing the volume of evidence submitted. Decisions involve analysis of the evidence and assessment of the credibility of witnesses. For the most part, legislation and judicial decisions have settled the technical issues of burden of proof as they relate to Title VII cases.

In each of the three types of discrimination cases, the plaintiff has the burden of coming forward with what is termed a prima facie case. A prima facie case is evidence that raises a reasonable inference that an employer's action, if unexplained, was based on unlawful factors. It is relatively simple to establish a prima facie case of discrimination. In a disparate treatment case, plaintiffs must show that:

(1) they are a member of a protected group;

(2) they either performed a job satisfactorily or were qualified

for a job being sought;

(3) they were disciplined, terminated, or rejected for a position despite having the objective qualifications for it; and

(4) either other employees of another Title VII class were disciplined less severely, or after rejecting an application, the employer continued to accept applications of people who were no better qualified.

These principles make the employers' rationales for their actions highly significant, since reasons must be plausible and consistent. An employer who maintains that the reason for discharge is poor performance, rather than discrimination, will face credibility problems if all the plaintiff's evaluations are highly positive. Although a jury as a whole may rely on legal principles, individual jurors are likely to evaluate an employer's reasons according to their own concepts of fairness. In reality, many cases are decided solely on the jury's idea of fairness.

Proof and Discrimination Suits

Are there ways in which employers can prepare for their potential burden in discrimination litigation? Certain steps may be helpful. Generally, employers are better protected if their decisions are based on objective, measurable criteria. Subjective decisions are more easily challenged as a pretext concealing discrimination. An employer is not well protected if an employee's termination is based on the unsupported subjective statement of a supervisor, such as that the employee has a poor attitude or demeanor, is not a team player, or has poor interpersonal skills. Although decisions based on subjective reasons are not illegal, the more subjective the reason, the easier it will be for a jury to decide that discrimination is the real reason.

A health care employer's documented reasons for putting someone on the fast track may include terms such as "dedication to work" or "good team spirit." If the rationale is based on personality factors rather than on performance, an employer will find it more difficult to convince a jury that the distinction between the favored and the less favored employee is not race, sex, or age. Plaintiffs can characterize such evidence as demonstrating that the favored individual is part of the club because of a difference in race, national origin, gender, age, or disability. This potential vulnerability leads some lawyers specializing in employment law to advocate that management eliminate or reduce subjective factors in their decision making.

Companies that consistently apply a policy of progressive discipline and maintain records of employees' performance and deficiencies are in a better position to defend themselves against discrimination claims than those that do not observe these practices. Clear policies on the nature of unacceptable employee conduct also assist with the burden of proof.

In health care, as in every other industry, there are pressures that tend to favor leniency toward those who are in the decision-making hierarchy of the workplace. If the workplace has the traditional racial composition, favoritism of this kind tends to excuse white males while other groups are held accountable. If highly placed and lower level employees are not treated consistently for the same conduct, lawsuits by minorities and women are bound to raise knottier questions than they would otherwise. A risk manager seeking to protect an organization against liability would do well to keep the necessity for consistent treatment in the forefront of the minds of management.

Affirmative Action

Affirmative action and reverse discrimination embody two concepts that are controversial and require definition. Often these terms are used to represent different concepts in the workplace.

Voluntary Affirmative Action

Voluntary affirmative action plans by employers are permissible if they have the same remedial purpose as Title VII and open employment opportunities for protected groups in traditionally closed occupations. Plans must not unnecessarily infringe on the rights of others. Affirmative action plans must be justified by a demonstrable imbalance in historically segregated job categories. To determine if an imbalance exists, an employer compares the proportion of women and minorities in its workforce to the area labor market, or if appropriate, to the general population. Many employers have affirmative action requirements that mandate the reporting of workplace statistics to government agencies. A review of these available reports allows for an organizational comparison of the racial, sexual, and ethnic composition of the workforce. Since 1989, the federal government has paid its employees at least $87.4 million, mostly for back pay, as a result of equal opportunity lawsuits.

Reverse Discrimination

Reverse discrimination is "discrimination against groups historically favored in employment, such as whites or men." Importantly, reverse discrimination is lawful only if it is pursuant to a valid affirmative action plan.

Sexual Harassment

Sexual harassment law is relatively new, has grown in importance, and has imposed completely new obligations on employers. Specifically, sexual harassment law emphasizes the employer's obligation to anticipate and to prevent illegal behavior. Employers are required to have an explicit policy addressing sexual harassment; a general policy on harassment is not sufficient to meet the employer's responsibility. Generally, an employer is well advised to make efforts to prevent sexual harassment and to address actual cases of harassment. Employer-initiated efforts can reduce liability. Court decisions have found the employer not liable if prompt, effective steps to investigate and stop sexual harassment were taken.

To guard effectively against the risks of sexual harassment, we must understand what sexual harassment means. As defined by the Equal Employment Opportunity Commission, sexual harassment is unwelcome sexual advances, requests for sexual favors, or other verbal or physical conduct of a sexual nature when

- Submission to such conduct is made either implicitly or explicitly a term or condition of employment.

- Submission to or rejection of such conduct by an individual is used as the basis for employment decisions affecting that individual.
- Such conduct has the purpose or effect of unreasonably interfering with the individual's work performance or creating an intimidating, hostile, or offensive working environment.

A nationwide survey of hospitals documented a rapidly increasing rate of sexual harassment charges within the health care industry. Although the vast majority of sexual harassment complaints are made by females, the concept applies equally to males. In addition, sexual harassment may occur between members of the same sex as well as across genders.

Frequently, there is a fine line between sexual harassment, and flirtation or romance. The same behavior can be illegal if unwelcome, or legitimate if the affected person is gratified by the behavior. If that person is displeased by the behavior, and the behavior is repeated, it will generally be considered sexual harassment. Harassment actions run the gamut from the use of seemingly innocuous terms such as "honey" or "babe"; to unwelcome printed material in the workplace such as sexual posters, photographs, or calendars; to physical conduct such as sexual assault or even rape.

Subtleties involved in distinguishing sexual harassment from welcome sexual attention make this issue difficult for an employer to recognize and address.

When confronted by a possible case of sexual harassment, the employer's representative should attempt to determine if the behavior was welcome. If the allegedly harassed individual was pleased to receive sexual attention from the particular person accused of harassment, the attention was welcome. On the other hand, if the individual merely tolerated the sexual behavior and went along with it voluntarily, sexual harassment occurred. Even if the questionable behavior was welcome to the direct recipient, it may offend other persons, such as employee bystanders, who have the right to challenge the conduct.

Two Categories of Sexual Harassment

Aside from determining if the challenged behavior is welcome or not, the employer should be prepared to distinguish between the two basic categories of harassment: quid pro quo harassment and hostile or abusive environment harassment. This distinction is meaningful because the employer's liability for quid pro quo harassment is absolute, while responsibility for hostile environment harassment is less clearly defined. Intriguingly, the same conduct can be challenged as constituting both types of sexual harassment.

Quid Pro Quo Harassment

This type of harassment involves a bargain or exchange of sexual conduct to obtain a workplace benefit or avoid a workplace detriment. Areas of concern for health care facilities include "operating rooms where sexually abusive remarks are exchanged in tense moments; labs, in which hugging and kissing are commonplace; medical staff that have little respect for nurses; and work units where sexual graffiti is present."

A supervisor insists that an employee have sex as a condition of receiving a positive evaluation, a promotion, or a favorable work assignment.

A supervisor threatens to fire someone who will not go out on a date or refuses to reveal details of his or her sex life to the supervisor.

Hostile or Abusive Environment Harassment

This type of harassment is a more difficult concept to grasp than quid pro quo harassment. A 1993 U.S. Supreme Court decision, Harris v. Forklift Systems, Inc., explained the standard to be followed in deciding whether a particular case constitutes hostile or abusive environment harassment: "When the workplace is permeated with `discriminatory intimidation, ridicule and insult'... that is `sufficiently severe or pervasive to alter the conditions of the victim's employment and create an abusive working environment,'... Title VII is violated."

To prove hostile environment harassment, an employee need not suffer any tangible economic loss. Employees can sue their employers for harassment even when they have benefited from the harassment.30 Victims need not show that they suffered psychological harm to make a case. However, hostile environment charges may be more difficult to prove, since subjective interpretations are involved. For example, males and females may have differing notions about what is hostile, intimidating, or offensive.

A hostile or abusive sexual harassment environment occurs when a person writes unwelcome love letters or sends unwelcome gifts to a colleague, when groups of males congregate near an entrance lobby to make unappreciated comments about the body parts of women entering the building, when supervisors brag about their sexual prowess, and when off-color jokes are allowed to continue in the office after employees complain that this conduct makes them uncomfortable.

Since sexual harassment includes so many routine behaviors, how can a health care employer be expected to control such behavior or be held liable for it? Realizing the breadth of the problem, persons learning about the law of sexual harassment for the first time often suggest that employers adopt no-fraternization rules as a means of avoiding illegal conduct. However, laws against sexual harassment do not require employers to adopt no-fraternization policies. Employers are not responsible for stopping all flirtation and romance in a work environment.

Nevertheless, risk managers should make sure their organization takes certain steps in this regard. Employers should have a specific sexual harassment policy indicating that sexual harassment will not be tolerated. This policy should provide that more than one person is authorized to receive sexual harassment complaints. Among the most important steps an employer can take to minimize liability is to ensure that employees and supervisors understand sexual harassment and believe that the company is serious about controlling it.

Stephanie Adams, a regional resource administrator for Burroughs-Welcome Company, sued her employer, charging the company with sexual harassment creating a "hostile work environment and defamation." Five of six assessors evaluating her for a promotion to hospital sales manager were men who "subjectively" rated her "poorly." She was denied the promotion and given menial tasks. Adams was "defamed" when a manager told others that she was demoted because of management problems. She suffered when male colleagues showed a pornographic video at a meeting and had sexually explicit conversations. Other female employees will testify about the "fraternity house atmosphere."

Managers and supervisors should be informed that they may be held personally liable for acts of sexual harassment.

Employers must respond promptly and effectively to harassment complaints. It is essential to investigate all complaints as soon as an employer becomes aware of them.

Any sanctions imposed on harassers should be calculated to bring the harassment to an end.

A prompt, thorough, and effective effort to eliminate harassment may shield an employer from hostile environment liability. Even if the employer's actions do not prevent liability in a particular instance, a credible enforcement program should have a deterrent effect on the workforce. Fear of potentially costly sexual harassment lawsuits has spawned a new cottage industry: A four-part interactive computer course teaches every employee the do's and don'ts of sexual harassment, tests the employees for mastery of the concepts, and awards certificates to those who pass. This education is accomplished at a fraction of the cost of using professional trainers.

The development of sexual harassment law makes it advisable for an employer to take proactive measures to publicize the company's antiharassment stance and to enforce its rules. In addition to legal liability, there is a significant public relations risk. A manager's worst nightmare concerns accusations of sexual harassment in the mass media. Prevention and quick remedial action are the best approaches.

AIDS AND THE HEALTH CARE WORKPLACE

Disability discrimination is a developing area of legal concern. Inevitably, the subject of disability leads to questions about AIDS and HIV in the workplace environment. Because of morbidity and mortality statistics, employers have become increasingly concerned about the effects of AIDS on the workplace. AIDS carries a special set of issues and obligations in the health care context because there are patient-related treatment implications as well as employment concerns.

These obligations stem not only from the Americans with Disabilities Act (ADA), a relatively new statute, but from a variety of other sources as well. Many states have passed legislation prohibiting employers from discrimination based on AIDS or HIV status. A majority of states have passed laws protecting the confidentiality of persons who are HIV positive or who have AIDS.

Obviously, an employer's first question is whether the ADA or other antidiscrimination statutes apply to individuals who are HIV positive or who have AIDS. In discussions about the ADA legislation, Congress debated this question and decided in favor of coverage of AIDS and other contagious diseases. 35 ADA provisions bar an employer from discriminating against an individual with a contagious disease, including HIV, unless it can be demonstrated that the employee poses a direct threat to other employees.

ADA regulations indicate that someone who is HIV positive is not automatically considered a person with a disability. However, individuals who are suffering physical effects are apparently covered. Persons who are HIV positive may fit the definition of individuals with a disability if they are perceived as disabled. Depending on the circumstances, a full range of possible accommodations must be made available to HIV- or AIDS-infected employees. When an HIV-positive employee is a person with a disability, what is the employer's obligation to accommodate that individual? In Cain v. Hyatt, the court found that the employer must accommodate HIV-infected employees by

- Not terminating them during their first AIDS hospitalization.
- Permitting them to take their sick and vacation days at that time.
- Placing them on medical leave until they are able to return to work or until the employer can prove that the situation imposes an undue hardship.
- Additional applicable accommodations include, but are not limited to
- Making facilities used by employees readily accessible to and usable by individuals with disabilities.
- Job restructuring; part-time, modified work schedules; or reassignment to a vacant position.
- Acquisition or modification of equipment or devices.
- Appropriate adjustment or modification of examinations.
- Training materials or policies.
- Provision of readers or interpreters.
- Other similar accommodations for individuals with disabilities.

Prejudice and fear among other individuals in the workplace does not justify an employer's discriminating against those who are HIV positive or who have AIDS. The safest recourse for employers, including health care employers, is a comprehensive program to educate employees. To dispel the myths and rumors, employers can provide employees with scientific information confirming that they are unlikely to contract AIDS through casual contact with someone who is infected. Of course, a health care employer has the added obligation to adopt reasonable protective measures to prevent HIV transmission from patients to employees. Failure to initiate appropriate preventive measures can cause a health care employer to be held liable for negligence. Generally, health care employers must comply with standards promulgated by the federal Occupational Safety and Health Administration (OSHA) to prevent the transmission of HIV. A major controversy among health care employers is whether employees who are HIV positive or who have AIDS should be pre vented from performing invasive procedures. This argument also applies to the private practice of medicine and dentistry. Steadfastly, the American Medical Association (AMA) has refused to require health care professionals to disclose their HIV status to patients before undertaking specifically identified invasive procedures. Similarly, the federal Centers for Disease Control and Prevention recommends leaving disclosure up to each doctor's professional judgment. These standards may change as the law regarding AIDS develops in the legislatures and in the courts.

Workers' Compensation

In a ten-state comparison, the most commonly specified injuries in workers' compensation claims were strains (38%), fractures (14%), ruptures (9%), sprains (7%), and other (16%). By percentage of injuries to the body, the most common workers' compensation claims involved lower back (40%), complex joint (15%), upper extremity (14%), multiple body parts (12%), lower extremity (6%), trunk (6%), head (3%), neck (3%), and central nervous system (1%). About 40 percent of injuries were caused by strain-related jumping, carrying, lifting or pushing, pulling, reaching, or using a machine or tool. Slips and falls (30%) and being struck by falling objects (11%) were next most frequent causes. Almost 63 percent of the cases involved surgery, and 68 percent of the costs were attributed to inpatient care. Workers' compensation costs have grown to $60 billion per year and are projected to increase to $140 billion by the year 2000. From a cost containment point of view, with these statistics in mind, workers' compensation emerges as a topic of increasing importance to risk managers.

Workers' compensation is a social welfare program that exists in every state. Although the programs differ in specifics, the basic concept is constant throughout the nation: Employees who are injured or become ill as a result of an accident arising out of and in the course of employment receive compensation, regardless of fault. This concept of no-fault compensation is fairly new to the

U.S. legal system. Traditionally, the law allowed recovery from another person when that person had caused an injury to someone else. Workers' compensation is an exception to this traditional approach because the program reimburses for medical expenses incurred as a result of the accident and provides limited income to the disabled employee. Typically, the income benefit is one-half to two-thirds of the employee's salary. The program's objective is not to fully compensate the employee for all losses connected with the injury or illness, but to give employees enough sustenance to prevent them from requiring public assistance. In return for these modest, but definite workers' compensation benefits, employees sacrifice the right to sue their employer for their injuries.

Whether the injury is caused by the employee's own negligence, the employer's negligence, or an act of God, the employee is entitled to workers' compensation benefits. Employees are not permitted to waive workers' compensation coverage, choosing instead to sue their employer for a particular injury, or for all injuries. Generally, workers' compensation is the exclusive remedy available against an employer for injuries caused by accidents arising in the course of and as a result of employment. This concept of exclusivity provides an employer with a defense to many actions that employees attempt to bring on the basis of workplace injuries. In Texas, however, employers are statutorily allowed to opt out of the state's workers' compensation system to provide for injured workers' disability needs. About twelve hundred companies are members of the Texas Association of Responsible Nonsubscribers, which began in 1990. Significantly, nonsubscribing firms lose the statutory protection afforded by workers' compensation, leaving them vulnerable to a variety of negligence suits.

Certain exceptions to the exclusivity of workers' compensation are built into most versions of the program. First, if an employer intentionally inflicts injury on an employee, the employee may sue the employer. Intentional acts of the employer are not covered by workers' compensation, since they are not considered to be "accidents" within the meaning of the law. Usually, this exception is confined to instances in which the employer had a "specific intent" to cause injury.

Where a wrong is committed that does not have a significant connection to the work itself, such as defamation and retaliatory discharge, and in some jurisdictions, sexual harassment, a plaintiff may be permitted to sue the employer. Another traditional exception to the concept of the exclusivity of workers' compensation coverage is the private feud that causes injury in the workplace.

Employers may be liable for employee injury if they had actual or constructive knowledge that certain equipment was unsafe and, despite that information, required the employee to do the work, because the job necessitated the use of the unsafe equipment. An injury that is not intentionally inflicted usually is covered by workers' compensation if it arises out of and in the course of employment. This means that the injury and/or illness must occur during the time and at the place of work while the employee is engaged in an employment-related action.

Workers' compensation, as an employee's exclusive remedy against an employer, does not always mean that the individual cannot sue. An employee injured at work by a piece of equipment may have a basis to sue the manufacturer for negligence. An individual who is injured in a contractor's parking lot may sue the contractor for damages.

A small-business owner was outraged at an employee's behavior. He deliberately and intentionally pushed a cart at the employee. Any resulting injuries would not be covered by workers' compensation because the owner took the action with the purpose of causing injury to the employee.

Risk managers are actively involved in controlling workers' compensation costs. Before efforts to contain medical costs, workers' compensation was a bastion of uncontrolled health care expenditures. The cost of workers' compensation insurance soared so high that a number of insurers stopped writing compensation policies.48 Experts maintained that the lack of cost controls had resulted in ballooning workers' compensation costs, in contrast to intensive efforts to monitor health care costs overall. This financial squeeze, along with related factors, motivated states and employers to adopt workers' compensation cost containment measures. These measures include steps to reduce accidents and injuries, and to monitor treatment and administrative costs.

Preventing Accidents and Injuries

Efforts to prevent accidents and injuries focus on safety analyses and safety training. Experts recommend that employers identify areas where injuries occur most frequently and include incidents where injury is possible. Studies indicate that out of three hundred accidents without visible injury or damage, such as slipping on a slick floor, thirty will produce property damage, ten will result in minor injuries, and one will result in a "serious disabling injury." A panel of insurance experts has concluded: "Investigating even minor accidents thoroughly and promptly is the key to preventing more serious accidents and to achieving loss control savings." Lessons learned from lucky near misses can be used to identify and reduce risks.

Employee training is highly recommended on topics such as safe lifting practices, safe work techniques, protective equipment, and safety rules. In some states, legislation requires employers to provide safety education. Training can begin with employee orientation and include continuing refresher courses. Safety committees to review workplace hazards, including committees that incorporate line employees, also are recommended and, in some states, required. An independent audit is one method of assessing safety practices; the audit may be provided by a state agency, the compensation insurer, or a private company.

To prevent injuries, changes in safety rules, work equipment, protective equipment, and job structure may be necessary. From a medical viewpoint, attention should be given to the detection, treatment, and prevention of technology-related work injuries and illness such as exposure to electromagnetic radiation, repetitive use syndromes, ear and eye injuries, respiratory difficulties, and skin disorders. Ergonomics, the process of adjusting the work environment to meet the physical and psychological needs of the workers, should also be considered. Ergonomic changes to reduce hazards can include remedies such as the redesign of work areas and/or lighting or the institution of frequent, short breaks to address a host of work-related problems: VDT (video display terminal) workstation eyestrain, chronic headaches, and fatigue; cumulative trauma disorders; repetitive strain injuries; and stressful postures.

A technological revolution has spawned a litany of computer injuries that focus attention on the need for an ergonomic analysis of the workplace. Typically, the upper extremitiesthe shoulders, arms, hands, and wristsare affected. Common diagnoses include tendinitis, tenosynovitis, ulnar nerve compression, cervicobrachial disorders, and carpal tunnel syndrome. When lower back injuries were found to account for 31 percent of the claims at Western Temporary Service (Walnut, California), at an average preclaim cost of $24,000, the company's risk management office took action. The company purchased therapeutic back supports, each one matched to the individual's anatomy, working environment, and job parameters. Its risk management program includes employee awareness, practice claims management, safety procedures, and training. Through multiple methods, including the use of back supports, the company lowered its workers' compensation costs by $500,000 per month.

Another prevention technique offers incentives for adherence to safe practices. Usually such incentives are monetary and include prizes for periods with no injury. Another way to create incentive is to make adherence to safety rules a criterion included in employee and supervisor evaluations.

Wellness Programs

Wellness programs are an essential component of risk management because they protect the company's most valuable asset: its workforce. In 1980, the city of Glendale, Arizona, placed its wellness program under the director of risk management and used this quote to explain the reasoning for the "preventive maintenance" effort. Glendale's twelve hundred employees and their families receive free annual mammograms, participate in health screenings, and use a wellness center. If employees participate in the wellness program, the city waives the group health insurance deductible, which is $150 for an employee and $300 for a family. Similarly, Coors Brewing Company (Golden, Colorado) operates a wellness center with twenty-four professional staff for its sixty-five hundred employees. Services include cardiac testing and rehabilitation, well-back programs, mammography, smoking cessation, and screening for cholesterol, skin cancer, and blood lipid.

A ten-year study of eight thousand Steelcase, Inc. (Grand Rapids, Michigan) employees confirmed that the average medical cost for an employee with two or more high risk behaviors (smoking, being overweight, being sedentary, consuming alcohol) was 75 percent higher than for an employee who followed a healthy lifestyles. There was a more than $500 difference in average medical cost between high and low risk employees specifically with regard to alcohol consumption, physical health, physical activity, life satisfaction, and age over 45. Steelcase's employees take voluntary health risk assessments, receive a confidential report, and are encouraged to consult with one of the company's health care professionals. Employees at risk are offered preventive activities such as nutrition education, exercise programs, or rehabilitation. If all the Steelcase employees adopted healthy lifestyles, the company estimates a savings of more than $20 million over a three-year period. A compilation of health promotion programs details the activities of many organizations engaged in wellness-type preventive programs.

MONITORING TREATMENT AND ADMINISTRATIVE COSTS

To minimize the adversarial environment that often permeates workers' compensation claims, employees should be informed about this benefit during their orientation. If they lack such knowledge when an adverse event occurs on the job, employees may be frightened and become antagonistic. In addition to assisting with this educational effort, risk managers can be helpful to an employer by developing a program to return disabled employees to the workplace at the earliest possible date. Studies indicate that employees are more likely to return to work if the employer maintains caring communications with the injured worker. Often, the most effective contact is from the employee's supervisor. Sending cards, visiting an employee in the hospital, calling the employee periodically, requiring the regular submission of medical documentation, and providing transitional light-duty assignments all appear to have a salutary impact on an employee's early return to work. Firms could establish an integrated approach to disability management with three goals:

- To reduce the number and severity of work-related and non-work-related injuries and illness.
- To decrease the length of disability associated with such situations.
- To reduce the likelihood of adversarial, and costly, legal encounters with employees.

Financial savings can result from steps to control administrative insurance costs. Risk managers can assist in evaluating insurers by comparison shopping for premiums and by examining insurance company reserves, the amount of money needed to cover open claims. An insurance company that overstates its reserves may overcharge an employer as a result. In states where it is permitted, some employers opt for self-insurance. Some states allow employers to self-insure in combination with a pool of other companies.

Reducing Costs Through Managed Care

Managed care as a remedy for soaring workers' compensation costs is receiving considerable attention. Medical cost management involves proactively administering the medical component of a workers' compensation claim. On the basis of an analysis of 76,612 workers' compensation claims compared with 71,248 group medical claims, the California Workers' Compensation Institute found disparities. Workers' compensation medical care averaged 21 percent more: $954 per claim as opposed to $789 for group medical claims. Furthermore, workers' compensation provided more intensive medical servicesmore treatments, medical procedures overall, and medical procedures per treatment, and a higher frequency of treatmentthan those of group medical care. A poll of four hundred risk managers revealed that 66 percent predicted that by 1999 "all medical care delivered under workers' compensation programs would be through managed care delivery systems." This survey identified six major cost issues:

1. Excessive medical treatments and attendant costs (67%).
2. Litigation over compensation for claims (61%).
3. Inconsistent state regulations (59%).
4. Increases in "difficult to diagnose as work-related" claims (50%).
5. Fraudulent claims (41%).
6. Increases in stress/mental health related claims (41%).

A director of risk management services for Lawley Service, Inc. (Buffalo, New York) was instrumental in initiating an employer-sponsored managed care program. That program included hospital precertification, contracting with the hospital's occupational health services, safety training, back training, a union/management safety committee, utilization review, follow-up with each injured employee, and daily monitoring of claims. Over a three-year period, workers' compensation premiums were reduced by $523,000 and claims dollars by $290,000. Adding $1,869,000 in direct and indirect cost savings, the company averaged $797,333 per year in savings.

State legislatures have been actively working to produce savings in workers' compensation through measures such as elimination of benefits for facial scars that do not affect employability, a requirement that occupationally induced stress result directly from a physical injury, elimination of coverage of voluntary sports or recreation, elimination of benefits for accidents occurring while under the influence of alcohol, limitations on the use of medical experts in legal compensation proceedings, a requirement that claimants pay their own attorney's fees, streamlined hearings, caps on the amounts of reimbursement, and requirements of antifraud measures.

Fraud in Workers' Compensation

Critics of workers' compensation attribute the nonstop rise in expenditures to fraud; one estimate avers that fraud accounts for 25 percent of workers' compensation costs. Employees who receive workers' compensation benefits for false or exaggerated injuries, or who prolong absences that are due to legitimate injuries, may be defrauding the employer and/or the workers' compensation insurance carrier. In addition to possible criminal penalties, employees who defraud their employers face possible dismissal. Risk managers should alert administrators who have disciplinary powers to monitor the workers' compensation program to determine if employees should be subject to workplace penalties for malingering or fraud.

Oregon succeeded in reducing its workers compensation insurance premiums by 23 percent over two years, while doubling payments to injured workers, by implementing many changes in its workers' compensation program, including a major antifraud effort. That effort resulted in prosecution of cases against claimants, physicians, and chiropractors. In August 1993, Pennsylvania's Workers' Compensation Reform Bill took effect, aiming to reduce fraudulent or excessive claims. Antifraud provisions were strengthened, billing for procedures and for an office visit on the same day was barred, utilization review was instituted, and physician reimbursement was capped. Actuaries conservatively estimated the fee-cap savings alone at $300 million, a 10 percent reduction in compensation medical payments.

Employee Assistance Programs

Research studies attest to the effectiveness of workplace health promotion activities in improving employee well-being, in reducing the risks of illness, and in lowering employers' health benefit costs. Employee assistance programs (EAPs) are employer-sponsored efforts to aid employees with personal problems. About 26.6 million

Americans, including the families of employees, are covered by full-service EAPs. Approximately 76 million people have access to more modest EAP services. EAPs have grown by 50 percent since 1992. About 120 large companies provide their own EAP services, but the majority use external EAPs funded jointly by several employers.

EAPs deal with personal problems such as alcoholism, emotional health, family relations, marital stress, mental health, physical health, stress, and substance abuse. Estimates indicate that about 80 percent of current EAP telephone calls are related to substance abuse. There is little research available that assesses the actual costs and benefits of an EAP. Nevertheless, many employers, particularly large ones, believe that their EAP programs reduce absenteeism, decrease on-the-job accidents, increase productivity, and boost morale. In a cost analysis, one company with more than five thousand employees saved as much as $3 million, while a fifty-person firm discovered no identifiable savings.

Employees access EAP services either through voluntary self-referral or employer referral. Self-referrals may account for two-thirds of the individuals who seek aid from full-service EAPs, and about one-third are referred by supervisory personnel who believe they have identified a personal or health problem affecting the employee's performance. EAP records should be treated in the same manner as confidential medical records, and with knowledge of this confidentiality, employees are more likely to seek help.

After an EAP referral, workers in substance abuse or other treatment programs often receive services covered by the employer's health insurance. As more health insurers initiate managed care coverage, the benefits available to employees tend to decrease. The result can be shorter hospital stays and greater use of clinical mental health services that supplement EAP counseling. Importantly, depressive disorders are among the most common in the workforce and seriously affect productivity.

Some experts believe that EAPs can help prevent stress-related lawsuits and workers' compensation claims. In addition to their counseling and referral services, EAPs can train supervisors and coworkers to recognize signs of substance abuse and to confront other employees constructively. In this context, a constructive confrontation involves an approach focused on job performance, not a diagnosis of the employee's problem.

EAPs often are an employer's sole resource dedicated to addressing personal problems as they affect the workplace. Although there is no conclusive evidence of their effectiveness, many organizations now consider the EAP essential to their operations.

Americans with Disabilities Act

The Americans with Disabilities Act of 1990 (ADA) provides broad-ranging protection for individuals with disabilities against employment discrimination. A fundamental provision is the following "general rule":

No covered entity shall discriminate against a qualified individual with a disability because of the disability of such individual in regard to job application procedures, the hiring, advancement and discharge of employees, employee compensation, job training and other terms, conditions and privileges of employment.

If found guilty of violating the ADA, employers face civil damages of up to $50,000 for the first infraction and $100,000 for subsequent violations. What constitutes a disability will require legal and judicial interpretations, since the U.S. Bureau of the Census estimates that 49 million Americans have a disability.

Medicaid and the ADA

Aiming to control the rising costs of Medicaid, Oregon devised an approach bordering on rationing. An ADA analysis concluded that the plan rested "on the premise that the value of the life of a person with a disability is less than the value of the life of a person without a disability." After revision, Oregon eliminated mentioning an individual's functional limitations when considering the medical effectiveness of treatment. This Medicaid discrimination issue still has to be played out.

As with most complicated legislation, regulations, and standards, risk managers can consult available resource material. The article "A Core Collection of ADA Information" provides a guide to resources, and a videotape is also available.

The ADA mandates require employers to consider each person with a disability on an individual basis to determine if the person is capable of performing the job in question. Making a distinction between individuals on a basis other than their ability to carry out a job is clearly not permissible under the ADA.

A bus company's medical standards prohibited persons with hypertension or epilepsy from working as bus drivers. Obviously, the employer's main concern was to lower the risk that sudden heart attacks or seizures would affect a driver, causing an accident. However, a person with controlled hypertension or epilepsy may present only a very remote risk to bus passengers. That risk may be no greater than that of the average person, who may be subject to an unpredictable heart attack or seizure at any time.

In 1955, Herb Ditzel III was diagnosed with a rare kidney cancer, Wilms' tumor, before he was one year old. He survived life-threatening surgery and illness and in 1988 was manager of publications for the University of Medicine and Dentistry of New Jersey (UMDNJ). Almost all of his performance ratings were superior. On January 31, 1994, he was fired for allegedly poor work. Ditzel claimed that UMDNJ fired him on a pretext because it no longer wanted to pay cancer survivors' health insurance. He sued for $4.5 million for violation of his ADA rights.

A disability is defined as a physical or mental impairment that substantially limits one or more major life activities, or a record of such impairment, or being regarded as having such an impairment. Major life activities are defined as "functions such as caring for oneself, performing manual tasks, walking, seeing, hearing, speaking, learning and working." A person is not covered by the ADA merely because a disability prevents him or her from performing one specific job. Any physiological disorder or condition, including cosmetic disfigurement, is included. Mental and psychological disorders, including mental retardation, special learning disabilities, and many forms of emotional or mental illness are also covered.

Psychological Stress as a Disability

A study of about thirty-five hundred people indicated that an employee will be absent from work 3.2 to 9.4 days per year for an emotional reason. Depression and panic disorders (44% each) constituted the largest percentage of these instances. Categories of workers who may file stress claims include the following:

- Replicated family workers regard the workplace as an extended family.
- High achievers expect that maximum effort will be directly rewarded.
- Assaulted superego workers balance alleged unethical tasks with survival and morality.
- Maligned workers need acceptance and feel that supervisors wrongly fault and control them.
- Outcasts are nonconformists who don't fit into the social aspects of the job.
- Constant turmoil workers bring multiple preexisting conditions and conflicts to the job.
- Malingerers believe that the world owes them a living and seek something for nothing.

More than half of the Fortune 500 companies offer programs to assist employees with psychiatric problems. Studies estimate a cost of $3,000 per year per depressed worker in diminished productivity. 87 Psychologists believe that much of the emotional stress on the job can be attributed to a lack of employer awareness.

Once identified, personnel who pose a potential stress liability can be aided by a six-component claim prevention model: an employee assistance program (EAP); job selection and placement programs; concrete personnel policies and record keeping; communication policies regarding employees' job expectations; supervisor training; and a strategy for treating an existing stress claim as a form of valuable feedback.

A Conference Board survey of 121 institutions found that many leading corporations were helping workers meet the needs of their children, parents, or other dependents through non-job-related activities such as providing support for day care, child care centers, emergency child care, holiday and vacation care, and before- and after-school programs.

Exclusions and Other Conditions

Certain conditions that relate to sex are excluded from the definition of disability: homosexuality, bisexuality, transvestitism, transsexualism, pedophilia, exhibitionism, voyeurism, gender identity disorders not resulting from physical impairments, and sexual behavior disorders. Some other conditions that might be considered mental illness also have been omitted: compulsive gambling, kleptomania, and pyromania.

Furthermore, psychoactive substance disorders resulting from current use of illegal drugs are excluded from the definition of a disability. Although alcoholism is a covered disability, employers are entitled to impose the same performance standards on people with alcoholism as on any other employee.

If alcoholism impairs the individual's ability to do the job, the person does not at that time qualify as disabled. About 96 percent of organizations have had direct experience with employee substance abuse, alcohol, cocaine, or marijuana on the job.89 A person under the influence of illegal drugs is not covered by the ADA, but a person who has a history of addiction to drugs but who is not currently using them cannot be excluded from employment.

Personal characteristics are not covered disabilities. Height, hair color, or a preference for a slow pace of work would not be termed disabilities under the ADA.

Essential Functions

If an individual meets the criteria for disability, employers must consider if that person can perform the essential functions of the job with reasonable accommodation. In deciding if a duty is essential, the following specific questions should be asked:

1. Would removing the function fundamentally change the job?
2. Does the job exist to perform a particular function?
3. Are there a limited number of employees available to perform the function?
4. Is the function highly specialized?
5. How much time is spent doing the task?
6. What are the consequences of not requiring a person in the job to perform a function?
7. Are there applicable terms in the collective-bargaining agreement? (Information in the agreement may be evidence of a position's essential functions.)
8. What is the experience of people who currently perform similar jobs or who have performed a job in the past? (Answering this question should involve observation of employees doing the job.)
9. Are there any other relevant factors? Examples include the nature of the operation and the organizational structure. In an assembly line operation, the essential function may be one task only. By contrast, a team structure may require all team members to carry out different functions on a rotating basis.

Although the ADA does not define "essential functions" specifically, there are certain factors to consider in deciding if reasonable accommodation is possible. First and most significantly, the employer should determine if the employee actually is required to perform the particular task. Only those tasks actually carried out are considered essential functions.

Reasonable Accommodation

A Job Accommodation Network survey found that about 67 percent of business respondents stated that it cost less than $500 to meet the ADA mandates; only 4 percent said it cost more than $5,000. Under the law, employees must make reasonable accommodations to enable an otherwise qualified job applicant to perform his or her duties.

Employers must use an interactive process to determine reasonable accommodation. First, they must determine the job's purpose and its essential functions. Next, they must find out the individual's specific limitations and determine if there are barriers to performing essential functions. Employers are entitled to request written documentation of the individual's limitations to support an accommodation request.

Part of the accommodation process must involve a discussion with the employee in question.84 An employer must consult with the individual to identify appropriate accommodation and to assess its effectiveness. Technical assistance may be useful at this stage in the process. A list of possible accommodations from the ADA Technical Assistance Manual enhances a practical understanding of accommodation:

- Making facilities readily accessible to and usable by an individual with a disability.
- Restructuring a job by reallocating or redistributing marginal job functions.
- Altering when and how an essential job function is performed.
- Instituting part-time or modified work schedules.
- Obtaining or modifying equipment or devices.
- Modifying examinations, training materials, or policies.
- Providing qualified readers or interpreters.
- Reassigning the employee to a vacant position.
- Permitting the use of accrued paid leave or unpaid leave for necessary treatment.

- Providing reserved parking for a person with a mobility impairment.
- Allowing an employee to provide equipment or devices that an employer is not required to provide.

Employers need not accommodate employees if such accommodation would mean undue hardship, but the ADA does not define "undue hardship." Factors that should be considered in determining if an undue hardship exists are the employer's size, the resources available, and the nature of the operation. Notices of ADA provisions, including reasonable accommodation, must be conspicuously posted. Medical examinations for employment are prohibited until after a conditional offer of employment is made. Furthermore, medical examinations are permissible only if they are given to all persons in the same job category. In addition, all medical information must be treated as confidential and kept in a separate medical file. Even though the ADA considers alcohol testing a medical examination, the testing is not preempted where it is a business necessity. Courts have supported alcohol testing in regulated industries, safety sensitive positions, and in private sector workplaces. A legal expert contends that "the ball is rolling toward making alcohol testing an accepted part of all workplace substance abuse programs."

During any medical examination following an offer of employment, an employer may ask wide-ranging questions. However, any information obtained during the examination may be used to disqualify an applicant only if there is a high probability of substantial harm to that employee or to others, as documented by current medical evidence. An employee's personal physician may challenge such medical disqualification.

Employment Interview

Many questions commonly asked during preemployment screening are prohibited by the ADA's rules. Whether on a written job application or during an oral interview, the following are prohibited questions:

- Do you have a disability that would interfere with your ability to perform the job?
- How many days were you sick last year?
- Do you have a physical or mental impairment?
- Have you ever been treated for any of the following: AIDS, cancer, diabetes, epilepsy, heart disease, high blood pressure, or any other disease?
- Do you wear corrective lenses?
- Do you take any prescription drugs? If so, what?
- Have you been hospitalized in the past five years?
- Are you currently under the care of a physician or other medical practitioner?
- Have you been treated by a psychiatrist or other mental health practitioner?
- Have you ever filed a workers' compensation claim?
- Have you ever sustained a work-related injury?
- Have you ever been treated for drug addiction or alcoholism?

An interviewer may ask if the applicant can perform the essential or marginal functions of the job, with or without reasonable accommodation. An applicant also may be asked to describe and/or demonstrate how he or she would perform those functions.

If the examination following the job offer reveals a disability, the employer may refuse to hire the person. Importantly, acceptable rationales for not hiring someone on the basis of a disability must relate specifically to the job, must demonstrate why the absence of such disability is necessary to the business, and must show that no reasonable accommodation is possible or that accommodation would impose an undue hardship on the employer. An applicant who poses a direct threat to the health and safety of others may be disqualified from the job:

The employer must show a significant current risk of substantial harm; the specific risk must be identified; the risk must be documented by objective medical evidence or other factual evidence regarding the particular individual;... that a genuine significant risk of substantial harm cannot be eliminated or reduced below the direct threat level by reasonable accommodation. Post-offer medical examinations cannot be used to disqualify someone with a disability who is currently able to perform essential job functions because that disability may cause a risk of future injury.

Suggestions for ADA Compliance

Risk managers can minimize ADA liability by making sure that a written statement of policy on the ADA exists and that it is distributed regularly to all employees. Employers can initiate a review of job descriptions to identify essential functions in advance of any controversy.

Policies on interactions with disabled employees should be evaluated in light of the ADA mandates. Policies and practices pertaining to the medical documentation of physical examinations should be reassessed in view of ADA regulations. If a collective-bargaining agreement exists, it is useful for unions to negotiate a provision stating that nothing in the contract will prevent the employer from complying with the requirements of the ADA. Without such a provision, the act's requirements may very well conflict with seniority stipulations.

Significantly, the ADA compels health care employers to be careful to fit the individual's abilities to the job in question. Risk managers must try to ensure that the ADA provisions are

understood and enforced throughout the organization. By the end of 1994, almost three thousand ADA complaints had been filed with the Justice Department.

Changing Workplace Risks

Workers' compensation remains a major area of concern for risk managers, as attention to wellness and prevention activities, along with deliberations about using managed care providers to render benefits, increases. However, other contemporary problems of the workplace also engender considerable potential liability for health care organizations. Significantly, risk managers must be concerned with reducing claims for age or sex discrimination, wrongful dismissal, affirmative action, sexual harassment, and disability violations.

To have an impact on potential liability claims, the risk manager must be involved with policy development, management and supervisor education, record keeping, analysis of trends and practices in the institution, and following of due process procedures. Employees, including risk managers, have rights that are protected by federal, state, and local legislation and regulations. Health care institutions should be aware of employee rights and observe the letter of the law to avoid the financial drain of liability claims.

5

Patient/Consumer Communications to Reduce Risk

An editorial in the Journal of the American Medical Association commented that "breakdowns in communication between patients and physicians and patient dissatisfaction are critical factors leading to malpractice lawsuits." An earlier Harvard Medical Practice Study found that about 1 percent of hospitalized patients suffer significant harm because of an adverse event and negligence. However, less than 3 percent of these patients or their families instituted a malpractice claim. Logically, risk managers need to examine why patients sue, observe the therapeutic milieu, listen to patients, and use communication skills. Applying appropriate communication skills to informed consent procedures and to patient education can result in meeting patient expectations and satisfying the customers. Satisfaction also raises the burgeoning issue of grading health care providers via "report cards." With these aspects in mind, it is relevant to remember that some communication difficulties may be the result of changes in the health care industry.

A NEW AGE IN HEALTH CARE

Health care providers seem to be adopting the culture of corporate America as they utilize the commercial creativity flowing from the nation's business schools. Critics of the "medical-industrial complex" argue that the profit motive is inappropriate and corrupts the entire health care industry. With competition in mind and the business approach touted as the answer, supporters declare that they will have to go out of business if they don't keep pace. If health care is a business, it is logical to assume that not all health care consumers are patients. Is it time to relabel the patient a customer?

Medical City in Dallas, Texas, is part of a mall-hospital that has twenty-two retail stores including a dry cleaner, a bank, an auto mechanic, a bookstore, an optician, a clothing store, a pharmacy, and several restaurants. There are two atria with water fountains and marble floors with bright lighting and airy spaces.

Insured customers/patients may pay little out-of-pocket money for health care. Some people have the attitude that the insurer's money is being spent when health care resources are used. However, health care is not subject to the usual business/customer relationship. Does a health care customer ultimately reign supreme? As César Ritz, the famed luxury hotel magnate, stated: "Le client n'a jamais tort." If health care is a business and the customer is never wrong, why is there a need for malpractice insurance?

Why do Patients/Customers Sue?

In talking about rude physicians, Dr. Sidney M. Wolfe of the Public Citizen's Health Research Group stated: "A doctor can't get away with being a technical whiz and an interpersonal jerk." This quote was a reaction to an American study concluding that doctors are more likely to be sued if a patient feels they are rude, rush visits, or fail to answer questions.9 A plethora of additional litigation rationales are identified in Medicine on Trial, "the appalling story of ineptitude, malfeasance, neglect, and arrogance." Using professional literature, authors from the People's Medical Society, a voluntary association primarily of nonphysicians, cited evidence and expert testimony related to abuse of patients. An investigation in England of why people sue doctors highlighted four familiar themes as reasons for litigation:

- Concern with standards of care: Both patients and relatives wanted to prevent similar incidents in the future.

- A need for an explanation: People wanted to know how the injury happened and why.
- Compensation: People wanted compensation to cover actual losses, pain, and suffering or to provide care in the future for an injured person.
- Accountability: People believed that the staff or organization should have to account for their actions.

An editorial in The Lancet rephrased the rationales into blunter, if skeptical, language: "Suing the doctor: altruism, naked truth, or recompense?" using anecdotal reports from Action for Victims of Medical Accidents. Examples of specific incidents indicate that the underlying issue is still communication, or the lack thereof.

More than five hundred potential plaintiffs in malpractice litigation were interviewed In a study of four risk factors: (1) being kept informed by provider; (2) rapport with provider; (3) availability of provider when needed; and (4) referral when needed. These litigation risk factors were related to eleven medical specialties, as well as dentistry and nursing. Patients felt that none of the thirteen provider groups kept them well informed. Obstetrics, family

"After the death of my grandchild, the obstetrician said by way of an explanation, `It was just one of those things.' That's not good enoughpeople need more than thatI hope they [my son and daughter-in-law] get the answers they need."

"They [the doctors] have admitted negligence, they have offered compensation, they want to make amendsbut they won't give me an apology`Yes, we did it but we're not sorry!' sums up their attitude."

practice, and pediatrics were rated highest for attaining rapport with their patients; nursing, orthopedic surgery, emergency medicine, and radiology were the worst. Emergency medicine physicians and pediatricians ranked as most available, and nurses were rated as least available. When patients felt that a referral was appropriate, all the providers were rated poorly except for internal medicine, pediatrics nursing, and neurosurgery. More than half (53%) of the potential plaintiffs griped, frequently in irate terms, about a poor relationship that existed with the health care provider even before the alleged negligence incident. Researchers concluded that "miscommunication between patient and provider is clearly a major contributor to calls received by attorneys."

In New York City, the Health and Hospital Corporation decided to spend at least $1 million in a mass media campaign to recruit 300,000 Medicaid patients into a managed care entity. If the multiyear goal is achieved, the MetroPlus Health Plan would gain $60 million a month. MetroPlus's advertising slogan is "We Really Care" and reflects praise for city hospitals documented in marketing studies. This publicity blitz aims to attract Medicaid patients, who often receive second-class treatment at private health care facilities. Professional literature is replete with references confirming that the synergistic interaction between curing and caring yields a more satisfied patient and/or customer. If a caring physician is so important to patients, it is understandable that patients, in conjunction with physicians, would sue a managed care organization to keep their preferred doctors from being deleted from the specified providers. This litigation risk factor emanating from patients is known as "deselection" and entails alleged antitrust and consumer protection violations.

Syndicated columnist Ann Landers commented on lawsuits for damages that address a diverse range of issues: injury from a cup of hot coffee, bleeding to death while undergoing cosmetic surgery, exposure to secondhand cigarette smoke defined as a form of battery. With possible litigation risk factors so directly correlated to the consumer/patient/customer trilogy, what can providers do to reduce the risk? How can risk managers assist health care providers in this endeavor?

Observe, Listen, and Communicate

Malpractice researchers identified four types of communication problems present in more than 70 percent of plaintiff depositions: (1) deserting the patient; (2) devaluing patients' views; (3) delivering information poorly; and (4) failing to understand patients' perspectives. These communication problems require health care providers to listen and talk to patients and to do so in a nonnegative manner. In a study of 160 adults, Lester and Smith19 demonstrated that the use of negative communication behaviors by the physician increased litigious intentions. Participants were shown two videotapes of office visits to a physician. In each videotape, the patient had an identical complaint, and the physician made the same diagnosis and performed identical treatments. The difference was the communication behavior of the physician.

Positive communication: Physician behavior included eye contact, a friendly tone of voice, smiling, shaking hands, appropriate praise, information presentation and requests for information, acknowledgment of verbalizations, and a five-minute twenty-five-second encounter.

Negative communication: Physician behavior included no eye contact, harsh and clipped tones of voice, criticism, nonsmiling expressions, no friendly physical contact, no praise, minimal shared information or request, and a two-minute two-second encounter.19

Fiesta agrees that words and attitude are important aspects of positive patient communication that establishes rapport and reduces liability. After an adverse event, Fiesta recommends an apology to the patient and family, without admitting negligence. Such apology is set forth as a matter of good manners, common sense, and an extremely important risk management tool.

To decrease the risk of a malpractice suit, Husserl suggests that effective communication is a powerful risk management tool. Two complementary communication models, known as E4 and F2, incorporate psychological, sociological, and behavioral aspects of medicine.

F2 involves the traditional interview tasks of finding the problem and fixing it. Initial letters of the E4 model specify the communication skills engage, empathize, educate, and enlist. These communication skills decrease the likelihood of malpractice suits and improve patient outcomes and greater patient compliance.

Engaging the Patient

Engaging the patient results in improved diagnostic ability, an understanding of the patient's perspective, and the development of a physician/patient partnership. Owen urges providers to listen to what is not said, by observing body language, voice inflection, appropriateness of complaints, and nonverbal responses to questions. Physicians tend to interrupt patients within 18 seconds after the initial complaint. When appropriate, the doctor should ask the patient, "Is there anything else you would like to talk about?"

Three skills aid in securing information: Knowing terminology: Medicine has its own language, and providers must adapt their words to the level of the patient with appropriate questions and explanations. In addition, the cultural background of the patient must be integrated into the terminology. Taking the funnel approach: Encourage the patient to communicate freely during the interview. Follow up with closed-ended questions designed to garner specifics and to organize the data.

Bridging the information: Acknowledge everything the patient said and explain which symptoms are most important or pertinent.

Displaying Empathy

Empathy can be communicated verbally and nonverbally. Patients can be greeted by name, preferably while they are still fully clothed. Avoiding inhibiting behaviors, such as sitting behind a desk or holding and reading a medical record, improves rapport. To show acceptance, for example, the doctor might say, "I understand how important it is for you to get back to work." Although a display of empathy generally elicits a positive response, providers must balance their concern for a patient's emotional needs with objectivity. If a patient feels that the physician has heard and understood their aches and pains, that individual is likely to confide in the provider. By displaying empathy, the health care provider lowers patient anxiety, increases compliance, and achieves higher levels of patient and provider satisfaction.

Educating the Patient

A random survey of the health-promoting behavior of 1,262 people revealed that a large percentage of Americans need to be educated, ideally by their health care providers, about maintaining good health. Nearly seven out of ten adults (68 percent) exceeded the recommended weight range for their age, sex, and body type. Only 37 percent exercised strenuously for twenty minutes or more at least three days per week. Overall, the "Prevention Index" of twenty-one health-promoting behaviors was only 65.6 out of a possible 100. "Consumer information is the most basic of all consumer rights," according to an American Association of Retired Persons publication that suggested opportunities and recommendations for lightening the load. Health care experts contend that an informed consumer is the key to quality, cost, and competitiveness. If people exit a provider/patient encounter without having had their questions answered, the result is anger and dissatisfaction. An angry, dissatisfied patient may certainly be a lawsuit waiting to happen. While information desires vary among patients, anticipating and answering basic general questions about procedures and outcomes will meet the information needs of most patients.

Enlisting the Patient

Noncompliance with therapeutic regimens is more the rule than the exception. Obviously, if harm results to the patient, litigation risk factors arise. Five communication techniques can improve adherence to the physician's instructions and reduce the risk of lawsuit:

1. Arrive at an agreed-upon physician/patient diagnosis through open discussion.
2. Keep the regimen as simple as possible.
3. Give the patient written instructions in understandable language.
4. Motivate the patient with benefits, personal goals, and individual ability to achieve them.

5. Discuss potential risks, possible side effects, and costs.

These E4 and F2 communication models are inexpensive, flexible, and applicable to all health care encounters. As a risk management tool, effective communication becomes a powerful tool to reduce litigation and improve patient satisfaction.

COMMUNICATION SKILLS AND MALPRACTICE HISTORY

Most cases of patient dissatisfaction stem from deficient communication on the part of medical care institutions and providers, rather than from patients' personality quirks. Relating this fact to the choice of an injury prevention approach or a human relations approach gives risk managers reason to reflect. It has been suggested that the malpractice problem is essentially a human relations problem and that greater attention to the human components is the only sure solution. Communication is a basic human component.

In a poll of seventy thousand readers, Consumer Reports identified five conclusions critical to the physician/patient relationship:

1. Physicians' communication skills were faulted as poor.
2. Physicians did not discuss the side effects of prescriptions.
3. Patients with chronic diseases were the most dissatisfied.
4. Female physicians performed better in terms of caring, communication, and thoroughness.
5. Patients were noncompliant when communication was poor.

The article told patients to ask crucial questions about the problem, the diagnosis, the prognosis, the diagnostic tests, medications, treatments, side effects, lifestyle changes, and preventive actions. The following specific guidelines for patients in encounters with physicians suggest a proactive communication skills strategy for risk managers:

1. Be prepared. Plan the visit. Bring a list of problems.
2. Bring memory aides such as a notepad or small tape recorder.
3. Reserve time to talk. Request no interruptions.

4. Clear up uncertainties. Ask the physician to repeat, to define, to use diagrams.
5. State your doubts. Ask for alternatives.
6. Ask to see your medical chart.

Investigators examined the relationship between patients' opinions of their physician's communication skills and the physician's malpractice history. This study, which included physicians and 2,030 of their patients, revealed a complex relationship. Women and better-educated patients gave higher ratings on communications and explanations to physicians with fewer claims. In contrast, men and lesser-educated patients rated physicians with more claims higher on these two dimensions. Patients gave higher ratings to general surgeons and obstetrician/gynecologists and poorer ratings to orthopedists and anesthesiologists. In conclusion, the researchers stated, "Physicians must learn to adapt their communications to the individual variations in their patients' intellectual and emotional needs." This leads to an exploration of the risks associated with informed consent.

Consent, Informed or Otherwise

"The subject of informed consent is to a hospital risk manager what the concept of a black hole is to an astronomer." Risk managers should advise physicians that informed consent is an unequivocal, nondelegatable duty. Consent implies a discussion of all the elements. As comprehensive as the informed consent process seems, the patient is not entitled to the entire body of medical knowledge.

An expanded checklist, marketed under the name PREPARED®, helps physicians cover the essential points that enable patients to make informed decisions. Guidebooks and videotapes augment the checklist where each letter in PREPARED® is associated with a discussion point.

In McGeshick v. Choucair, a federal appellate court in Wisconsin said that the doctrine of informed consent was meant to apprise a patient of risks inherent in a proposed treatment. It did not require that a physician provide a patient with all the knowledge he may have regarding the patient's condition or all other possible methods of diagnosis.

Kapp proposed expanding the informed consent concept to allow the patient to decide about the provider's "defensive medicine" practices, thereby shifting the decisions about "unnecessary" medical tests and procedures from the physician to the patient. A New England Journal of Medicine editorial commented on defensive medicine: "There can be no doubt that fear of litigation drives many physicians to wasteful styles of practice."

Misconceptions of providers may blur their perceptions of informed consent and lead to increased risk situations, as indicated by some of their typical quotes:

"Patients don't want a lot of information. It only makes them anxious."

"If patients want to know more, they will ask."

"I know what's best in this situation."

"This patient needs and wants me to make the tough decisions."

The Basic PREPARED? Checklist

Recommended Procedure, Plan, or Prescription.

Reason for the recommendation.

Expectation of preventing or reversing the harm stated in terms of the patient's reason for wanting the procedure.

Probability of achieving the patient's expectations.

All reasonable alternatives to what has been recommended.

All significant risks associated with what has been discussed.

Direct and indirect expenses associated regarding the recommendation and alternatives.

An informed collaborative decision.

Regarding the content of what a physician tells a patient, the California court decision in the Arato v. Avedon case instigated informed consent debates.

(1) Patients are generally ignorant of medicine.

(2) Patients have a right to control their own body and thus to decide about medical treatment.

(3) To be effective, consent to treatment must be informed.

(4) Patients depend on their physicians for truthful information and must trust them (making the doctor/patient relationship a "fiduciary" or trust relationship rather than an arms-length business relationship).

In reviewing this case, Annas felt that the court ruling was "an affirmation of information sharing and patient-centered decision making in the context of a physician-patient relationship based on trust." Nonetheless, Annas argued that existing law and good medical practice required that the critically ill patient be told the success rate of the proposed treatment relative to survival, as well as to the anticipated quality of life. He declared that the issue is not whether to tell, but how to do so. In American immigrant cultures, certain immigrant groups saw such directness as being cruel and bypassing family involvement. Nevertheless, patients and/or significant others must be given adequate information to make an informed decision. A related informed consent issue concerns people consenting to participate in experimental research therapies.

Miklos Arato had cancer of the pancreas, underwent surgery to remove the tumor, and died about a year later. His family sued, claiming that the physicians breached their duty to obtain informed consent by failing to tell the patient the statistical data about his projected life expectancy. Had the patient known, he would have foregone costly therapy and gotten his finances in order.

Informed Consent in Experimental Research

Does misinformed consent take place in research experiments? Federal regulations mandate that eight key elements be included in the consent forms:

(1) details of the research study;

(2) any reasonably foreseeable risks;

(3) likely benefits;
(4) alternative treatments;
(5) extent of confidentiality;
(6) rules governing compensation;
(7) a contact point for further questions in the event of research-related injury; and
(8) a note indicating the voluntary nature of any participation and the ability to withdraw.

Rarely do informed consent guidelines mention an investigator's potential conflict-of-interest financial disclosure to patients. La Puma and Kraut recommend that the prospective research participant ask the investigator a blunt question: "How much do you get paid if I volunteer?"

People with chronic hepatitis B received fialuridine in an experimental study. Patients were told that the drug caused the virus to "disappear completely" and was well tolerated. Participants were not told that an earlier research study had shown that patients still remained HBsAG positive and that 75% of the participants had had adverse reactions. Patients were not told that the purpose of the study was to test drug safety and that there was a risk of the drug worsening underlying liver disease and other symptoms. Five patients died in this experimental research.

Types of Informed Consent

Emergency situations when the patient is unable to give consent have led to several alternatives to informed consent: deferred consent, compassionate use, implied consent, consent at hospital admission, and waiver of consent.

In deferred consent, consent is given after the individual enters into the research study, and it is not real consent. Compassionate use without informed consent applies in emergency and/or life-threatening situations for which recognized treatment is available. Implied consent, a similar concept, is based on the rationale that a reasonable person would give consent in an emergency.

In recognition of the difficulty in some cases of obtaining informed consent prospectively, facilities may seek a waiver of consent. Health and Human Services permits the waiver of informed consent, provided that:

(1) The research involves no more than minimal risk to the subjects;

(2) The waiver or alteration will not adversely affect the rights and welfare of subjects;

(3) The research could not practicably be carried out without the waiver or alteration; and

(4) Whenever appropriate, the subjects will be provided with additional pertinent information after participation.

FDA regulations are akin to emergency situations:

(1) The human subject is confronted with a life-threatening situation necessitating the use of the test article;

(2) Informed consent cannot be obtained from the subject because of an inability to communicate with, or obtain legally effective consent from the subject;

(3) Time is not sufficient to obtain consent from the subject's legal representative; and

(4) There is generally no alternative method of approved or generally recognized therapy that provides an equal or greater likelihood of saving the life of the subject.

Problematically, health care providers may apply liberal innovative definitions of regulatory wording to explain a waiver of informed consent.

Potential payoffs from improved informed consent can be substantial in terms of compliance, outcomes, and satisfied patients. If informed and educated patients have more realistic expectations, they are less likely to be disappointed and less likely to sue. Risk managers might do well to promote patient education activities. In addition, risk managers should assure periodic physician and house staff education regarding informed consent, to reduce potential liability from misunderstandings and ineffective communications with patients.

Managing Risk Through Patient Education

A professional conference on communicating risk to patients suggested that risk information should be (1) provided in writing, (2) tailored to the patient, and (3) prioritized by the health care provider. A review of patient education in the health care industry concluded that "patient education is good patient care and good business." An analysis of twenty-five patient education programs found that for every dollar spent, the institutions saved an average of $3.50.46 In addition to saving money, patient education can influence whether or not litigious situations arise.

Barriers to patient education from the physician's point of view include lack of time, lack of adequate reimbursement, provider forgetfulness, physician doubt, and the effects of the provider's personal life. Computer programs allow physicians to generate inexpensive customized patient handouts to deal with drug information, health risk appraisal, diet planning, anatomy, and the question "What's wrong with me?"48 Electronic data links allow physicians to monitor the patient's health automatically and to provide proactive care to individuals with problems such as asthma, diabetes, heart ailments, high risk pregnancy, and kidney failure. Providers can help patients become medication risk managers, actively participating in their own care, by following these guidelines:

1. Encourage patients to keep a list (medication log) of their medications, their over-the-counter nutritional supplements, and/or other remedies.
2. Remind patients to tell providers about allergies and/or sensitivities.
3. Remind patients to tell providers how they take their current medications.
4. Encourage patients to be active partners in care by asking the name and purpose of medications.

5. Explain how to prepare each day's medications in advance and to review and check them.
6. Encourage patients to examine medications for size, color, shape, and dosage form.
7. Remind patients to ask questions before any intervention.
8. At discharge, verify patients' understanding of medications by asking questions.
9. Advise patient to select a single pharmacy and to know the pharmacist.

According to Kinnard,51 nurses classify patients into six categories of people who are likely to sue:

Patients who take notes and write everything down.

Patients who have a lawyer in the family.

Patients who are lawyers, accountants, or other professionals.

Patients with certain injuries or illnesses (e.g., head injuries, backaches).

Patients who have serious injuries or illnesses.

Patients who always want to know more.

Patient education offers an opportunity to prevent the patient from becoming dissatisfied, disappointed, and/or enraged. Robert White, director of claims and loss prevention for the Physicians Protective Trust Fund, appraised the situation bluntly: "Patient rapport and good documentation are the only two things that matter in loss prevention." Relative to documentation, Cordell devised a streamlined form to document the patient teaching that was being done but not being charted. Providers can check off appropriate boxes or add brief comments in three areas: educational assessment, educational goals, and knowledge or skill criteria to be met by discharge. Each item is dated and initialed when taught.

Consumer Information Strategy

To provide information on choice and utilization of health care services, the federal Health Care Financing Administration (HCFA) created the Consumer Information Strategy (CIS). This service is intended for Medicare and Medicaid beneficiaries and for care providers, and seems to combine patient education and informed-consent principles. Using modern communication and education techniques through the CIS, the HCFA aims to help beneficiaries:

- Stay healthy, by encouraging them to take full advantage of preventive services that have been proven effective.
- Understand their health care provider and treatment options and execute their preferences.
- Make the best and most informed health care choices for their own individual health care needs.

A foundation supported by pharmaceutical firms urged improved patient education and suggested that the minimal information to be provided by the physician should include the name and dosage of the drug, and its purpose and benefits; instructions on how to take the drug properly; any special precautions regarding age, sex, occupation, or concurrent medications. Patients should be warned about the probability and seriousness of any adverse effects and advised on actions to take if problems occur.

Patients' Rights

Do patients have any rights similar to the usual consumer/ manufacturer/retail store relationship? Toward that end, the American Civil Liberties Union (ACLU) published a guide to the rights of patients. Annas discussed the patients' rights movement, informed consent, human experimentation, medical records, confidentiality, organ donation, malpractice, living wills, refusal of treatment, and how to use medical and law libraries. 56 Regarding risk management, Annas pointed out that risk managers should educate health care personnel about the issues of patients' rights and patient safety to benefit patients generally. European countries have also identified the rights of patients.

During the health care reform debates on managed care providers, the AMA proposed the Patient Protection Act. Goals of the act were to ensure due process for patients and doctors, to provide up-front information for patients, to allow physician input into managed care plan standards, and to ensure a quality-based selection process for physicians. Dr. James S. Todd, executive vice president of the AMA, explained why the patient protection bill was needed: to provide people with a list of exactly what the insurers will and will not pay for; to give clear instructions on whom to call before seeing a doctor; to give patients survey information on how other patients feel about the health plan; and to detail a choice of plan options. Although the AMA's proposal received bipartisan legislative support, there were critics. A Group Health Association of America statement responded, "The Patient Protection Act is a disingenuous name for what is a provider protection act."

Access to the information in the federal National Practitioner Data Bank (NPDB) could allow consumers to see which physicians have been sued and/or disciplined by professional boards. U.S. Congressman Ron Wyden contends, "At the very least, consumers have a right to know which health care providers they should avoid or ask more questions about." Believing that the data may be misinterpreted, the AMA opposes public disclosure, while the Public Citizens' Health Research Group favors disclosure, so that "the public can be warned about a potentially dangerous practitioner."

After a series of hospital mistakes in Florida that seriously harmed or killed patients, the Association for Responsible Medicine was formed. This patient advocacy group urged state legislators to force disclosure and to impose criminal penalties on physicians and hospitals. Legislators responded and proposed a Patients' Right to Know bill.

Patient education leads directly to the topic of patient satisfaction, again integrating the rationales for lawsuits: communication and informed consent.

Satisfying the Patient Stops the Suits

Patient satisfaction may be a measure not of what actually happened during the physician/patient encounter, but more of an individual's perception of what took place. Critics of patient satisfaction as an evaluative measure argue that patients lack the scientific background to evaluate care, that patients' health status may make them incapable of judgments, that patients don't have a comprehensive grasp of their care, that providers and patients have different goals, and that definitions of quality care vary greatly. With these conflicting views and vagaries in mind, studies identify three measures of health care that consumers value:

- Science of medicine: technical competence, knowledge, and skills to resolve the problem.
- Art of care: interpersonal, expressive, and communicative attributes of "caring" for the individual.
- Amenities of care: comfort, courtesy, privacy, and promptness in the setting in which care is rendered.

"Satisfied patients will heal better, complain less, be more likely to return, and less likely to sue." A marketing professor at a business college advises that the quality of care provided and the level of patient satisfaction are emerging as the core of many marketing strategies in health services. Strategic marketing by health care providers should aim to establish, in the minds of consumers, that their institution's service quality and customer satisfaction is the "best in the world."

To achieve that lofty "best" status, a thirty-four-chapter, four-hundred-page book, reminiscent of high-powered sales manuals, takes providers through a step-by-step approach to prove that patient satisfaction pays. Four key elements are identified for a patient satisfaction effort: "The customer is the reason for all your efforts. Without commitment, you will achieve nothing that is meaningful. You must know your patient's expectations to satisfy, manage, or exceed them. Service demands continuity through daily attention and continual improvement." Payoffs include a reduced risk of a malpractice suit and greater profitability, in addition to improvement in referrals, compliance, productivity, collections, and efficiency. Medical Economics reported that "more than two hundred Texas physicians who have never been sued for malpractice credit their flawless records to positive patient relations." Why are positive patient relations important? Joel, a former president of the American Nursing Association, unflatteringly described the health care provider environment as one where "people feel intimidated, overwhelmed, and victimized as they try to muddle through a mean-spirited delivery system." She recounted that customers "encounter unjustified paternalism, heavy-handedness, and confusing explanations." Patients can react violently to a provider's behavior.

Dr. Marcus Edelstein, a Brooklyn (NY) ophthalmologist, was shot and seriously wounded outside his office by a disgruntled patient. Mike Lombard said he had been treated three years earlier and was dissatisfied with the care he had received.

Patient Expectations and Patient Satisfaction

As expectations often have not been met, Freed asserts that society has become very dissatisfied with medical technology's cost and ineffectiveness. Public expectations of medical technology must be tempered by the following three considerations: (1) Medical technology does not behave by itself. (2) The ideology underlying medical technology does not operate independently of the availability of resources. (3) The expectation that medical technology is guided by an objective, omniscient medical establishment needs to be redefined. Medical technology, just like the health care system, no longer can meet every expectation of society. Initially, medical technology can satisfy consumers, but it bears the liability brunt when the technology fails. For example, Dow Corning Corporation was forced to file for bankruptcy after thousands of women who had received silicone breast implants filed lawsuits for injuries.

Conceptually, explanations for patient satisfaction can fit into discrepancy, fulfillment, and equity theories. These three theories measure differences between a patient's desires and experiences, between rewards desired and those received, and a consideration of a balance of inputs and outputs. Regardless of the theories about patient satisfaction, in 1994 a National Research Corporation national survey of ten thousand households ranked twelve characteristics for a satisfaction report card. The results:

- I had some tests done and I would like to find out my test results.
- I want the doctor to prescribe medications or refills for me.
- I would like the doctor to write a letter or fill out some forms for me.
- I want something to be done to relieve my physical discomfort or symptoms.
- I would like to be referred to a specialist or other doctor for treatment of my problem.
- I want the doctor to do something or have some tests done to find out what's wrong.
- I would like to tell the doctor my ideas and concerns about my problem (what I think my problem might be, what I think caused it, or how it's affecting my life and family).
- I would like to know more about my problem (what the name of my problem is, what caused it, what I can and can't do while I have the problem, whether it will get better or get worse).
- I would like some advice about how to stay healthy (diet, exercise) or about some personal health habits (how to lose weight, stop smoking, control my drinking).
- I want to tell the doctor about problems I'm having taking my medications on time.
- I would like to know more about my medications (how they work, what are the possible side effects).
- I want to tell the doctor about side effects or problems I think are caused by my medications.
- I want the doctor to make some changes in my medications (type, amount, schedule).
- I want something to be done to relieve my emotional discomfort (nerves, stress, worry).
- I would like help for some personal family, marriage, or emotional problems I'm having.

- I want to talk with the doctor about increasing or decreasing how often I come to the clinic.

SATISFACTION AS A RISK MANAGEMENT TOOL

Abeln assumes that consumers view the quality of their care on the basis of their own values and preferences. To the point, she contends that ensuring patient satisfaction does provide an edge in managing the risk of medical negligence claims. According to Abeln, consumers look for providers who quickly recognize a commonsense nursing care approach that uses four strategies for meeting, and even exceeding, patient expectations:

Percent Satisfied,[a] by Type of Health Plan[b] Variable

	Market Average[c]	Traditional	Hmo	Ppo	Medicare
Overall satisfaction	56%	55%	64%	50%	41%
Overall quality of care	70	74	69	71	60
Medical care outcome	65	69	65	64	57
Recommend doctor	87	90	84	89	78
Complaints and problems	73	74	73	70	71
Access to specialty care	60	70	53	53	41
Ease of seeing choice of doctor	61	75	50	52	46
Out-of-pocket costs	42	34	60	35	32
Claims forms/paperwork	61	57	75	55	44
Distance to doctor's office	58	60	60	55	54
Making appointment	58	61	57	57	54
Waiting to see doctor	44	47	45	41	38

a Satisfaction combines "completely satisfied" and "very satisfied" ratings.

b Researchers classified coverage as customers gave the name of their plan:

Traditional health plan is indemnity fee-for-service.

HMO includes IPAs, Medicare HMOs.

PPO includes insurer-designated plans.

Medicare is primary provider. Does not include Medicare HMOs.

c Market average is total satisfaction for all four types of health plans.

Customer Satisfaction with Health Care

Don't just assess your patients' needs; reassess them.

Try to exceed your patients' expectations.

Recognize that you own the problem, even if it's not your fault.

Remember that patients are health care consumersand like all consumers, they want good service.

A professional management consultant advocates a patient-centered practice to achieve patient satisfaction. Three aspects of care quality on the part of the provider are identified: technical (clinical skills); humanitarian (caring people skills); and transmissible (responsiveness and enthusiasm). All three elements can be measured by patient satisfaction surveys. Risk managers should help devise questionnaires and cooperate in surveys to investigate dissatisfaction issues in specific services or with particular providers. Once the dissatisfactions and potential liabilities are identified, risk management activities should be initiated to alleviate the problems.

With reference to older patients, satisfaction in initial medical encounters revealed positive associations with the length of the encounter, the physician's engagement with the patient, the provider's use of questions worded in the negative, shared laughter during the encounter, physician orientations to the visit, and physician satisfaction. Furthermore, there was a positive relation between the quality of the physician's questions and topics raised by the patient, physician support on questions raised by both the patient and the physician, and provision of information to the patient on topics raised by both the patient and the physician.

Responding to the market influences in the health care industry, factors such as patient satisfaction, communication, informed consent, and patient education have led to the concept of "report cards" for consumers.

Grading Health Care for Consumer Report Cards

Health care providers can be rated in a similar manner, with a "report card" that helps consumers make informed choices about a provider's reputation and about disenrolling in a particular group. A report from the Massachusetts Health Care Purchaser Group did exactly that. Sixteen health plans were compared on a grid for six clinical indicators with five symbols ranging from better than average to worse than average for their 1992 performance. Measurements included mammography, prenatal care, cesarean section, hypertension, asthma (adult and child), and mental health (admissions and days). Similarly, Health Pages, a consumer magazine, rated twenty managed care providers in Sarasota, Florida; Milwaukee, Wisconsin; and in the St. Louis, Missouri, area. Criteria included the rate at which the plans perform childhood immunizations, PAP smears, cesarean sections, eye exams for people with diabetes, and mammographies.

Report card measurements by the providers include clinical and administrative performance variables such as mortality rates for surgery, immunization rates, cancer survival rates, patient satisfaction, and claims experiences. Presumably, consumers would use these report cards to choose health care providers with the best performance for the least cost. Although report cards could pose a threat to health care businesses, the president of the Group Health Association of America, the nation's largest managed care association, wholeheartedly endorses the evaluation concept.80 State legislative governing bodies also generally approve, and since 1991, California, New York, and Pennsylvania have released report cards to the general public about certain hospital services provided in their states. With assistance from federal agencies, Oregon aims to build a better report card.81 After a typographical error misled people into believing that there was a list of "death hospitals," Florida issued an updated corrected version of their report card.

On a voluntary basis, the Joint Commission on Accreditation of Healthcare Organizations (JCAHO) offers performance reports, for $30 each, on providers accredited by them. Eventually, report cards will be available on more than eleven thousand providers, including hospitals, nursing homes, clinics, surgical centers, home care agencies, and mental health units. Entities accredited by JCAHO will receive a numeric score from 0 to 100 based on twenty-eight categories ranging from medication use to dietary services to patients' rights. Comparison figures indicate how other institutions measure up. Separate scores are provided for areas such as patient care functions, service providers and staff, environment and safety, organizational leadership and management, and department-specific requirements. According to the JCAHO: "The new reports are designed to tell consumers not only how providers have scored in a given category... but to give the information in a useful, easy-to-understand format."

Although it has been difficult to define the quality of health care, most experts now agree that assessing quality includes measuring attributes related to three variables:

- Appropriateness: providers giving the right care at the right time.
- Accessibility: patients being able to obtain care when needed.
- Acceptability: patients being satisfied with care.

These attributes are measured using indicators that represent (1) the structure of careresources and organizational arrangements in place to deliver care; (2) the process of carephysician and other provider activities carried out to deliver the care; and (3) the outcomes of carethe results of physician and provider activities. Outcomes are the most difficult to interpret, and "research has not clearly demonstrated correlations between some commonly used measures of structure and process and desirable outcomes."

It is commonly accepted that a board-certified physician provides better care than a non-board-certified physician. However, an Office of Technology Assessment review of seven studies indicated that "no one has proven that the patients of board-certified physicians have better results than other patients."85 Clinical factors and patient characteristics such as age or prior health status could affect the results significantly. "Risk adjustment" methods may be necessary to rectify the outcomes. Alarmingly, risk adjustment systems have not been perfected yet. A review of the literature reveals that "risk adjustment systems may not be able to predict whether patient characteristics or poor quality of care is the reason for a poor outcome."

No matter what attributes are used in health care report cards, the data will not be comparable unless the performance indicators are standardized. Under the aegis of the National Committee for Quality Assurance (NCQA), the Health Plan Employer Data and Information Set (HEDIS 2.0) emerged.86 More than sixty indicators are included in HEDIS 2.5 that describe performance in five areas: quality, access and patient satisfaction, membership and utilization, finance, and health plan management activities. These indicators include:

- Childhood immunization rates, low birthweight rates, and asthma inpatient admission rates.
- Number and percentage of primary care physicians accepting new patients.
- Percentage of members who are "satisfied" with the plan, according to health plan survey information.
- Membership enrollment and disenrollment information.
- Frequency and average cost of certain high-occurrence, high-cost procedures.
- Inpatient utilization rates.
- Compliance with statutory requirements.
- Descriptive information about provider recredentialing.
- Financial liquidity.
- Premium trend information.

Administrative databases and medical records constitute the primary sources of information for the report cards. These sources might be inaccurate, incomplete, or misleading. Administrative data are designed to speed accurate and timely payment to providers; limitations in such a database may be that it is (1) incomplete because information about a patient's condition or the results of services rendered required for report card indicators are not collected; (2) misleading because numerical codes are used to represent undefined diagnoses, procedures, and treatments; and (3) inaccurate because data have been entered carelessly.

In medical records, providers may knowingly or unknowingly enter incorrect information or neglect to document certain information. A variety of health care professionals can type, write, or scribble clinical and non-clinical notes on the voluminous pages of a medical record. Trained personnel are required to retrieve report card indicators from medical records. This data collection process can be expensive and time-consuming and still not deal with the underlying problem of misleading or inaccurate information.

HEDIS measures will be revised and clarified continuously. An ongoing NCQA study involved twenty-one different health plans serving 9.6 million members in a pilot project to standardize how they specify, calculate, and report a subset of HEDIS 2.0 measurements for report cards. Analysis of the data from this study found that no single plan was a high performer in all areas. All of the participating plans showed individual strengths and weaknesses. "A clear lesson from the project is the need to rapidly improve health plan information systems, and in particular, clinical information systems."

Investigators analyzed forty studies of patient judgments on general practice care. Measurements dealt mainly with the accuracy of the practitioner's professional performance, humaneness, informativeness, and availability. Minimal data were collected on effectiveness, mutual trust and cooperation, accountability and autonomy, and continuity of care. Managed care organizations use patient report cards to award financial incentives to their physician providers. A medical journal asked if patient satisfaction report cards have turned up the heat on doctors.

In contrast to the emphasis on the quality of care, consumers do have enlightening opinions regarding a choice of a health plan. A national public opinion poll of 750 adult health care consumers selected the most important information in choosing a health plan: choice of physician (49%), benefits package (20%), patient satisfaction

(13%), easy access (10%), and standardized quality measures (9%). More than half (55%) said that they considered a provider's reputation among friends, neighbors, and coworkers more important than satisfaction surveys and standardized quality ratings. This consumer attitude was reinforced in a JCAHO marketing investigation using a focus group. Participants revealed that "a gap existed between the kind of information employers and policy makers consider important and what consumers want." In view of the diversity of professional desires, the views of policy makers, and the stated needs of consumers, report cards could raise troubling questions. A commentary in American Medical News was filled with speculative queries and exclamations related to patient satisfaction polling. Pointedly, Adelman highlights the dilemma: "Will the surveys turn an encounter with a doctor into a popularity contest? Will doctors have to be good-looking, dressed in suits and smiling?"

Strategic Caveat

Risk managers must navigate the boundaries separating professionals, politicians, policy makers, and consumers in the communication quagmire. Specific occurrences such as the following require immediate attention: an increase in malpractice claims, a decrease in cash flow, a diminished reputation of the organization in the community, an increase in the movement of patients to other providers, a decrease in provider participation in the plan, the aftermath of quality assessment reviews, unfavorable information collected for data banks, and the impact of varied surveys. Strategically, all the vested interests have to be satisfied while the financial stability of the institution endures. Risk management activities must be integrated into the responsibilities of personnel in quality assessment, education, medical records, and administration. Scientific report card measurements will be required to meet professional demands and to assure reimbursement. If the consumer opinion polls are reliable, a combined, cooperative effort will be required to maintain a bottom line profitability and to enhance the institution's reputation in the community.

6

Financing of Risk and Insurance

Risk managers must identify each of the many areas of risk exposure and determine how best to manage their financial consequences. Identification of these various exposures is an organized process that includes using insurance company loss data, in-house adverse incident reports, Occupational Safety and Health Administration (OSHA) reports, complaints from guests and visitors, financial statements, accreditation and licensure inspections, and professional periodicals. A matrix of incidents can be distinguished and coordinated based on variables such as employee shift, location in the facility, type of incident, and outcome. Once a pattern is recognized, appropriate solutions can be identified and implemented. Cooperation of the administration and the medical staff is essential for effective implementation. Any risk reduction plan also includes the education and training of medical care personnel, executives and administrators, nonprofessional staff, and volunteers in the procedures for controlling loss, for reducing incidents of patient injury, and for identifying and avoiding potentially injurious events and taking appropriate corrective actions.

When formulating a plan, risk managers must carefully evaluate the potential loss in terms of frequency of adverse events and severity of financial consequences. This analysis is central to the choice among the alternatives for dealing with risk exposure.

Frequency refers to the number of times an event occurs and can be gauged in relation to any relevant period of time or areaper patient day, per discharge, per year, per procedure or in the emergency room area, per operating suite, or per intensive care unit. Areas of the organization should be studied individually and comparatively over periods of time. Typically, the most frequent adverse occurrences are of a minor nature, such as the loss of eyeglasses or false teeth. One of the difficulties in gathering accurate data is that many very minor occurrences may go unreported. However, an "occurrence screen" procedure that requires employees to report specifically listed events may yield increased data about minor incidents. In essence, the "occurrence screen" is an integration of quality assessment and risk management.

Severity refers to the cost of the loss in dollars. Financial payouts can range from insignificant to catastrophic. A risk exposure that is infrequent and catastrophic can be one of the most difficult and time consuming to assess. Losses of that nature are difficult to plan for because their likelihood always seems remote and the size of the loss may distract attention from preventing other more prevalent, though less costly, potential losses.

Daniels and Lynch argue that all reasonably predictable losses should be retained and covered by the health care organization using financial ratio analysis, actuarial review, and cost benefit analysis to determine the optimal risk retention. This disciplined methodology to calculate the amount of risk to self-insure or retain should replace the notion of applying unscientific "rules of thumb" in the decision-making process.

A facility that suffers from a combination of high frequency and high severity financial losses will generally find itself facing high costs and limited options unless the administration makes significant changes in the scope and manner in which it operates. For organizations willing to undergo rigorous self-examination and implement necessary changes, however, a 1993 survey of almost seven hundred members of the Risk & Insurance Management Society showed risk management budget reductions of 22 percent and staff reductions of 11 percent. To achieve this type of cost reduction, all levels of management must address the critical problems. According to a Wall Street Journal article, U.S. firms are spending less to guard against risk for the first time in years.

Five reasons were given for these lower costs:

(1) development of more efficient ways to finance the cost of insurance,

(2) improved safety,

(3) utilization of managed care to cover health insurance benefits,

(4) effective back-to-work programs, and

(5) changes in workers' compensation laws.

The first addresses insurance cost, and the other four address loss prevention and reduction. In essence, the larger companies found ways, including insurance, to affect real savings. Until risk managers consider all innovative alternatives, meaningful cost savings cannot be achieved and/or sustained.

Options in Implementing a Plan

Traditionally, the purchase of insurance has been the key ingredient in a risk management program. Insurance is an effective alternative and can be implemented quickly; the cost is fairly predictable, major exposures are usually covered, and the insurance company offers services that complement its programs. However, the cost of insurance tends to be the highest among all alternatives. The cost is high because insurance companies pool premiums from all participants and use the pooled monies to pay claims. Exposures not covered by the insurance carrier are not the carrier's responsibility or concern. If such events occurred, the facility could still be exposed to substantial financial loss. In addition, part of the cost goes to insurance company expenses and profit.

In addition to fully insured guaranteed cost programs, there are other various "loss sensitive" plans available from insurance companieswith deductibles, retrospectively rated plans, and dividend plans, to name a few. Loss-sensitive plans may respond to a good loss experience with return of a dividend to reduce the premium.

Before choosing any insurance plan, the organization should undertake a historical analysis of claims and premiums for a period of five years, if possible. This analysis should consider the time value of money and loss costs, prospectively and retroactively.

One of the techniques in analyzing the potential financial loss in terms of frequency and severity is "benchmarking." A benchmark is comparable to a standard or norm. Flores concluded that "benchmarking should be... a problem identification tool, not a performance indicator." His company utilized the frequency rate published by the U.S. Bureau of Labor and Statistics (BLS) and each operating plant was compared to BLS statistics. Certain statistics predicted financial losses that could be incurred as a result of medical care, employee time off, and productivity reductions. Each accident has ramifications beyond the immediate incident. With the benchmarks in use, improvement was possible because a measurable standard existed, allowing management to evaluate performance.

Insurance Options Based on Premium Size

An anticipated premium level can be determined by the size and complexity of the health care organization or facility. In addition, the premium depends on factors such as payroll, physical plant, number of beds, utilization statistics, specific programs, and other variables. Health care consultants commented on the risks of ignoring insurance risk management and the factors contributing to the resulting uncertainty: "Health care insurers face financial risks when they assume liability for the difference between premium revenues and their estimates of future claims costs for a group."8 Although there is no definitive rule that states when each alternative is feasible, the greater the premium, the more alternative risk financing methods are available.

In this exhibit, the number of types of plans that can be considered increase as the premium levels advance. Each of the common alternatives to a conventionally insured program is indicated in the exhibit. In a small hospital with a premium of $200,000 to $450,000 for workers' compensation alone, many alternatives are available. However, if the premium is at $50,000for example at a home health agency then fewer alternatives are realistically available; certainly self-insurance and captives are excluded. This example refers primarily to workers' compensation and cites options regarding captives, self-insurance, self-insured groups, large deductibles, and retrospectively rated plans.

In addition, at higher premium levels the cost becomes less predictable as the cost savings opportunity increases, because in larger insurance programs the costs are driven by losses rather than by premium payments.

Captive Insurance Companies

A single owner captive is an insurance company owned solely for the benefit of an individual health care organization to insure its own risks, whereas a multiowner captive is established jointly by more than one health care organization of like size and exposure for the purpose of insuring the risk exposures of the participating institutions. In exchange for the policy, the health care organization is charged a premium reflecting the charges to issue the policy and to pay the claims.

Typically, the domicile of the captive insurance company is Bermuda or the Cayman Islands because the capitalization costs and assets needed for operation are much lower there than those required in the United States, and there are certain tax advantages.

Self-Insurance

When a health care organization assumes the risk of a loss within its own financial structure, it is considered self-insured. Simultaneously, the health care organization develops a plan to accumulate reserve funds in escrow to pay for any loss that occurs. Most organizations combine an escrow account with an "excess insurance" policy purchased from a commercial carrier. Up to a specified dollar amount, the self-insured organization pays the claims, and the insurance carrier picks up the losses in excess of the designated expenditure level.

Pools, or Self-Insured Groups

A group of similar health care organizations may pool their funds to finance a trust fund that is used to pay claims. This single entity trust fund develops, adopts, and follows a formal financial plan to accumulate funds with which to pay the cost of loss-producing events of the members of the pooled self-insurance fund. These pools are attractive to small or medium-sized organizations, which may not be able to self-insure economically and have the advantage of group pooled experiences. Pools are not legal in all states.

Large Deductible Insurance Policies

These insurance contracts provide "coverage" from the first dollar. Insurance companies handle the claims and then assess the insured up to the agreed-upon deductible. This is not self-insurance, but it helps the insured meet the requirements of statutory coverages (for example, workers' compensation) without having to be a licensed self-insurer. The amount assessed tends to be $50,000 or more; thus it is considered "large deductible."

Retrospectively Rated Dividend Plans

For retrospectively rated plans, the loss experience of the current year is evaluated. If there are few losses (a "good" experience), there is a potential credit or dividend. If the losses are high (a "poor" experience), there is a potential debit to be assessed. At the initiation of the contract, the rating formula is agreed upon and usually includes commissions, taxes, assessments, loss adjustment expenses, and administrative costs.

Considerations in Choosing an Alternative Insurance Program

In any review of the financial consequences of these alternative insurance programs, the philosophy of the health care organization's management should be considered. If the health care organization is conservative, a gradual approach should be used. Additional considerations involve portability, flexibility, services, and protection.

To assist in structuring any contemplated alternative insurance, costs should be evaluated.

Portability

For multistate organizations or networks, the portability feature is extremely important. If the insurance coverage is statutory in nature, such as workers' compensation or automobile liability, the ability to operate with a single insurance plan program in multiple states outside of conventional insurance is limited. In self-insurance, the states require the insured to become licensed in each state for statutory coverage and to comply with all state laws. An alternative is to be "fronted" by a licensed insurance carrier, which would issue the policy and then reinsure with the self-insured program. Captives and their variations also can be used to address portability.

Flexibility

Many financial programs, including some insured programs, require letters of credit or a bond to guarantee that the claims will be paid by the insured. Typically, the letters of credit must be collateralized. Often, programs require that each policy period have its own letter of credit or bond until all claims are liquidated. This makes changing insurance carriers more difficult. Additionally, there should be a consideration of whether there is flexibility when services are purchased individually.

Services

Evaluation of the claim handling, investigation, claim payment, and loss control services is critical. Except for full insurance programs, the health care organization has an opportunity to choose the company, or third-party administrator, to service its claims or to perform loss control services.

Choosing a Third-Party Administrator

Since claim costs are key in all programs, an effective preloss and postloss plan must be in place. Factors to consider in choosing a third-party administrator include:

Experience: Line of coverage, type of business, and references should be provided.

Staffing: Consider the number of claims per adjuster, turnover, presence of RNs or nurse practitioners on staff, and geographic location.

Technology: Are they fully computerized? Can they tie into the facility's system? Is there a twenty-four-hour reporting system?

Procedures: Is there twenty-four-hour turnaround? Is the reporting system cumbersome? Can they modify for each facility? What are their short term and long term case management procedures?

Costs: Per-claim and flat-cost projections should be analyzed. Third-party administrators should offer a proposal that provides service until the agreement is severed and adjust claims until they are closed.

Protection: Since all the risk financing alternatives involve elements of insurance, the contractual obligations set forth affect the scope of coverage. These include the definition of retention, how the limits are applied per event or per occurrence, and what the limits are. In addition the financial strength of the carrier, claim practices, and reputation should be evaluated. A comparison among all competitors should be comprehensive.

Structure of Risk Exposure Management

A risk manager has the task of identifying exposures to loss and managing the potential effects of those exposures. This is a dynamic process that must be systematically approached on a daily basis. The nine key areas of exposure are:

Property: structures, their contents, and goods in transit.

General liability: injuries to third parties arising from operations.

Professional liability: injuries to third parties arising from medical incidents.

Automobile liability and physical damage: usual automobile coverage.

Employee/volunteer injury and illness: occupational accident and disease, as well as disease or injury transmitted to family members.

Directors and officers liability: management errors and omissions.

Fiduciary liability: financial injury to others arising from an employer's acting in a fiduciary capacity. Most arise from employee benefit plans.

Aircraft liability: injuries sustained while loading or unloading aircraft.

Crime: employee dishonesty and theft.

The risk manager must understand each area of exposure. Obviously, this is not a solo task; other professionals in administration and finance will be needed and should be available to assist in assessing the risks.

Property

For many institutions, physical property is the largest asset. Before examining insurance programs or alternatives, property insurance underwriters usually require basic information about buildings, contents, electronic data processing equipment, valuable printed material and documents, unusual property, personal property of others, boiler and other machinery, and business income. A property insurance contract should be for "all risks" of physical damage. Without this stipulation, the carrier can decline the loss if it is specifically excluded from the contract. Another way to insure property is on a "named peril" basis. This requires the insured to identify perils before the loss and to link the exposure to the financial loss when an adverse event occurs. A court ruling in Garvey v. State Farm Insurance 11 clarified the issue:

In determining whether insurance coverage exists under an "all-risk" homeowner's policy, when loss to an insured property can be attributed to two causes, one of which is a nonexcluded peril, and the other an excluded peril, the courts are to find coverage only if the nonexcluded peril is the efficient proximate cause of the loss, rather than finding coverage whenever a nonexcluded peril is a concurrent proximate cause of the loss.

In large organizations, the insurance valuation of various types of property can be a very difficult task. An initial review has to identify the types of property to be protected and the various risk exposures to be insured against. The following sections address each type of property individually.

Buildings

Valuation of the physical plant is primarily a function of the total square footage and the cost per square foot. Generally, the cost per square foot is based on the type of construction, local labor costs, and safety features such as automatic sprinklers. A facility's engineering department should be able to provide the analysis of square feet by fire division, by the age of each part of the building, and by how the building is protected against loss. Factors to be considered are: "(1) specifications, (2) materials, (3) labor, (4) overhead, and (5) profit."12 With this information, an engineer from the loss control service or insurance company can usually determine the value of the building. However, the insurance company appraisal is not guaranteed by the company. Prudent risk managers will consider an independent appraisal. Risk managers need to select insurance coverage based on replacement cost or depreciated value in the event of loss. A survey of business owners revealed that although 76 percent thought they had purchased replacement cost insurance coverage, only 9 percent actually had such coverage.

Contents

Since the contents of buildings are so variable, this type of property is difficult to value, especially in a large facility. In part, the reason for the difficulty is that the amount of materials purchased and deleted is hard to track. In addition, either the replacement cost or the original cost must be determined and verified. Physical contents of buildings include materials such as furniture, fixtures, and equipment. Disposable contents include inventories of medical supplies, spare parts, and housekeeping materials. Typically, the valuation of these contents is set at replacement cost. An appraisal company can help place a value on contents. However, special contents may prove more difficult to insure.

ELECTRONIC DATA PROCESSING (EDP) EQUIPMENT: HARDWARE, SOFTWARE, AND PCS

Electronic data processing is the "nerve center," if not the "brain," of the health care organization. Every part of the organization is affected, and EDP is vital in a risk management program.

Valuation difficulty stems from the rapidly changing technology, which causes obsolescence in a short period of time. Data processing managers must constantly calculate the cost of purchasing state-of-the-art equipment. As the organization becomes more dependent on computers, there is a greater exposure to loss. Furthermore, the types of losses the computer can suffer compounds the insurance coverage difficulty.

A computer data system is best insured on a specific EDP "floater" to the policy. This floater addresses the specific valuation and causes of loss associated with computer equipment.

Valuable Papers, Books, and Documents

This risk includes the re-creation of critical documents such as medical records. Loss control companies can make a predisaster assessment of the cost to restore valuable papers, books, and documents. Of course, a simpler alternative is to maintain a duplicate set of records.

Experience indicates a special need to protect records that have been requested by a plaintiff attorney or government agency. If these records are scheduled to be used in a hearing or trial, they must be complete and unaltered. Risk managers should consult with the director of medical records concerning the state of the art in record protection and retrieval.

Unusual Property

Some general examples of unusual property are items of sophisticated technology, of extremely high value, of an essential nature, or of intrinsic value; high technology communications equipment; movable property; and exhibits. Specific examples include magnetic resonance imagers, linear accelerators, paintings and collectibles, satellite dishes and mobile radios, and equipment on ambulances. Property that emits X-ray radiation or has the potential of nuclear exposure should be insured for contamination and toxic remediation of the occurrence site. After these items are identified, they must be appraised appropriately. If the property is essential, a replacement or backup must be locatable and available prior to a loss. Unique property should be insured separately on an inland marine "floater." This coverage is usually broader and easier to adjust in the event of loss.

Personal Property of Others

This category consists primarily of leased equipment and the personal property of patients, guests, employees, and volunteers. Risk of such loss can be controlled by not allowing patients to keep highly valued personal property on the premises. Guests and volunteers should be alerted to protect their valuable belongings. Employees should accept full responsibility for their own goods.

Boiler and Other Machinery

Boilers or pressurized machinery that is located in the basement or the main building represents a potential catastrophic exposure. Proper maintenance and an effective backup system are an absolute necessity. If the boiler is insured separately from the general property coverage, the property carrier and the boiler carrier should sign a "joint loss agreement."

This agreement resolves any discrepancies between the two carriers in the event of a loss.

Pressurized machinery is frequently underinsured, because an inspection service is the primary focus and the law does not require other equipment to be inspected. In most cases, insurance is the best way to meet this risk exposure because of the relatively low rates and the low frequency, high severity nature of boiler losses.

Business Income

An organization can suffer a loss in business income as a direct consequence of a physical property disaster. In addition to a general loss of revenue, losses include continuing operation costs, extra costs (overtime, rented telephones, heaters, etc.), and opportunity costs. These potential business income losses should be identified and quantified in a written disaster plan.

Additional Property Exposures

Risk exposure related to construction activities and in connection with rental property are common liability risks for health care organizations. The initial process is to design the structure and to hire a contractor.

Model contract forms contain specific wording regarding "hold harmless" and "assumption of liability" conditions. Such wording transfers the risk to the architect and the contractor. "Builders Risk" is the insurance policy that addresses this situation and sets dollar limits based on the completed value of the construction.

Along with the building, off-site property, property in transit, contractor's equipment, and installed equipment must have proper coverage.

Since either the contractor or the building owner is responsible, the construction agreement should indicate acceptable coverage limits for automobile liability, workers' compensation, and general liability, naming the facility as an additional insured. If this is not done, the health care organization will be responsible for supplying the protection.

When renting property from another entity, the terms of the lease should delineate who is responsible for damage or injury. In many leases, a partial demise of the premises does not necessarily decrease the rent.

General Liability

A health care organization faces exposure to loss from various areas arising from the law of torts. A tort is a failure to act in a responsible, prudent manner. This standard of prudence constantly changes as society changes, a dynamic process that must be constantly monitored. Risk managers should strive to be continuously aware of laws and court decisions that affect the health care industry. When a tort is committed, various subdivisions of the law can impose a penalty. Jurisdiction is determined as follows:

Common law: judicial interpretation of law.

Statutory law: legislative acts.

Civil law: suing another for damages.

Criminal law: societal punishment for intentional violations of law.

Contract law: violation of written or oral agreements.

Civil actions are the most common actions taken against health care facilities. To be awarded damages, a plaintiff must show negligence on the part of the defendant. Costs for the health care institution involved with any civil action may be divided into at least five categories:

Settlement or judgment: Three awards may be determined: general, noneconomic loss such as pain and suffering; specific, such as medical bills or lost income; or punitive, such as punishment for acts considered reckless or unusually harmful by the courts.

Defense costs: Defense costs may exceed the settlement and may include lawyers' fees, court costs, transcription fees, and various other legal costs.

Loss reduction: These are the costs to change work practices to avoid future losses.

Morale: Continuous losses cause employees to question work safety, the professionalism of the health care facility, and the management. Thus, the institution may need to spend money to boost morale.

Opportunity costs: When a facility takes too long to decide on new projects or abandons them altogether, the opportunity dissipates and incurs costs.

Although criminal actions can have ramifications of tremendous proportion, they are typically uninsurable. In some cases, unintentional criminal acts can be insured. Risk managers can address only imputed liability to the organization. Internal controls and procedures can deal with this type of exposure. Loss of public or consumer confidence as a result of real or perceived safety concerns can lead to a significant loss of business and income.

Risk Transfer

Organizations generally arrange for some form of insurance, either primary or excess, to cover the catastrophic cost potential associated with general liability. Key terms and conditions in the insurance contract need to be fully examined. For a health care organization, the following will typically be included in the contract, and should be applied per location: bodily injury and property damage; products/completed operations; fire damage legal liability; employee benefits liability; and patients' property. General aggregate coverage applies to everything except products/completed operations/employee benefits. Medical payments should be endorsed in the policy to cover guests and volunteers, on and off the premises. Professional liability limits are usually stated separately on a per loss or aggregate basis.

Insuring Agreements

Insuring agreements state that the insurance company "will pay those sums that the insured becomes legally obligated to pay." This means that the law imposes an obligation on the insured. Further, the insurer responds to bodily injury or property damage inflicted upon a third party. Even if the lawsuit alleges uninsured acts along with a covered act, the insurance company has a "right and duty to defend" the health care organization. Inclusion of an insured act obliges the insurance company to defend the entire lawsuit. However, the insurance company reserves the right to settle or to defend. Exclusions enumerate the coverages specifically taken out of the contract, such as work-related injuries, pollution, aircraft, and automobile liability. Personal and advertising liability in the general liability contract covers offenses such as libel, slander, invasion of privacy, and false arrest. When allegations affect a loss of reputation or loss of employment status, the employee may claim that unfounded slanderous or libelous remarks of various insureds caused the termination.

An ice cream manufacturer produced a contaminated product, and a settlement in the resulting lawsuit of $24 million was reached with the U.S. Food and Drug Administration. This firm supplied its own defense because the primary general liability carrier and excess carrier denied coverage. A court ruled that the carriers must pay the policy limits, but not the cost of the defense. An appeals court decided that the insurers had breached their duty to defend. It said that the insurers were contracted to defend the entire action, even though some allegations might be out of the scope of coverage.

Because of the dynamic and complicated legal structure of a health care organization, the "named insured" can include the entity, its owners or active directors, officers and stock-holders, employees, and real estate managers. A conditions section of the policy outlines the "named insured's" duties, rights, and responsibilities and the rights of the health care organization under the contract. Failure to properly review the conditions could mean restriction or denial of coverage.

Professional Liability

Professional liability coverage can be written either as an endorsement or as a separate contract. To avoid "gray areas" in the event of a claim, the general liability and the professional liability insurance are often written by a single carrier. Liability coverage is triggered by a "medical incident." This term is explained in the definitions section of the policy and should include at least the following four types of liability:

Liability from finding by an accreditation survey, review board, or committee.

Liability arising from any and all services provided or not provided by an insured or someone for whom the insured can be held liable.

Liability from the dispensing of drugs and supplies.

Liability from any and all postmortem procedures.

These liabilities can result in "injury," but bodily injury is not a requirement for coverage. If physicians are included in the program, dollar limits can be applied per location or per provider. Provided that a legal liability exists, the duty to defend still applies.

A "consent" provision in an insurance contract relates to whether or not the insurance company needs the insured's consent to settle a claim. This clause obligates the insurance company to pay up to the covered amount of any pretrial settlement or posttrial judgment. If the insureds refuse to settle, they are personally responsible for any judgment amount in excess of the proposed settlement. This option can cause a tremendous personal liability to the health care provider.

Liability insurance differentiates between "occurrence" and "claims made" coverage. "Occurrence" policies cover all injuries that occurred during the policy period, regardless of when they were reported. "Claims made" policies cover injuries reported during the policy period that occurred after the retroactive date stated on the policy's declaration page.

An advantage of an occurrence policy is that it will cover all injuries during the policy period until the agreement is exhausted. A disadvantage is that medical malpractice claims may be made many years after the event. Any awards resulting from such claims are applied against dollar limits that seemed adequate at the time the insurance was purchased, which may be woefully inadequate at the time of settlement. Occurrence limits should be negotiated with the realization that their financial adequacy may be tested twenty years later.

Automobile Liability

Health care organizations can use conventional automobile liability insurance to provide coverage for vehicles. Only vehicles licensed for Without having been properly notified of a lawsuit resulting from a complicated birth, a hospital changed its insurance coverage to a claims made policy. The incident in question had occurred prior to the retroactive date of the new insurance. Solely on the basis of the dates of coverage, the carrier denied coverage. In its defense, the hospital relied on the fact that the carrier knew that the hospital had poor risk management procedures. road use qualify for coverage. Service vehicles used solely on the premises are covered under the general liability policy. Unless the organization has an automobile fleet that generates enough premiums to justify alternative risk techniques, it is not cost effective to go beyond conventional insurance. Auto liability is statutorily required, and evidence of financial responsibility must be documented.

A business auto policy has several sections. In all states, auto liability is mandated, and some states require uninsured motorist and personal injury protection. Auto liability is offered on a per occurrence basis with no aggregate limit. A large emergency ambulance fleet has a much greater exposure to severe loss than does a fleet of autos for executives. Automobile physical damage is an optional coverage that can be purchased for any vehicle.

Employee/Volunteer Injury and Illness

Workers' compensation is statutorily required in all states. This insurance policy is composed primarily of two coverage parts. Part A affords statutory benefits as allowed by state law. This policy covers medical payments, indemnity, and legislatively mandated benefits. Part B insures employees not included under part A and covers injuries to family members arising from the employee's injuries. In a health care setting, part B is critical coverage, since a disease could be transmitted from employee to family members.

Litigation regarding injury and illness of employees and volunteers is increasing on the basis of two legal arguments:

(1) Dual capacity "means that the employer can be held liable for supplying the means to incur the injury in the course of doing business." For example, an employee is injured mowing the lawn while using a lawn mower manufactured by his own employer.

(2) "Third party over" means that an employer has improperly instructed an employee on how to use a particular product. If an employee is injured while using the product and sues the manufacturer, in turn the manufacturer enters the employer as a codefendant in the lawsuit. Health care organizations, in some states, may purchase coverage "ex-medical," which allows the organization to provide the required medical services.

Experience modification is another factor that must be reviewed. Experience modification is an actuarially determined premium factor that applies either a debit or a credit to the premium. A mistake, such as an overstatement of an insured loss, can result in unnecessary premiums. Loss information and the workers' compensation experience data work-sheets must be reviewed on a periodic basis. In a fully insured program, the procedure takes four steps:

1. A claim is reported to the insurance company by the employer.
2. An insurance company adjuster receives the claim and sets a reserve. This reserve represents the estimated gross severity of the claim and is called an incurred loss.
3. Incurred losses are reported to the state workers' compensation bureau.
4. On the basis of the first three of the previous four years, the workers' compensation bureau makes calculations. Earned premiums and incurred losses are used to determine the experience modification. Other factors in the formula include a loss limitation and frequency.

Risk managers should check the state laws regarding the reporting of small claims. If legal, small claims should be paid directly to the employee by the employer. This will keep claim frequency down and reduce overall costs. In fact, any cost controls allowed by law should be implemented immediately.

Directors and Officers Liability

A ranch foreman was seriously injured and left with a permanent partial disability. Unable to return to physical activity, he refused to be retrained, despite strong academic and mental abilities. A district court denied him a lump sum payment for permanent and total disability, finding that the benefit was only economic. An appeals court upheld the denial, on the basis of his unwillingness to be retrained.

Significantly, risk managers should be aware that "D&O insurance is the only coverage that is triggered solely by an action against an individual" of the health care institution. Since D&O contracts are not standardized, all contract proposals must be scrutinized carefully. Risk managers should be aware that a D&O contract does not include the coverage normally found in a general liability policy. There are additional distinctions between D&O coverage and general liability insurance:

Typically, D&O insurance does not "pay on behalf" of the insured any legal defense costs. The insured must pay the settlement and legal costs first and then wait for reimbursement.

D&O insureds employ their own legal counsel, and the insurance company has no "duty to defend." Since there is no duty to defend, the company can "allocate" defense cost and coverage based on the allegations in the lawsuit. These allocated legal defenses can be costly and cause an additional lawsuit against the company.

A D&O contract covers only nonphysical injury, and aims to protect against management errors and omissions. An action that alleges pain and suffering is different from a suit that claims wrongful acts not involving bodily injury. Lawsuits must be evaluated carefully with the aid of legal counsel, because allegations can be categorized into the general liability and/or workers' compensation policy, or into the D&O policy, depending on the type of claim.

Beneficiaries of a hospital association established to provide benefits to railroad employees sued the hospital board of trustees to prevent the dissolution of the association.

Trustees of a charity sold an old building used to house the homeless and invested in a newer, better building. They were sued for wasting the trust's assets.

A D&O contract is on a "claims made" basis, and an extended reporting period is offered after the policy is canceled or not renewed. The cost, the duration, and the terms of the extension should be checked.

A D&O insurance application contains warranties by the purchaser. An application for a D&O policy requires the insured to guarantee specific facts to be literally true, to their best knowledge and belief. Failure to do so voids the coverage. Warranties relate to prior and/or pending litigation, knowledge of circumstances that could result in a claim, and whether prior D&O insurance had been canceled or was not renewed.

D&O insurance came into prominence in the United States in the 1980s. Today it is a worldwide problem. In an international review of D&O liability, three top financial management executives cited examples of litigious societies in Australia, Canada, China, France, Germany, Hong Kong, Japan, Taiwan, and the United Kingdom.

If a health care organization plans to offer stock to the public, the organization should have a three year Securities and Exchange Commission (SEC) liability contract along with the D&O policy. This SEC liability agreement protects the health care organization from lawsuits that arise from misstatements in its prospectus.

Fiduciary Responsibility

In another burgeoning area of litigation and risk exposure, fiduciary responsibility liability addresses risk exposures that the health care facility faces as a result of the handling of money for employees. Primarily, the insurance covers employee payroll deductions for pension plans, savings plans, and various employee benefit options. Exposures arise from the loss of funds or benefits by the implementor and/or fiduciary of the plans, the employer. Even in fully insured plans, a failure of a designated provider of a benefit can result in a vicarious loss. An employer must select benefit providers that are not only financially sound, but also operationally adept.

Aircraft Liability

A general liability insurance policy excludes bodily injury arising from the loading or unloading of any aircraft. Since many health care organizations have helicopter landing pads on site, it is prudent to have a helipad liability policy to cover the loading and unloading of patients, supplies, and passengers.

Crime Insurance

A crime insurance policy can be included with the property contract or written separately. In its most common form, the blanket crime contract includes five insuring agreements:

1. An employee dishonesty agreement covers theft by an employee and is in the form of a bond. A bond is written as a guarantee of an employee's faithful performance of duties. Should a loss occur, the bond carrier tries to recover the value of the stolen items or money from the individual(s) responsible. If necessary, a bond endorsement can cover theft by an employee from third parties. If the health care organization has employees rendering services to patients in their own homes or in the community, or performing similar off-site activities, this is necessary coverage. To comply with the federal Employee Retirement and Income Security Act (ERISA) regulations, the amount of the bond should be at least $500,000 or 10 percent of pension assets. As an insured plan, the exact name of the pension plan should appear on the bond.
2. A loss on premises agreement covers robbery or theft.

3. A loss off premises agreement also covers robbery or theft.
4. A counterfeit money orders and currency agreement loss is extremely rare and may be unnecessary for many health care organizations.
5. A depositors forgery agreement covers the theft and alteration of negotiable instruments.

Protection for a Rainy Day

Health care organizations cannot operate without a cash flow and a positive profit-and-loss accounting. Risk managers can assist in protecting the financial assets of their organizations against devastating liability losses.

A knowledge of the options and key areas of risk transfer and insurance helps build a comprehensive risk management program. Within health care organizations, there are experts who can help with everything from overviews of insurance coverage to an entire restructuring of the risk management program.

These experts could be personnel of the health care organization itself, such as financial and accounting managers, plant engineers, electronic data processing managers, nurse supervisors, directors of volunteers, organizational auditors, insurance brokers, and numerous others who have the expertise in some or most of what the risk management plan proposes to do.

A risk management process affects every aspect of the health care organization in varied ways. Finances of the organization can be crippled by an uninsured or underinsured loss. Benefits can accrue through cost-effective improvements in the overall program. Employee morale increases if losses go down. Operational efficiencies are realized when the health care organization's assets are properly protected. If a health care organization has a commendable safety record and reacts to losses with little, if any, effect on the services, the community recognizes that the organization is well run.

Top management must be solidly behind risk management efforts. A demonstration of visible, quantifiable results is the best way to garner management support. If results are presented in general terms, management may not fully understand the impact of proper risk management. As a technique, "benchmarking" creates optimistic outcomes and shows quantifiable results that demonstrate quantifiable financial outcomes.

As complex as the risk management mission in financing and insurance seems currently, the dynamic nature of the health care industry can only lead to a higher level of sophistication with newer options to minimize losses.

7

Total Quality Management, Continuous Quality Improvement

No challenge in risk management is more immediate than the imperative of demonstrating that the evaluation of the risk management program makes a difference to the organization and its bottom line. An evaluation process helps determine how well risk management is doing within the organization while the process of total quality management and continuous quality improvement enables institutions to make the transition to higher levels of performance. Risk management focuses on an institution's exposure to financial loss. In minimizing this exposure, risk managers make a contribution to quality patient care by assuring that hazards and injuries are less likely to occur.

MEDICAL INJURIES ARE NEITHER NEW NOR UNCOMMON

Kaiser Wilhelm II, the emperor of Germany during World War I, had a withered left arm acquired as a result of a nerve injury during his birth in 1859. His birth was a difficult breech delivery that required a number of exacting obstetrical maneuvers and chloroform anesthesia. Most likely, the amount of oxygen was diminished for eight to ten minutes, resulting in "minimal brain damage."

As a prince, Kaiser Wilhelm II was hyperactive and emotionally unstable. If not for his difficult birth, the Kaiser might well have been an entirely different person. Although speculative, an obstetrical loss prevention/risk control program might have prevented World War I. However, the monarchy at that time could not have embraced such radical ideas as risk management. In addition, physicians were not knowledgeable enough to intervene effectively during young Prince Wilhelm's formative years.

Even the vast amount of medical knowledge that has been acquired since World War I, however, does not preclude medical accidents. A 1991 Harvard Medical Malpractice Study estimated that roughly 1 percent of patients discharged from New York State hospitals were victims of medical negligence resulting in injury. A larger number of patients experienced an injury not caused by negligence but obviously causing patient dissatisfaction. This study concluded that injuries happen with significant frequency during hospitalization.

Injuries and Lawsuits

Most of the injured patients in the Harvard study did not initiate a lawsuit. Most of the actual claims did not result from adverse events caused by negligence.3 Paradoxically, many claimants seek redress in the courts for injuries that are not really appropriate candidates for compensation. One rationale for the rapid rise in malpractice lawsuits could be the steady increase in the number of lawyersabout 50,000 new attorneys each year.4 Compared to other countries, the United States has more than three times the number of lawsuits. Generous awards from professional liability insurance coverage create a major incentive for malpractice litigation.

Injuries happen and so do lawsuits. A challenge for risk managers is to effectively minimize the injury side of the equation. Claims do require skillful management, but control of the future lies in prevention.

The Challenge of Prediction

If science and mathematics eventually permitted predictions about hazards and malpractice, risk management would be very different. Risk or hazard could be appreciated before the fact and eliminated before an adverse event. Importantly, predictive methods are statistical in nature. An equation cannot tell you that something will happen, only that there is an increased likelihood that it might happen.

A patient who likes a particular practitioner is less likely to sue that physician in the event of a bad outcome.5 To some extent, a physician's likability is determined by cultural attributes, although the reason could be as simple as giving a patient quality time. Cultivating a personal style acceptable to patients is an important loss prevention technique for today's physician. Physicians need to be enlightened, and the risk manager is in a unique position to identify those who need help, because the risk manager knows which physicians have been sued.

Statistical Predictive Models

Gibbons developed a statistical model for predicting medical malpractice claims for individual physicians.6 Insurers can use this model to "predict an individual's claim vulnerability." Investigation revealed the following:

- A sizable random physician effect exists.
- Risk of a claim increases for physicians between the ages of 40 and 60 years.
- Surgical specialists are at increased risk of a claim.
- Male physicians are at greater risk for a claim than their female colleagues.
- Following an initial claim, risk increases, particularly in the first year after the claim.
- Risk management education has beneficial effects on physicians with a prior claim history, particularly in anesthesiology and obstetrics/gynecology.

In addition, the researchers noted that even if the risk management education did not reduce the number of claims, the payout was often less because the education "may equip the physician to be a better defendant in the event of a claim."

How can this information be utilized? Should middle-aged male physicians in surgical specialties be targeted for intensive review and remedial education? Given the lag time between an adverse event and the receipt of a claim, it's likely that the damage or injury alleged in subsequent claims occurred prior to the arrival of the first claim. If a risk management program is to be proactive rather than reactive, the risk management activities to be emphasized must be predetermined. Post-claim risk management education for professional staff seems like a good bet, but don't expect to see immediate positive results.

Cindynics

Cindynics, literally "the science of danger," is concerned with the new discipline of hazard identification. This technique attempts to describe the basic assumptions about the "operating systems" of complex organizations and to identify mechanisms to allow risk management professionals to understand the nature of the hazards. Methods are mathematical and involve complex reasoning to describe hazards and catastrophes. Cindynicians see systems that are subject to hazard as occupying a cindynic hyperspace.This hyperspace is composed of five related spaces that describe the nature of the system and the effect of a hazard on that system:

(1) statistical space and statistics and numbers,
(2) epistemic space for modeling,
(3) teleological space for goals and objectives,
(4) deontological space for rules and ethical considerations, and
(5) axiological space for values. Complex systems may require more than a single hyperspace to describe them. These, in turn, are linked in a network.

For a hazardous condition to exist, at least one of the following abnormalities must occur: an absence of one of the five elements of cindynic hyperspace, a gap within one of the five spaces, a dislocation within the defined hyperspaces, a lack of organization within a space, or obstacles to regulations that govern the interactions of the spaces within the hyperspace. Following a catastrophe, a dissonance forms that is viewed as a change in or near one or more of the five spaces. A change in the statistical database, the knowledge base, the goals, the rules, or the values is possible. Risk managers attempt to reduce the dissonances before disaster results. In the future, financial issues such as the quantification and transfer of risk will be determined by mathematical analysis and cindynics.

EFFECTIVENESS OF RISK MANAGEMENT

Risk managers may have to prove the value of the services they provide.8 Does a risk management program in health care have value? Assuming merit, which programs are the most valuable? It is vital to illustrate that a risk management program materially contributes to an institution's survival and to the quality of care delivered. A study in Maryland hospitals demonstrated significantly better claims experience in hospitals with certain risk management policies or activities.

One pivotal activity for the risk manager focused on regular formal education programs to teach physicians and nurses about risk management and the role of the risk manager. A key to success involved the handling of information and interventions following an adverse event. Information must get to the upper-level administration and, most importantly, to the clinical chief or chiefs as quickly as possible. Although controversial, the study supported the beneficial influence of a policy to inform affected patients and families of adverse events. Investigators identified "highly productive" areas for quality review and risk management oversight in ambulatory care that included hospital discharge diagnosis, procedure codes, length of stay, and cancer staging.

Risk Management Process

Traditionally, the risk management process consists of five steps that are similar in other disciplines, such as quality assessment or nursing:

1. Identify and analyze the exposures to loss.

2. Examine the feasibility of alternative techniques: for example, risk control to stop losses, risk financing to pay for losses.
3. Select the apparent best technique(s).
4. Implement the chosen technique(s).
5. Monitor and improve the risk management program.

In the last step, the program is evaluated as the particular operation, assumptions, and interventions are reanalyzed. Subsequent improvement of the process can follow this evaluation.

To ensure excellence, Penchansky developed a reconceptualization of the linkage between quality assessment, risk management, and utilization review. The "organization must have continuing processes to (1) define and/or change the desired goals and related standards of performance; (2) measure performance; and (3) maintain performance and/or change inadequate performance." There can be no doubt of the direct linkage between the risk management process and quality assessment.

Quality Assessment

"As a systems approach to preventing malpractice claims, organized risk management identifies, analyzes, and treats risks which quality assessment works to eliminate." However, quality care may be influenced by ulterior motives and result in blaming others. In blaming the "bad apple," the traditional view indicated that problems of quality are caused by poor intentions.

Martin defined quality assessment (QA) as a "formal, systematic program by which care rendered to patients is measured against established criteria." Ongoing monitoring of systems is necessary to ensure that problems are identified early and appropriate intervention is initiated. Inspection improved quality and established thresholds for acceptability. Under specific circumstances, oversight and disciplinary measures are necessary. There must be a mechanism for identifying dishonest or poorly performing practitioners. Sanctions or limitations in privileges may be necessary. Standards of care cannot be left to chance when a patient's safety is at stake. If health care is to improve beyond these artificial thresholds that discourage peak performance, the concept of quality improvement must be introduced.

Administrators trained nurse assistants to take vital signs, to measure blood pressure, and to draw blood so that the patients could have their needs met immediately. A hospitals' professionals union leader said, "Patients don't know they're at risk. They just assume that the person caring for them is qualified to do so." A union report accused management of putting budgetary concerns above patient welfare.

Although quality assessment is individualized for each patient, QA professionals routinely seek to aggregate information to identify recurring quality problems. Data from QA, utilization review (UR), infection control, and risk management departments must be reviewed as a whole. This synergistic amalgamation of data enhances the common desire to improve quality. LDS Hospital (Salt Lake City) combined the QA, UR, and risk management departments into a single unit, the Quality Management Department, to simplify the task of information management. A group of thirteen registered nurses accomplish the department's shared functions. Anyone involved in assessing the quality of patient care requires a basic understanding of quantitative methods and information management systems.18

Sophisticated technology raises thorny questions about quality of care. For example, when is it appropriate to evaluate a patient via telemedicine? According to the Center for Health Policy Research: "Telecommunications technology for most routine consultative purposes is acceptable." Thus far, telemedicine has escaped a malpractice suit. Nobody has argued that a diagnosis was missed because the physician couldn't touch the patient. Nevertheless, the liability risks are complex, since telemedicine can cross state lines, can join two physicians in a common practice, and can make it difficult to determine who's at fault in a suit, because of the variance among state malpractice laws. Standards and practice guidelines are being developed by the American Telemedicine Association.

TOTAL QUALITY MANAGEMENT

After World War II, the modern quality movement began with the work of W. Edwards Deming in Japanese industry. His 85-15 rule states: "When something goes wrong, 85 percent of the problem is related to systems failures; 15 percent is the fault of the people involved." This powerful concept rejects the traditional approach to problem solving that aims to identify those at fault and punish them. While the threat of dismissal or of a poor evaluation can be motivational, the 85-15 rule posits that such interventions may not be the most effective way to solve a problem or to prevent its recurrence.

A better approach, total quality management (TQM), focuses on the system and not on the individual. Stratton urged management not to give employees the impression that they are responsible for the 15 percent. Management must take responsibility for the entire problem. However, employees may have a good idea of how to fix the process or system, the other 85 percent of the problem. Suggestion boxes have proved that it pays to ask employees. Three working premises about quality emerge:

- Quality is important and can be measured.
- People are a critical part of the solution and not necessarily the problem.
- Change is fundamental and always present, but change can be managed to improve any organization.
- Kim discussed implementing TQM in the health care industry while Goonan described applications, with an emphasis on clinical quality management, along with practical advice for establishing a TQM program.
- Total quality management is a broad business concept that includes the continuous quality improvement (CQI) process. CQI initiatives occur simultaneously in many areas and are overseen and guided by the TQM process.

Lynn stated that TQM is the process organizations use to improve their ability to satisfy customer expectations. A key to understanding TQM changes in health care is the recognition of the central importance of the customer. In business, a customer buys services from a vendor and is free to choose to buyor not to buy. Patients/customers of health care institutions can select services that meet their expectations and reject services that do not. This approach will be the measure of the health care organization's success in the future. The following fundamental beliefs form the basis of the TQM approach:

- TQM is a positive strategy for growth and should be integrated into the organization's strategic business plan.
- Top management must be committed to and actively involved in the TQM process.
- TQM is a process, not a program.
- Quality improvement processes must be applied to all levels of the organization.
- Quality improvement benefits everyone, both internal and external audiences.

A WORD OF CAUTION

Youngberg cautioned health care professionals that quality improvement methods are not a "quick fix." Several factors are necessary for success:

- A strong commitment from senior-level management, including resources and time.
- Careful modification to the health care setting, with consideration of the nature of the product to be delivered. (Health care is not automobile manufacturing.)

Avoiding a retreat by health care professionals and managers into technical methodology such as gathering statistics, diagramming flow patterns, and developing "Pareto" (vertical graphing) and "fishbone" (pointed arrows) diagrams to the detriment of the reason for this new strategy.

If, after correcting all the systems and solving all the problems, patients and employees are still dissatisfied, the time and effort spent on quality improvement initiatives can be of questionable value. Organizational culture of health care institutions may create obstacles to implementing CQI initiatives.

Separation of administrative functions that are usually performed by non-clinicians from the medical functions performed by professional staff makes efforts to involve physicians in CQI more challenging. Physicians tend to focus their attention on patients and not on what they perceive to be administrative responsibilities. It is imperative for the success of CQI to help physicians understand how the process will benefit their patients.

Furthermore, the hierarchical and bureaucratic structure of larger health care organizations makes the empowerment of the employees on CQI teams, a fundamental tenet of CQI thinking, even more difficult. "Hot groups" may allow an organization to bypass resistance to change. Hot groups are those that managers cannot control; individual members are self-motivated and see themselves as moving beyond their own limits. Neatly organized institutions often suffocate the initiative of this kind of group, but these groups are well worth cultivating as quality improvement teams. An entrenched cadre of middle management, resistant to change, further hinders the process.

ASSESSMENT OF TQM ACTIVITIES

When planning TQM activities, it is advisable to consider how efficacy will be assessed after TQM is implemented. To perform properly, TQM activities demand considerable organizational resources. Assessing the impact of these TQM activities is a valuable exercise because the program may not be cost effective or changes may increase cost effectiveness. One complex audit procedure examines TQM activities relative to efficiency and effectiveness in financing, operations, and human resources, with marketing added to the effectiveness audit. This audit uses process and outcome measures for each of these dimensions. However, the specific measures must be developed for each TQM activity by each organization.

CONTINUOUS QUALITY IMPROVEMENT

As a management tool, the concepts of continuous quality improvement (CQI) are an integral part of the thinking of health care administrators. CQI directs attention to the fundamental mechanism that drives a process or system being reviewed. Furthermore, CQI focuses on techniques to accomplish positive change by assessing a process that leads to an intervention. In selected hospitals, CQI actions have decreased unnecessary intravenous catheter use, improved preventive services in primary care, decreased hospital costs for patients with chest pain, and improved the timeliness of preoperative radiologic reports.

Birnbaum discussed the use of sentinel events as an important component in managing the quality of care through CQI. A sentinel event is a single occurrence of sufficient concern to trigger a systematic response. Parisi urged implementing a CQI approach to incident reporting to improve health care systems and processes.36 Regardless of the technique, evaluating the process after the intervention to further refine or change the strategy begins the cycle again. This cycle should be viewed as a spiral through time, rather than as a static circle. After each subsequent turn, the intervention will never be quite the same. In a letter to employees, the president of Beth Israel Medical Center (New York) stated that the enhancement of quality on a broad scale results from the cumulative impact of the success of numerous, individually focused quality improvement projects. He added that by systematically studying the delivery of medical care, an organization can approach optimal quality in clinical and operational performance.

QUALITY IMPROVEMENT TEAM

In the improvement process, the Quality Improvement Team (QIT) is the effector of change. Staff members appointed to a team should be the employees who actually do the work within the company or institution. A QIT should be of manageable size, with one member designated as recording secretary to ensure a written record of the proceedings. Traditional group dynamics theory projects that the ideal team has five to seven, and generally no more than ten, members. A QIT may need to be somewhat larger to encompass the organization's various areas and disciplines. In addition, the team needs a leader to provide direction and vision for the group. In experienced groups that have developed a cohesive structure, any member can serve as the leader.

A facilitator, who is not a member of the QIT or part of the problem in the organization, acts in a guiding role when the team loses its focus or veers off track. This key role combines the traditional task roles of clarifier, summarizer, and reality tester with maintenance roles of harmonizer, consensus taker, and compromiser. The facilitator is primarily an observer and is in a unique position to provide feedback to the group regarding its progress or lack of progress. A QIT should meet regularly to carry out the CQI process.

With the prospect of numerous teams simultaneously moving in many directions, central guidance certainly is necessary. There is a need to coordinate the QITs, to focus team efforts on strategic priorities, to transfer learning from one set of projects to another, and to focus quality improvement work on the organization's strategic priorities. A steering committee should approve QIT projects and monitor the teams' progress. This committee can help remove obstacles to implementation and change.

CQI QUESTIONS

As a process, CQI implies that an organization knows what needs to be improved. If resources are limited, making the correct choice may be unlikely. The following pertinent questions need to be asked:

1. Is there a corporate strategic plan or mission statement that sets the organization's general direction?
2. Which operations are fundamental or critical to the organization?
3. What are the needs of the external (community) and internal (employees, volunteers, attending physicians) customers? What do they expect from the organization?

4. How is the organization spending its money? Where is the money going? Can less be spent?
5. What existing problems have been identified?
6. From current data, what can be done better and more efficiently?
7. Which activities would benefit from simplification? Which activities seem so complicated that it is obvious there must be a better way?
8. Where can the organization put its resources and expect a reasonable outcome or return?

Undoubtedly, more than one problem will be isolated in the group's initial brainstorming session. Deming listed questions contributed by an executive of the Ford Motor Company to help a QIT start the process. Those questions provided initial direction in thinking about the organization's structure, what the organization does, and where the individual team members fit into the organization, and they are directly applicable to health care institutions and agencies.

AN ORGANIZATION'S MISSION STATEMENT

A CQI team begins by reviewing the organization's mission and/or vision statement, such as the following:

Beth Israel Medical Center will be recognized as a premier health care system in New York City. We will strive consistently to surpass professional quality standards, exceed patient and physician expectations and promote an exceptional work and healing environment.

By focusing on the critical few objectives, rather than on the trivial many, this CQI review ensures that the organization's design for its future and direction is incorporated into the team's planning. Then, the quality improvement team can write its own mission statement to set its direction. Next, the team's goals and objectives must be developed. In particular, the objectives must be specific to the problem, and they must be measurable. Archibald's examples of a mission, goal, and objective for a team working on the problem of medication errors demonstrate the increasing specificity of the statements.

Mission: The quality management program at the medical center has the mission of supporting the mission of the hospital as a whole by providing our community with services including consultation and support for TQM activities.

Goal: To ensure that treatments provided to all patients at the medical center are administered in a timely, caring, and professional manner.

Objective: Medication errors on inpatient units will be decreased by 15 percent by the end of June 1995.

A FOCUS ON THE CUSTOMER IS VITAL

Driven by the needs of the organization's customers, the quality improvement process recognizes the customer as being central to its purpose. Nine quality improvement factors define the process:

1. State the objectives: Decide what your mission will be, consistent with that of the company; state your objectives in relation to this mission.
2. Identify the customers: Determine what the customers want. What are their needs? What do they require from the organization to meet those needs?
3. Understand how the process works now: Identify the process components and perform a flow analysis to locate the problems within the system. Problems may be identified for further study and subjected to CQI.
4. Collect the data: Focus on the problem and subject the data to analysis to determine cause and effect.
5. Decide on a solution: Develop an appropriate plan of action to solve the problem.
6. Implement the plan: Initiate actions to solve the problem.
7. Evaluate the plan: Determine the success or failure of the plan of action.

8. Improve the process: Redraft the objectives or mission, if necessary; determine the effect on the customer; and reconsider the plan.
9. Create a new plan: Incorporate learning from prior efforts.

Juran created a quality planning road map that was customer driven and designed to meet the needs of the organization. He explained the flow process:

- Identify our customers.
- Determine the needs of those customers.
- Translate those needs into our language.
- Develop product features that can optimally respond to those needs.
- Develop a process that optimally is able to produce the product features.
- Transfer the process to the operating forces.

It is important to know who the customers are, as well as their relative importance to the operation. Specific operations must be examined in some detail to identify all of the customers. Internal customers belong to the organization, either as employees or through some other relationship, such as volunteers or private contractors (for example, attending physicians). These people help produce the product: health care. External customers, such as the community, do not belong to the organization but use or purchase its goods and services or are affected by the organization in some other way. In health care, the patient is the primary external customer. Juran described customers as belonging to two groups:

The vital few, all of whom are of "great importance," because of the amount they buy (for example, a health maintenance organization) or because of the amount they contribute (for example, a successful surgeon who brings many patients into a hospital).

The useful many, who are a relatively large number of customers, but each of whom is of only "modest importance" to the organization (for example, a patient or a nurse).

How does the organization discern a customer's needs? Simply, customers can be asked about their likes and dislikes either in an interview or through a written questionnaire. Indirectly, an organization can examine the products or services that customers actually use and in what relative quantity.

In the case of a product, analysis of what is returned or discarded is helpful. A customer may have a need that has not yet been perceived; these needs may be discovered in the details as the process is subjected to flow analysis. A pilot project can be instituted to meet the unperceived need. If successful, the pilot program results in the identification of a particular customer need. Juran contended that customers' needs are a "moving target," not static, but requiring continuous evaluation and prioritization over time to ensure that they are met.

Juran referred to the concept of replanning to give direction to the retrospective analysis performed at the conclusion of a project. This "Santayana Review," as Juran labeled it, reinforces positive actions and prevents the repetition of mistakes.

A SAMPLING OF POTENTIAL RISK MANAGEMENT CQI PROJECTS

Health care institutions might benefit from the application of CQI intervention to analyze the following readily identifiable potential risks:

- Excessive delay in responding to fetal distress.
- Excessive number of missed emergency room diagnoses of cerebral or spinal injuries, myocardial infarction, appendicitis, ectopic pregnancy, or meningitis.
- Slow response time to trauma patients requiring surgery for orthopedic, abdominal, or head injuries.
- High, unplanned return rate to the operating room within forty-eight hours of initial surgery.
- Intubation mishaps, such as failure to maintain an airway.
- High suicide rate among psychiatric patients.

- Frequent failure to monitor/observe adverse effects of psychiatric or other medications.
- Improperly obtained informed consent.
- High rate of central nervous system complications during or within two days following administration of anesthesia.
- High rate of adverse occurrences/claims involving HIV/AIDS patients.
- Inadequate credentialing and privileging policies and procedures.
- High rate of institutional review board-related occurrences/claims.
- High rate of claims for which the risk identification/reporting system failed to provide warning.

A recent study yielded an unexpected result relating to the appearance of postoperative infections at several medical centers from 1990 through 1993. One would normally expect these infections to result from the surgical intervention, but close examination revealed that the handling of the anesthetic agent, propofol, was at fault. This particular agent is lipid based and capable of acting as an excellent culture medium for bacterial growth. Lapses in accepted aseptic technique by anesthesia personnel had resulted in contamination of the propofol and unintentional inoculation of patients with infectious agents.

QIT RISK MANAGEMENT EXAMPLES

Quality improvement team activities with risk management implications can be illustrated by specific actions performed at Bethesda Hospital (Cincinnati, Ohio) and by process action teams at Wright Patterson Medical Center (Dayton, Ohio).

The initial selection of CQI projects that evaluate processes of direct concern to the medical staff may engender participation. If physicians realize that CQI makes their work more effective and less frustrating, they may become willing participants in the CQI process. In one institution, a CQI team that included physicians significantly decreased the time between ordering and performing diagnostic imaging scans. Team members must be clear with themselves and others about why they are interested in the activity of a particular team. To promote individual self-awareness of these factors, the team should discuss the issue of self-interest and bias. In addition, a basic tenet of TQM holds that top management must be committed to the process.

CQI AND LABOR RELATIONS

Two recent decisions by the National Labor Relations Board (NLRB) raise the possibility that TQM/CQI employee management teams may violate the National Labor Relations Act (NLRA) of 1935. Such a violation would occur if the TQM/CQI teams were judged to be labor organizations dominated by the employer. In reality, most employee participation programs, including QITs, are problematic under the criteria set forth in the NLRA. A two-part test would have to be satisfied in any complaint of unfair labor practice:

(1) The employer-employee group would have to be consistent with the definition of a labor organization and

(2) It would have to be shown to be unlawfully dominated by the employer.

To be considered a labor organization, the group would have to meet all three of the following conditions:

(1) Employees participate.

(2) In part, the organization exists for the purposes of dealing with management.

(3) Dealings concern conditions of work, grievances, labor disputes, wages, rate of pay, or hours of employment; conditions of work can be broadly defined and would include work-related issues with which a CQI team might be concerned.

A corporate health team sought to improve the transfer process referring patients to and among various Bethesda Hospital facilities and to ensure continuity of care for corporate health clients and their employees. Client satisfaction was increased by 73 percent. Satisfied clients and improved continuity of care can reduce the risk of malpractice actions. A QIT was formed to improve the timeliness of surgical pathology reporting. A quick and accurate process of delivering diagnostic information to the patient's physician is a critical risk reduction intervention.

A process action team improved the outpatient physician consultation system by simplifying procedures. This change shortened the consultation time, reduced misplaced consultation forms, and improved feedback to the provider, patient, and consultant.

A process action team found ways to decrease the time required to obtain mammography results on patients at risk for breast disease and to eliminate delays between the diagnosis of breast cancer and surgery. If the group is identified as a labor organization, the second part of the test is invoked: is the group dominated by the employer? Unlawful domination exists if only one of the following conditions is met:

(1) An employer interferes with the labor organization's formation.

(2) An employer interferes with the labor organization's administration.

(3) An employer provides the labor organization with financial and other support.

Depending on interpretation, almost any group could be considered to be in violation of any one of these three conditions. Three specific characteristics of CQI programs appear to make them allowable:

(1) Information sharing with management is the purpose of the group.

(2) Employees, not management, retain the right to make decisions, by majority rule, to implement proposals. Management can participate in the decision but not control it. Management cannot administer the CQI team.

(3) The collective bargaining process offers an alternative solution for establishing "legal" CQI teams.

Risk managers should insist that the structure, mission, and objectives of CQI teams be reviewed to be allowable under the NLRA. Care must be taken to avoid even the appearance of management interference in the group process of these teams. In the early planning, the structure, goals, and objectives should be developed in partnership with the employees who will do the work. Team members must be volunteers, not acting on behalf of other employees, and must not address employee discontent. Areas such as those involving safety and health must be approached with caution to avoid conflict with the NLRA. It is possible to have a team whose sole function is to make recommendations to management.

Benchmarking Comparisons

Benchmarking is a process whereby one organization's operation is compared to that of another, usually an organization that happens to do it better. A limited internal type of benchmarking can compare different units of the same organization to discover the "best" practices. However, there is no assurance that any particular unit will be doing any better than any other unit. To gain the most from benchmarking, it is advisable to go outside the organization to find the best within the industry, or even outside the industry, to find others who excel in similar processes.

Benchmarking is a thoughtful, introspective process that goes beyond simply touring another organization. First, risk managers must know their own organizations and have an idea of what they want to accomplish. Next, organizations that are appropriate for comparison need to be identified, assessed, and compared regarding their operation.

Risk managers must then formulate a plan to bring their operations closer to the best practices of the other organization. Evaluation and replanning must follow the implementation of any changes in the organization. This is not a process to be undertaken without a firm commitment in resources by upper-level management.

Community Quality Management

With the emphasis of health care shifting from large centralized institutions, there is a natural growth in the importance of community-centered quality management activities. Contemplating the shared activities of diverse community groups produces variations in planning. The following guidelines may be helpful:

1. No single organization can meet all the needs of all the customers.
2. Respect for diversity of organizational culture helps everyone and assists the collaborative process necessary to solve common community-based problems through the application of scientific thinking.
3. An infrastructure for interorganizational communication of data results and continued improvement efforts should be developed.
4. Control over variation in the processes of complex and interdependent health care services is possible through hard work and cooperation.

PROGRAM EVALUATION ISSUES AND METHODS

In health care risk management, program evaluation traditionally has been considered difficult. Unlike quality assessment, program evaluation does not focus on what is normal. Risk management deals with abnormal events or aberrations that expose financial structures to loss.

In health care, a major professional liability exposure may be unrelated, or only slightly related, to the quality of care rendered by a physician to a patient. A jury may disagree with expert reviewers who judge the standard of care to be acceptable. Despite the facts, the well-known sympathy factor contributes to a jury's liberal monetary awards in malpractice cases. These unrelated factors make it difficult to form objective conclusions based on the data. Standards, evaluations, and checklists contribute to resolution of the difficulty.

Standards as Guides

What are the standards? The standards are whatever an organization says they are. It is the responsibility of each institution to determine its own standards. A definition of standards begins with the corporate mission statement or a similar declaration of organizational goals or strategic objectives. To have meaning, standards must be a reflection of the company's goals. A standard must be reasonable, capable of being achieved, and measurable. In health care, specific standards may be imposed by government regulatory requirements. Antidumping provisions of the federal COBRA statute necessitate establishing a standard and monitoring the disposition of patients arriving at the emergency room.

Outcome measures use a standard or norm to arrive at a risk-adjusted expected value for a patient outcome.48 This expected value is compared to actual patient outcomes to determine whether a problem exists. Outcome measurement ensures that quality has been maintained or indicates to what degree quality has been compromised.

Problems are identified and referred to quality improvement for a process and systems review. The first step is to review and confirm the accuracy of the data documenting the substandard condition. There is a tendency to assume that data must be correct because the measurements are quantitative, but there may be problems with the measurements. The JCAHO issued a call for collaboration in performance measurement defined "as an interrelated set of process and outcome measures that, when used together, provide a meaningful performance profile of the organization to which the measures are applied."

Standards may be described either as results standards, which refer to what is accomplished, or as activity standards, which refer to the means by which something is accomplished. Outcome measures, such as patient mortality or survival, are results standards. An activity standard could specify the number of staff education sessions on basic or advanced cardiac life support for different levels of professional staff. Carroll classified more than 140 outcome indicators of patient care into fifteen clinical areas for quality evaluation review.

Evaluation

Evaluation is the process that determines to what degree the standard was or was not met. Evaluations may be done on a regular basis, as part of the ongoing monitoring of a process, or in response to a problem within a process.

In all cases, standards are assessed for compliance, and their reasonableness is reviewed.

If a standard is not being met, the fault may be with the standard rather than with individual performance. Systems problems may prevent a reasonable standard from being achieved. For example, even if the standard specifies that single-cut frozen section results will be available to the surgeon in the operating room within a specified time period, specimen transport problems and clerical delays may prevent the meeting of that standard.

Checklists

In evaluating programs, risk managers need assurance that they have incorporated all possibilities into their risk management efforts, such as a checklist for evaluating an incident reporting system. This evaluation gives the risk manager valuable and comprehensive direction. Although part of the evaluation process is qualitative, the assessment may point out areas in which quantitative methods for monitoring are appropriate. A checklist is not a complete description, but rather identifies many components of the process.

External Evaluation

On occasion, the risk management program will be evaluated by organizations outside the health care institution. These external evaluators could include the Joint Commission on Accreditation of Healthcare Organizations (JCAHO), insurance companies, professional organizations, government entities, and legal groups.

JCAHO Evaluation

As part of its accrediting procedure, the JCAHO may examine the risk management program. The JCAHO requires the organization to collect data about risk management activities. Risk managers need a methodology for data collection, data analysis, and data transmittal to other departments and/or committees. Quality, risk, and safety groups are expected to share information toward the goal of improving quality. Aggregate data and information from risk management and these other areas must be applied to organizationwide performance/improvement activities.

Evaluation by Insurers/Underwriters

The primary role of the insurance company underwriter is to act as a gatekeeper. In this role, the underwriter has the greatest control over who will be offered access to the protection offered by his or her insurance company.

Underwriters are concerned about credentialing, peer review, screening systems, compliance with JCAHO standards, and related internal evaluation mechanisms. An underwriter can evaluate the soundness of a risk management program by considering the following vital program elements:

- Commitment: senior management involvement.
- Centralization and coordination: a designated individual responsible for the program.
- Committee structure: issues identified, analyzed, resolved, and monitored.
- Quality assessment integration: QA and RM mutually supporting and reinforcing.
- Medical staff involvement: active physician involvement.
- Informed consent: effective in reducing claim frequency.

Checklist for Evaluating Incident Reporting Systems

In evaluating an incident reporting system, the director of risk management should review the report form, the organization's policy on incident reporting, and the extent to which employees are complying with the policy.

POLICY EVALUATION

- Do hospital practices and procedures reflect the policy at all stages in the incident reporting process?
- If so, could the policy and/or the practices be modified to improve the responsiveness of the system to the hospital's needs?
- Are the reports prepared and submitted promptly?
- If so, is appropriate follow-up initiated?
- Are the reports completed satisfactorily?
- If not, what proportion of the reports must be returned for completion?
- Is there a pattern to the type of missing information or the point of origin of incomplete reports?
- Does analysis of the incident reports indicate ways to reduce the hospital's risk?
- Is sufficient information available to make the incident report as useful as possible?

INCIDENT REPORTING EVALUATION

- Does the form secure adequate documentation of the circumstances surrounding the incident?
- Does the form provide information on which to base an evaluation of the hospital's potential liability?
- Does the system provide for reporting of physician-involved incidents?
- Is the reporting of physician-involved incidents complete and comprehensive? If not, why not?
- Are there system weaknesses that could be remedied by such measures as redesigning the form or training those who complete the form?

- Would another method of information gathering be more effective or easier to implement?
- Patient representation system: handling patient complaints.
- Disposition management/discharge planning: posthospital needs addressed (case management).
- Incident/accident reporting: essentially a reporting system but also very important to trend and to respond to adverse trends.
- Claims management: written policy of procedures to follow after a serious incident occurs or an actual claim is filed.
- Biomedical services and medical devices: test equipment prior to use; evaluate and remove defective equipment from service.
- Contract review: risk manager should be involved in reviewing contracts.
- Educational programs: provide education in risk management issues.
- If the health care institution is self-insured, the same evaluation process protects the assets of the self-insured trust fund, captive insurance company, or alternate risk financing mechanism.

Claims experience is one of the most critical elements an underwriter will evaluate. Underwriters want to review a minimum of five to seven years of claims experience, as well as the entire period for which coverage of prior acts is sought. Prior acts coverage insures the institution against events that occurred before the inception date of the policy. At a minimum, the risk manager should have the following information on every open and closed claim:

- Date of loss
- Closing date
- Evaluation of the allegations
- Date of notice
- Nature of the injury

- Who's involved; insurance coverage
- Reserve evaluation or final disposition

Practice Guidelines

Practice guidelines set a standard of care to which the practitioner will be held. These guidelines require continuous monitoring and/ or evaluation to ensure that the requirements are appropriate for the clinical area, are being used properly, and are reasonable. Risk managers must be aware of departures from the guidelines, because of the potential liability risk exposure. As such, practice guidelines can potentially reduce the number of malpractice cases and the costs of settling those claims. However, practice guidelines may cut in both directions. One study reviewed claims from two malpractice insurers and found that seventeen of 259 claims used practice guidelines but that in twelve (71%) of these cases, the physician was implicated in a charge of medical malpractice.

When guidelines are implemented, they should first undergo a multidisciplinary review by the affected clinical departments, risk management team, and in-house counsel. It should be assumed that plaintiff's counsel will review any guideline in use for their own purposes. Following the institution of standards for minimal monitoring during anesthesia, there was a decrease in anesthesia-related injuries. As intended, that practice guideline appeared to lower liability exposure and resulted in reducing the malpractice insurance premiums of anesthesiologists.

Malpractice Claims Data

Without access to a voluminous database, it may be impossible to derive statistically significant conclusions from an analysis of malpractice claims data. Nevertheless, the evaluation of malpractice claims is critical. Merely the fact that a physician has a claim may mean that more claims are forthcoming or that the physician's communication style is impersonal or abrupt and needs an overhaul. A physician's prior claim history could reveal the existence of complaints filed with the state licensing board. More importantly, malpractice claims data can be used to identify problem-prone clinical processes and suggest interventions to reduce negligence.

Targeting individual practitioners for education or sanctions on the basis of their malpractice claims histories is problematic from a medical perspective. However, the malpractice insurer may cancel a physician's insurance because of underwriting considerations, on the grounds that someone with numerous claims will cost the program too much money. At the very least, the risk manager needs to evaluate the individual claims to make sure a practitioner is not dangerously incompetent. For issues other than standards of care, a more thorough review is recommended. If physicians do the evaluation, the reviewer's knowledge of the severity of the outcome to the patient could negatively influence his or her judgment regarding the appropriateness of care. It may be advisable to withhold patient outcome information from the reviewers until the quality review process is complete.

In addition to the evaluation of individual claims and discussions with the clinical director, trend data for all malpractice claims should be examined. This tracks individuals, specialties, departments, frequencies, severity of injuries, and the nature of claims. At this time, loss prevention issues can be identified. When relevant issues are involved, risk managers may direct their efforts toward education and training.

High Risk Areas

High risk activities have accumulated a history of financial loss much greater than that in other areas. Clinical services of obstetrics, surgical anesthesia, and the emergency department commonly appear with greater severity on loss runs. Diagnostic services, such as radiology, require close monitoring by risk management. During a clinical consultation, communication between physicians demands ongoing scrutiny. Frequently, lawsuits mention the lack of informed consent. Other areas that need ongoing evaluation by risk managers include advance directives, do not resuscitate (DNR) orders, the withholding of treatment, credentialing, and confidentiality.

Medical records may be requested by a host of people, such as parties to lawsuits, state regulators, peer review organizations, and law enforcement agencies, and they may be troublesome. These individuals and organizations may not be aware of, or may choose to ignore, the health care organization's obligation to maintain the confidentiality of the medical records. Risk managers need procedures for monitoring medical record requests with respect to appropriateness and liability exposure. Two instances that should trigger risk management evaluation are requests by malpractice law firms before a lawsuit and requests by patients who wish to review their own records. Monitoring trends in requests for medical records, particularly by law firm and by department, is a critical activity for risk managers. Tracking these trends can help identify breaches of confidentiality. Breaches may occur innocently or through leaks to journalists or plaintiff's attorneys.

A risk manager should monitor credentialing policies that might tend to exclude or deny privileges to physicians. If physicians' admitting privileges are withdrawn or denied, the economic impact on their practice could be significant enough to cause them to seek compensation in court. If a patient is unable to respond, the belief by a patient's family or significant others about the patient's wishes regarding resuscitation or withholding of treatment is paramount. Effective monitoring by risk management can provide an early warning that the family is in disagreement and that litigation is being contemplated. From a liability viewpoint, the monitoring of high risk areas by risk management is a vital activity. Information on trends is particularly important for clinical areas because quality of patient care may be an issue. Procedures for monitoring whether informed consent has been obtained properly are necessary. Risk managers can track this through the claims incident reporting process. Auditing procedures also may help determine the frequency of lapses.

Risk Management Self-Assessment Manual

The Risk Management Self-Assessment Manual uses process and outcome measures to aid in evaluating the effectiveness of risk management programs and in planning actions to enhance their effectiveness. A chart in the manual indicates how evaluation and planning for part of the organization of the risk management program includes activities, process measures, outcome measures, and action plans.

Process measures assess whether these activities are being carried out as intended. Outcome measures assess whether the program is having the impact it was designed to have. Measures should be quantifiable, derived from experience, describe what should happen rather than what is happening now, and be trackable. When using this self-assessment process, the risk manager first identifies the structural components of the risk management program and the necessary activities for achieving those components. A quantifiable process measure or indicator measure is then identified for each activity. In this way, a risk manager can determine whether the activity was carried out as planned. Finally, an outcome measure is formulated for the activity This is a goal statement that includes a quantifiable measure of the outcome of the activity if it is successful. An example for the claims management structural component might include:

- Activity: Set up a written claims management policy that outlines the institution's claims management process.
- Process measure: Senior management develops a policy that is reviewed at least annually.
- Outcome measure: Seventy-five percent or more of the claims are investigated within twenty-four hours of the report of the incident.

Depositions

In an out-of-court setting, witnesses can be examined and can give testimony under oath before the parties in a lawsuit or their representatives. This examination process is called a deposition and provides an opportunity for the witnesses to tell their stories and to be questioned. Risk managers may assist in the preparation of institutional employees for deposition.

Importantly, risk managers should review depositions, or at least peruse the defense firm's summary, looking for areas of exposure. On the basis of such an investigation, Beckman devised a set of questions for deposition reviews. His study examined forty-five patients' depositions and classified fifteen categories of "relationship issues" found in the depositions to identify problems. As perceived by the patient, these issues were failures in the physician/patient encounter. Physicians confronting specific problems in patient relationships might benefit from educational intervention. Since depositions are taken under oath, the documents often reveal information about the practitioner's involvement that was not previously understood.

Risk managers should devise a structured approach to deposition review that individualizes criteria to the particular institution and its potential problems. If obstetrical residents are permitted to deliver infants without an attending physician under certain circumstances, all depositions in obstetrical cases should be reviewed to validate the location of the resident and attending physicians during labor and delivery.

Evaluation is an Appraisal

Analytical tools may assist in the identification of factors that could predict litigation or hazards that lead to injury. Statistical procedures can identify medical practice problems causing litigation. Cindynics allows for the conceptualization of hazard prediction. TQM is a process, not a program, and must be applied to all levels of the organization. CQI is a business concept and a management technique that views quality as something dynamic that can always be improved in a continuous process of evaluation and change. No matter what the initials TQM, CQI, or XYZ an evaluation follows the usual scientific method: defining the problem, collecting and analyzing data, formulating hypotheses, testing the hypotheses, and appraising the outcome before starting all over again.

All activities that reduce the incidence of litigation are of primary concern to risk managers. Of course, existing theories and approaches created or adapted from management experiences can be blended into a risk manager's program. A precarious predicament emerges as risk managers initiate liability reduction activities that may affect the quality and quantity of care delivered to patients. This catch-22 occurs if choices are made for economic reasons rather than for quality of care rationales. A relevant adjudication of this dilemma must consider the best of both approaches risk management and quality assessment. Evaluation and change are two constants that permit an organization to reach new levels of capacity. Whether through TQM, CQI, or reengineering, an organization must look at its critical processes, redefine its direction on the basis of that review, and meet the needs of the customers utilizing its services.

8

Ethical Issues for Risk Managers

A variety of forces have joined together to increase awareness of ethical issues in health care: patient's rights, sophisticated medical technologies, consumer demographics, non-traditional family settings, and the influx of managed-care organizations. On top of all these complicating forces, ethical issues also evolved related to the control of skyrocketing health care costs, even though "ethics is the discipline of determining right from wrong and is not directly governed by those who benefit and those who do not." Risk managers will confront many ethical issues in their daily practice. Where federal, state, or local legislation exists, it is vital that the risk manager be familiar with the law. Risk managers may need to develop policies or guidelines to apply the law to specific situations. At other times there will be no law, and the risk manager will have to adapt measures to resolve complex ethical problems. Guidelines regarding ethical issues in health care and examples of related law can help the risk manager develop appropriate procedures.

ETHICAL GUIDELINES FOR RISK MANAGERS

Autonomy, beneficence, and justice are three ethical principles that underlie the perplexing decisions that must be made by health care organizations as they render care.

Autonomy

Autonomy, or self-determination, is the core principle of American bioethics. In the United States, the Constitution builds a framework of respect for individual rights, as long as the exercise of those rights does not infringe on the rights of others. In a country as heterogeneous and culturally pluralistic as the United States, this can be quite a challenge. Adults have the right to make their own health care decisions, a change from former determinations based on paternalism. In a paternalistic system, clinicians tell patients what to do relying on what they think is right or best for them. Patients do what they are told to do without asking questions. Yet a clinician's decisions could be grounded in sound medical judgment or could be influenced by the clinician's own personal values or sense of what is right or wrong.

When decisions are based on a respect for autonomy, patients choose from the available options. From the clinician's perspective and values, the patient may make a "bad" decision. Despite the perception of others, individuals have the right to make bad health care decisions about aspects of their lives such as smoking or driving without a seat belt. However, the clinician has an obligation to inform the patient about available options, including no intervention or treatment, where appropriate. Respect for autonomy does not preclude the clinician's offering information or an opinion about the optimal option(s) for an individual patient. Nevertheless, the ultimate choice belongs to the patient, including "the final autonomy."

Beneficence

In health care, beneficence is interpreted as the obligation to do good for patients. When there are no good options, the clinician should, at least, do no harm as stated in the Hippocratic tradition of nonmaleficence. At times, a clinician's sense of what is good for a patient is compromised by an autonomous patient's choices. For example, conflicts may arise between a clinician's sense of beneficence and the patient's autonomy in caring for a Jehovah's Witness who refuses a blood transfusion or a surgical patient who refuses to consent to the suspension of a do not resuscitate order in the operating room. When respecting the patient's wishes would cause harm, clinicians are not obligated to violate their own set of values and act against their desire to be beneficent. In such situations, clinicians are entitled to a conscience objection. While physicians can't abandon a patient in an emergency, they can refer a patient elsewhere; clinicians can inform their superiors of their objections and ask that the patient be transferred to another provider.

Justice

Ethically, the principle of justice dictates that people should be treated in an equitable, or fair, fashion. Justice is adhered to, or violated, when the allocation of health care resources or access to health care is considered or rationed. In a "just" health care system, people would have access to the resources necessary to achieve a minimally acceptable level of health care. However, it is not clear that health care is a right, or an entitlement, in the United States, and a finite amount of health care resources is inequitably distributed. While resource allocation is important on a societywide level, clinicians are compromised when they have to allocate or deny access to health care resources at the bedside. In reality, providers are constantly allocating resources. When staffing is limited or inappropriate, clinicians may have to struggle with how to apportion their time.

Shortages of supplies or critical care beds must also be resolved. Over a considerable period of time, these allocation decisions and the associated stress can contribute to burnout in health care workers. However, a distinction should be made between insufficient resources for optimal care and situations where the resources are so insufficient as to lead to an unsafe health care environment. In the latter situation, the health care institution may be operating in an unethical or even an illegal fashion capacity to choose. People affected can include those who previously had the decision-making capacity and temporarily or permanently lost it.

Substituted Judgment

There is a consensus in American society, albeit an uneasy one, that adults with the capacity to make their own decisions have the right to do so. Clinicians have the obligation to respect the patient's autonomy. When the patient lacks the capacity to make an informed decision, the situation becomes more difficult. When a previously capable adult loses capacity to make decisions, the ethical standard of substituted judgment is applied to health care decisions. What would this individual have decided, given this set of circumstances? Individuals make decisions based on what's uniquely important to them: their own set of values, culture, religion, lifestyle, or life experiences. Examples of patient values include:

- I want to retain my capacity to think clearly.
- I want to avoid unnecessary pain and suffering.
- I want to be treated with respect.
- I want to be treated with dignity when I can no longer speak for myself.
- I don't want to be an unnecessary burden on my family.
- I want to experience a comfortable dying process.
- I want to be with my loved ones before I die.
- I want to be treated in accord with my religious beliefs and traditions.
- I want respect shown to my body after I die.

An advance directive makes substituted judgment much easier, by legally extending the patient's autonomy beyond the loss of decision-making capacity. A living will specifies a patient's wishes about medical treatment to prolong life and allows individuals to indicate what they would or wouldn't want in critical care situations. Most living wills focus on what the individual would not want to happen. One of the problems with a living will is that the statements are often not clear in relationship to the particular situation at hand. What does it mean when individuals say they wouldn't want to be on a ventilator? People might not want to be maintained on a ventilator if they were in an irreversible, ventilator dependent state. In contrast, they might not feel the same way about being on a ventilator for a few days after major surgery if their prognosis were good.

Since the patient lacks capacity when the living will is consulted, clinicians cannot have a conversation with the patient to clarify the meaning of the statements in the living will. Sometimes there is uncertainty about whether the patient would have changed their mind, given the specific circumstances. People may not want to live in a quadriplegic state, if given a choice. On the other hand, if there is no other alternative, they might adjust their feelings and live in that state rather than not live at all. In such circumstances, a surrogate decision maker, able to discuss the pros and cons of interventions, would be helpful in providing substituted judgment. Advance directives, such as health care proxies and durable powers of attorney for health care, allow for the designation of a surrogate decision maker to make medical decisions when the patient cannot. Health care organizations must ask about any advance directives.

Best Interest

When substituted judgment is not possible, the appropriate guideline is the standard of best interest, also known as the objective benefits/burden, or "reasonable person," standard. Best interest applies for individuals who have never had decision-making capacity, such as infants and children. There is no means to determine what a particular infant or child would have done with no advance directive and no identifiable surrogate decision makers. Thus, caregivers must ask the following questions: What is in the best interest of

this patient, given the critical circumstances? What would a reasonable person choose to do under the circumstances? Making the decision "requires morally imaginative and empathetic efforts to enter the experimental world of such patients." Despite the difficulties, this determination should be as objective as possible, holding the best interest of the individual uppermost.

Codes of Ethics

A code of ethics is one of the defining characteristics of a professional organization. Traditionally, the Hippocratic oath conveys a sense of the privileged roles and responsibilities of physicians over time. Almost every organization of health care providers has a code of ethics detailing the values, duties, and ethical responsibilities of their chosen professional membership. However, these codes of ethics contain broad statements that provide little assistance to the individual practitioner trying to interpret the applicability of the codes to specific clinical situations. Ethical codes are guiding principles, not directions for action in distinct situations. Although codes of ethics are open to interpretation, they remain important guidelines for health care professionals.

Confidentiality and Ethics

Every code of ethics emphasizes provider-patient confidentiality. Even though confidentiality is one of the most important ethical obligations of health care providers, it may be one of the most commonly violated. Health care providers have an undeniable obligation to respect the privacy of patients and to keep all information given to them in the strictest confidence. However, hospital visitors riding the elevator or sitting in the cafeteria can attest to breaches of confidentiality.

Violations of confidentiality are always ethically problematic. Breaches are even more unethical if the information is serious, has the ability to stigmatize the patient, or could lead to discrimination. Certainly, a diagnosis of HIV seropositivity should be treated confidentially.

There may be individuals, including health care providers, who the patients may not wish to inform. Discrimination against people with a positive HIV blood finding, although illegal in many states and a violation of the Americans with Disabilities Act, does exist. Patients may reasonably fear the loss of friends and support persons, housing, insurance, or job. This discrimination is extremely burdensome for individuals already dealing with a potentially devastating diagnosis. Health care providers and institutions should do everything they can to protect this sensitive information. Obviously, risk managers must be aware of the potential liability of the breach of confidentiality.

Some states, such as New York, have specific laws dealing with strict confidentiality regarding HIV test results. New York's legislation allows, but does not require, physicians to inform those believed to be at risk of exposure to HIV. Patients must be notified of the physician's intention and must be given the choice of allowing the physician or the health department to notify the contacts. Contacts are told only that they have been exposed, not by whom. Importantly, the only way to know who is really at risk of HIV exposure is to have the cooperation of the index patient. This New York State law is designed to relieve physicians from legal liability for breaching confidentiality. Disclosure is optional, to grant physicians discretion in encouraging patients to inform contacts themselves. It is hoped that this approach will not discourage patients from seeking needed care.

Informed Consent

Clinicians are obligated to provide autonomous adult patients with all the information they need, in a way that they can understand it, to allow them to make a fully informed decision. Patients must be given enough information to weigh the relative benefits and burdens or risks associated with the proposed intervention. Informed consent is a process, not just a signature on a consent form. While the signed consent form serves as documentation of the patient's understanding and consent, the process and dialogue between the clinician and patient are even more important. Can desperately ill patients be expected to weigh all the risks?

Conceptually, informing a patient about all the possible risks associated with an intervention or treatment is overwhelming to clinicians. How does the professional determine the extent of the discussion to fulfill the obligations associated with informed consent? Risk managers can profit from the court's reasonable approach to this question:

> The discussion need not be a disquisition, and surely the physician is not compelled to give his patient a short medical education; the disclosure role summons the physician only to a reasonable

explanation. This means generally informing the patient in nontechnical terms as to what is at stake: the therapy alternatives open to him, the goals expectably to be achieved, and the risks that may ensue from particular treatment and no treatment. So informing the patient hardly taxes the physician and it must be the exceptional patient who cannot comprehend such an explanation in at least a rough way.

Decisional Capacity to Weigh Risks

Decisional capacity refers to the individual's ability to weigh the relative benefits, risks, or burdens of proposed interventions and still have the ability to make a decision. In contrast to a psychiatric or legal determination of competency, decisional capacity is a clinical judgment. Importantly, an individual may have the capacity to make some decisions and not others and/or may have capacity at some times and not at others. Senile individuals may be clearheaded at times and understand and make choices. Sick elderly individuals facing Mrs. Schloendorff was admitted to New York Hospital in 1908 with a stomach disorder, later determined to be a fibroid tumor. She consented to an examination under ether but explicitly stated that there was to be no surgery. While she was under anesthesia, the fibroid was removed. Defense lawyers argued that the surgeon saved her significant mortality and morbidity risks associated with a second anesthesia. Judge Cardozo disagreed: "Every human being of adult years and sound mind has the right to determine what shall be done with his body; and a surgeon who performs an operation without his patient's consent commits an assault, for which he is liable in damages." This court held that the only exception to informed consent was an unconscious patient where an emergency operation was necessary before consent could be obtained.

Mr. Canterbury consented to and underwent a laminectomy in 1958. Postoperatively, he fell and was subsequently paralyzed from the waist down. He consented to a second operation, but after that he "required crutches to walk, still suffered from urinal incontinence and paralysis of the bowels, and wore a penile clamp." In the court's decision there was a discussion of "true consent" or the obligation of physicians to disclose information to patients. Mr. Canterbury had not been warned about paralysis resulting from falls.

An expanded version of "true consent" in the court's decision provides guidelines for risk managers involved with the informed consent process:

> True consent to what happens to oneself is the informed exercise of a choice, and that entails an opportunity to evaluate knowledgeably the options available and the risks attendant upon each.... the physician discharges the duty when he makes a reasonable effort to convey sufficient information although the patient, without the fault of the physician, may not fully grasp it.

difficult and complicated treatment decisions may understand that they do not have the capacity to make complex decisions but may be able to make simple decisions or designate a surrogate. Extremely sick patients or those undergoing surgery may temporarily lose their decision-making capacity and regain it after treatment or intervention. However, these people may have enough capacity to choose a health care agent or surrogate decision maker. A court appointed guardian can also make surrogate decisions. Acting as her guardian, Cindy Wasiek's mother consented to sterilization by laparoscopic tubal ligation for her twenty-six-year-old, severely retarded daughter. A prior legal guardian tried to stop the sterilization and the case went to the U.S. Supreme Court.

Judge David Souter found the sterilization appropriate where the woman "may experience severe or life threatening trauma if she becomes pregnant... is incapable of understanding reproduction or contraception... and is incapable of caring for the child... and is likely to engage in sexual activity."

Clinical Applications of Ethics

There are many clinical situations in which a risk manager should have knowledge about ethical approaches to problem resolution. Critics may contend that violations of ethical doctrines do not incur liability. Yet, as professional organizations publish codes of ethics that include current opinions with legal annotations, liability arguments could be bolstered with the codes of ethics data. A 177-page book published by the American Medical Association discusses a broad spectrum of issues and includes about 150 legal citations. Ethical considerations can be applied in routine health care services such as decision making for adults with capacity, surrogate decision making, perinatal dilemmas, pediatric care, geriatric care, organ transplantation, medical futility, and end of life choices.

Decision Making for Adults with Capacity

Adults with capacity have the right to make their own health care decisions, but they do not have the right to demand that clinicians take professional actions perceived as bad medical or nursing practice. In a nonemergency situation, clinicians are not required to do things that violate their personal values, such as perform abortions.

A common conflict arises in the care of capacitated adult patients who are Jehovah's Witnesses and refuse an appropriate blood transfusion. Jehovah's Witnesses believe that it is a serious violation of their religion to accept blood or blood products, 19 and most will risk death rather than imperil their eternal salvation. Clinicians may find their beneficence-based belief in saving lives violated by allowing a Jehovah's Witness to die if a transfusion could be life-saving. These clinicians should remove themselves from the care of Jehovah's Witnesses.

They are not justified in transfusing a known Jehovah's Witness who has expressed a conviction against transfusions. Doing so would risk liability, since the doctor would clearly be violating the patient's autonomy. Courts almost never issue an order to transfuse an adult Jehovah's Witness with capacity who refuses a transfusion, or a previously capacitated adult with a relevant advance directive. On the other hand, the courts almost always grant a court order to transfuse the minor child of a Jehovah's Witness against the parents' wishes. Older adolescents who express the same religious beliefs as their parents present a more difficult case; there is no consistent precedent for this situation.

Dilemmas faced by clinicians are magnified when a health care institution is geographically located in an area with a large number of Jehovah's Witnesses. In such situations, Jehovah's Witnesses may identify specific hospitals sensitive to their beliefs where the wishes of autonomous adults are routinely accepted and all measures possible are taken to avoid transfusions in children. However, court orders will be obtained to transfuse children if necessary. As a risk management initiative, health care institutions should probably identify professionals in surgery, anesthesia, and obstetrics/gynecology who are comfortable with the implications of the Witnesses' religious beliefs. Such planning avoids the ad hoc compromising of health care providers' values and beliefs, while respecting the religious beliefs and values of Jehovah's Witnesses.

Surrogate Decision Making

When a previously capacitated adult loses capacity, it is helpful to have a designated surrogate decision maker, even when an advance directive exists. This surrogate can participate in decision making just as the patient would have, had capacity not been lost. Critics attack the moral and legal rationale for surrogate decision making for three reasons:

(1) Interests of incompetent persons are different from those of the same person during their competent state.

(2) Surrogates often project their own desires and needs while neglecting the patient's preferences and values.

(3) The lives of vulnerable individuals may be undervalued when instructions are unclear and not comprehensive.

A surrogate may have intimate knowledge about the individual that assists in making a substituted judgment. In the absence of such information in an advance directive, the surrogate may participate with clinicians to determine which decisions are in the patient's best interest. Ideally, the surrogate should be chosen by the patient, when capable, and designated in a health care proxy or durable power of attorney for health care document. Appropriate documents vary from state to state. In some states, family members function as surrogate decision makers and are recognized by the law as such. In other jurisdictions, such as New York State, the family member has no legal authority to make decisions to withdraw or withhold life-sustaining treatment unless properly designated as a health care agent in a health care proxy. Often, end of life decisions need to be made for an incapacitated individual.

Respect for autonomy dictates that clinicians abide by the decisions made by a properly designated surrogate. Risk managers should understand the law in relation to surrogate decision making within their jurisdictions.

Perinatal Dilemmas

Perinatal issues constitute the most unresolved dilemmas in clinical ethics. While this is certainly true about abortion, it also holds for maternal-fetal conflicts and dilemmas in the neonatal intensive care unit (NICU).

Although not without controversy, abortion is a constitutionally protected right in the United States. Violence at abortion clinics and the debate over training residents in obstetrics/gynecology to perform abortions are evidence of the continuing emotionally charged controversy. Risk managers should understand the law in their state regarding abortion, including access and consent issues.

In obstetrical care, maternal-fetal medicine remains highly charged with ethical predicaments. Many clinicians practice as if they have two patients, the mother and the fetus, where only one of the patients speaks for herself. This emphasis on two patients was not always the case. In the nineteenth century, there was little discussion among physicians or midwives about the well-being of the fetus. Childbirth was dangerous for the mother, and little could be done for the infant, much less the fetus. During the twentieth century, childbirth became safer for the mother through the use of antibiotics, blood typing, cross-matching, and improved anesthesia. At the same time, technology evolved to intervene with high risk infants and fetuses. Ultrasound imaging allows for the visualization of the fetus and conveys a real sense of the fetus as an additional patient during the prenatal period.

Maternal-fetal conflicts arise only when the rights or behavior of the pregnant woman are not in the best interest of her fetus. Possible high risk behaviors of pregnant women include the abuse of drugs or alcohol, the refusal of a cesarean section indicated for maternal well-being and/or fetal distress, the refusal by a pregnant Jehovah's Witness to receive a necessary blood transfusion, and the failure by a brittle diabetic pregnant woman to adhere to her prescribed diet. These varying behaviors provoke differing emotional and ethical anguish in clinicians. A clinician may be able to accept the decision of a pregnant Jehovah's Witness to refuse a blood transfusion, on the basis of respect for autonomy. Clinicians may have much less tolerance for a pregnant woman addicted to crack cocaine.

A pregnant woman should not be treated any differently from other patients with respect to autonomy. Advocacy for the fetus requires a significant effort to help the pregnant woman understand the consequences if her behavior is not in the best interest of her fetus. Some physicians would seek a court order if a pregnant woman refused a cesarean section necessary for fetal well-being. Even stronger motivation exists if the mother is also at risk, as in placenta previa. On the other hand, some physicians would attempt to get a court order but would not tie the woman down and operate without her consent, even with the court order. These clinicians hope that going to court reinforces, for the pregnant woman, their serious concerns and the seriousness of the situation. From an ethical perspective, it is extremely serious to violate a woman's autonomy simply because she is pregnant.

Case law is inconsistent and not particularly helpful in maternal-fetal conflicts. While some courts have intervened on grounds of fetal interest, others have refused to issue court orders. In some cases, the patient has delivered while the court was still deliberating.

Decision making in the NICU raises profound ethical challenges. Prior to the regionalization of intensive perinatal care, clinicians and perhaps one or both parents made private decisions about imperiled newborns. Often, these decisions were not subject to public scrutiny or even to professional examination within a hospital. Imperiled newborns include premature births, congenital anomalies, genetic defects, and those who are very sick.

Mrs. Angela Carder had been diagnosed with cancer as an adolescent, and it was in remission. She was warned that the cancer could be exacerbated by a pregnancy. Nevertheless, she became pregnant and the cancer reappeared and worsened. Early in her third trimester she was dying as a court ordered delivery of her fetus by cesarean section. Her neonate died after birth, and she died shortly after the surgery. Surgery hastened her death by a few days. On appeal, the court reversed the earlier court's order, ruling that Mrs. Carder's autonomy dictated that her wishes be respected. This was particularly true in this case because her fetus was at only borderline viability.

A landmark article about decision making in the NICU appeared in the New England Journal of Medicine in 1973. Duff and Campbell argued that it is sometimes appropriate to withdraw or withhold life-sustaining treatment from seriously ill or anomalous newborns. They described a methodology employed in the NICU at Yale-New Haven Hospital (Connecticut) to attempt to achieve consensus regarding appropriate treatment for such newborns. Everyone involved with the baby's care or with an interest, such as the parents, was included in those discussions. Duff and Campbell contended that it was fitting to treat some of these severely compromised neonates less aggressively. Furthermore, parents had to be active decision makers with the team caring for the baby. Infants who were not aggressively treated were supported in a humane way during their dying days. In contrast, critics believed that nonaggressive treatment decisions could be problematic from a legal perspective and that grieving parents might not be in the best position to make such decisions for their children. An active debate regarding decision making in the NICU ensued among clinicians in pediatrics and neonatology.

In the early 1980s, the federal government became involved in public policy regarding neonatal decision making when the Baby Doe regulations were issued. On the basis of the Rehabilitation Act of 1973, the regulations established a telephone hotline and investigative procedures to deal with alleged discrimination against or inappropriate treatment of "handicapped" newborns. Although the regulations were overturned by the Second Circuit Court in the New York case of Baby Jane Doe, a public policy debate ensued. In addition, federal legislation was passed that required states receiving federal funds for child abuse and neglect prevention programs to create mechanisms to investigate suspected abuse or inappropriate denial of treatment for handicapped newborns.

Legislative amendments defined medically indicated treatment for newborns as "treatment, including appropriate nutrition, hydration, and medication, which in the treating physician's... reasonable medical judgment, will be most likely to be effective in ameliorating or correcting all such life-threatening conditions." Three exceptions are allowed in which treatment can be withheld: (1) infants who are irreversibly comatose; (2) infants for whom treatment would merely prolong dying, would not remedy all the infant's life-threatening conditions, and would be useless in ensuring survival; and (3) infants for whom treatment would be "virtually futile" and its provision would be inhumane. Many states utilized existing child abuse reporting measures to implement the federally mandated program. Risk managers should be aware of the specific procedures in their state.

Usually, parents are the appropriate decision makers for their children. They generally try to make decisions in the best interest of their children, and they live with the consequences. However, parents need information from health care experts to make these difficult decisions. In addition, parents may be comforted if they have a sense that those caring for their infant agree with their decisions.

On the other hand, it is quite apparent from the child abuse and neglect statistics that not all parents strive to or are able to make decisions in the best interest of their children. In such rare cases, society has opted to protect the vulnerable child. Such situations occasionally arise with infants in the NICU. When parents are clearly not making decisions in the best interest of their child, an ethics committee should be consulted and ultimately a court order may be obtained. For example, parents could refuse to consent to surgery for an easily correctable gastrointestinal anomaly in an infant with Down's syndrome. In other cases, such as with anencephaly, aggressive treatment clearly is inappropriate. Most would agree that supportive care during the process of dying is the appropriate course for such infants. In the Virginia case of Baby K, however, nonaggressive care was challenged. Baby K's mother demanded aggressive care for her anencephalic infant. Courts supported her request on the basis of legislation prohibiting discrimination against the handicapped and another law prohibiting "dumping" of patients from one hospital to another. Unsuccessfully, clinicians argued that it was medically futile to treat Baby K. The Supreme Court refused to hear the case, and Baby K survived for more than two years.

Many patients in the NICU fall into a gray area where it is appropriate for clinicians and parents to struggle to determine what is in the baby's best interest and to proceed accordingly. Many ethicists and clinicians believe that overtreatment, rather than undertreatment, is the major problem in the NICU. Fear of legal liability, a failure to understand legal requirements, and the inability to accept the limits of technological medicine contribute to overtreatment.

Pediatric Care

Decision making for children is guided by the same ethical standard as for neonates: the best interest. Identifying the individuals who are optimally suited to determine the child's best interest and the parameters to use can present real dilemmas. Strict objectivity is a vital component of any choice.

Generally, parents are able to determine their child's best interest. As with neonates, parents must live with the consequences for their children. To make fully informed decisions, parents require information from appropriate health care professionals. Children old enough to comprehend data about their health and proposed interventions should also be given information appropriate to their age and developmental level. Chronically ill children may be quite sophisticated about their health status and care. Although the legal decision-making authority generally resides with the parents, children should be given the opportunity to assent, if they are capable. Particularly difficult situations arise when the patients are adolescents. They may have a high degree of understanding and differ with the decisions of their parents. Some adolescents are considered emancipated by virtue of living independently and/or becoming pregnant or having children of their own. In this area, the law varies among jurisdictions.

In some circumstances, parents do not have the legal right to make health care decisions or their decision-making authority has been removed. It is extremely important for risk managers to have a clear understanding of the law in their particular state or jurisdiction. For example, in New York State, parents have a great deal of latitude about how they raise their children in areas such as education and routine health care decisions. However, there is no clear basis in New York State law for parents to make decisions to withdraw or withhold life-sustaining treatment for their children. This ambiguity may leave the child with no clear advocate, short of the courts.

All states have mechanisms for the removal or suspension of parental custody when child abuse or neglect is suspected or verified. The state has an obligation to protect the potentially vulnerable child. In addition, health care providers have an obligation to report suspected child abuse or neglect. Although reporting violates confidentiality and may damage the provider-patient relationship, the protection of this vulnerable population warrants disclosure.

Religion is a variable that may influence the decisions parents make for their children. Freedom of religion is constitutionally protected, and parents are free to raise children as they see fit. Yet sometimes religion interferes with what society perceives to be the best interest of children. Society may intervene and override the decisions of parents, such as when Jehovah's Witnesses refuse to allow a blood transfusion for their child. When parents pursue nontraditional remedies or refuse surgery on the basis of religious beliefs, clinicians or society may label the decisions "medical neglect." Communication with the parents and the child, as developmental level permits, is vitally important, whether or not a court order is pursued and granted.

The participation of children in clinical research and trials is controversial. Obviously, the potential vulnerability of children as research subjects is an ethical concern. Generally, clinical trials are not conducted on children unless the experimental drug has proven to be effective on adults. On the other hand, researchers in areas such as oncology and AIDS argue that ineffective agents in adults may prove to be therapeutic for children because of differences in physiology. Although this is a difficult and ethically problematic dilemma, some children may benefit from being enrolled in particular clinical trials. Risk managers should be certain that all appropriate approvals and consents are obtained and ensure that the clinical trials, as well as the subjects, are carefully monitored.

Significantly, children should not be submitted to clinical trials that may increase suffering and hold no hope of benefit, as in last-resort clinical research. This scenario may arise when parents have difficulty accepting the fact that their child is dying. Whereas an adult may choose to participate in a trial for altruistic reasons, children who can't consent should not be subjected to that experience.

Geriatric Care

Elderly people are quite vulnerable, and there is a heightened awareness of elder abuse in the United States. Risk managers must be aware of the legal requirements for reporting elder abuse. Elderly people can be victims of abuse from those caring for them in nursing homes, as well as in residential arrangements with relatives or friends. There are many ethical dilemmas specific to nursing homes and group living situations.

A common problem for elderly patients in hospitals and nursing homes is the inappropriate use of restraints. Confused or senile elderly patients have a tendency to fall, and a fractured hip may result in a total loss of mobility, as well as legal liability for the institution. Elderly patients who have capacity are prone to falls because they may fail to recognize their need for assistance and their limitations in certain situations.

Restraining elderly patients thus may seem like a beneficent action. However, there is a clear limitation to mobility and autonomy for patients restrained against their will. This is especially true when patients are restrained inappropriately or for the convenience of the staff. Because of restraint abuses, specific policies and protocols have been established, and restraints often require a doctor's order. Risk managers must be aware of administrative policies and work with staff to promote maximal safety for patients with minimal restriction of autonomy and mobility.

Frequently, elderly patients are ignored when health care decisions regarding them are made. Just because individuals are aged does not mean they lack the capacity to make their own decisions. Some are senile and never have moments of lucidity. Others have periods when they are more clearheaded. Some may not have the capacity to make complex decisions related to their health but may possess enough capacity to designate a surrogate decision maker. Elderly individuals who retain their capacity must be allowed to make their own decisions and should be encouraged to prepare advance directives and to appoint surrogate decision makers.

The appropriate use of limited health care resources for the elderly presents some quandaries. A large percentage of Medicare money is spent on elderly individuals in the last months of life. Ethicist Daniel Callahan suggested reconsidering the allocation of such resources. In specific cases, the extension of life through technological intervention may be inhumane and, by some standards, unethical. In other situations, a reasonable quality of life may be maintained. There is no societal consensus on guidelines for the allocation of health care resources to the elderly.

Organ Transplantation

The medical ability to transplant organs has engendered ethical issues such as the determination of "brain death" and the consent for the donation of organs. Moreover, there may be a fear that the potential donor will be denied care or treatment. Real or perceived religious and cultural prohibitions also play a role in diminishing the number of donors. Mass media promotes awareness of the need for transplantable organs. When celebrities such as baseball star Mickey Mantle or the governor of Pennsylvania receive an organ, public discourse on the subject increases.

Many potential organ donors die each year, many in catastrophic accidents, without actually becoming donors, as potential recipients die while awaiting a transplant. A British study found that although 63 percent of 218 respondents carried organ donor cards, estimates projected that only 40 percent of potential donors actually made donations each year. The low rate of donation is assumed to be due to the reluctance of clinicians to approach the family members of a potential donor. However, a study demonstrated that it is usually the family of the potential donor who is reluctant and refuses the request, as they are grief stricken and struggling to cope with a sudden catastrophic event.

State laws may "require request" when potential donors are identified, and family members of potential donors must be asked about the donation of organs. That mandate differs from a suggested "presumed consent" policy not routinely adopted, because of the obviously strong public opinion on the subject. Since laws differ among states, it is critical that risk managers be familiar with the relevant laws and policies in their jurisdiction.

A shortage of transplantable organs focuses controversy on how the waiting list is prioritized. The geographic locations of the potential donor and recipient are priority factors, since organs have a short survival time. The severity of the patient's illness is another variable. Social supports available to the patient may be a consideration, given the usually lengthy recuperation period and the need for follow-up care. Although economic considerations play a part in the decision, from an ethical perspective they probably shouldn't. In reality, money must be paid up front or there must be a third-party payer willing to reimburse for the transplant.

An especially acute shortage of organs for infants and small children exists, since they require organs commensurate with their body size and the pool of potential donors is limited.

Although not brain dead, anencephalic infants are born without their upper brain, and basic body functions such as respiration and heartbeat may be maintained for a short period of time by the brain stem. These infants are thought to have a universally dismal prognosis. Families of these infants might take comfort in knowing that their child, who will not survive, could benefit other children through organ donation. However, the use of organs from someone who is not brain dead is highly controversial. There is no consensus on anencephalic infants as organ donors, although the American Medical Association recently issued an opinion condoning such donations in certain circumstances.

If transplant services are available in the institution, it is imperative that appropriate policies, procedures, and staff training be in place to avoid risk. Each event should be tracked to ensure that actions were in concert with ethical principles for donor protection, and with maximum potential for a successful outcome.

Medical Futility

Many health care providers concur with the court's decision in the Gilgunn case. "Futile" treatment may deplete a significant amount of scarce health care resources and prolong suffering. On the other hand, determining exactly what is futile remains a real dilemma. Futility is a dangerous "slippery slope" and must be defined explicitly. Since there are no clear legal guidelines, the Gilgunn case may be the beginning of a legal framework for futility decisions.

Catherine F. Gilgunn became comatose and suffered irreversible brain damage. Her daughter, Joan, told attending physicians that her mother wanted everything medically possible to be done to keep her alive. Over the daughter's objections, doctors issued a do not resuscitate order. Joan sued, saying the doctors were obligated to abide by her mother's wishes. A jury found that the mother would have wanted to stay on life support but that it would have been futile and of no benefit. Therefore, the decision was in favor of the doctors.

Attending physicians could be constantly confronted with families demanding care. An emotional conflict arises between families who want every effort undertaken, no matter how futile, and doctors, applying the beneficence doctrine, wanting to do what's best for their patients and not prolong suffering. Some health care professionals indicated that it would have been disastrous if the jury had ruled otherwise in the Gilgunn case. Providers would have had to render whatever the family demanded, regardless of whether the treatment was of any benefit to the patient.

In a practical sense, a perplexing problem with the concept of futility is that there is no precise definition or legal clarification of what is futile. In the narrowest sense, if an intervention achieves its desired goal, it may not be viewed as futile. Administering antibiotics to cure an infection that is sensitive to a particular antibiotic may not be futile. On the other hand, if the patient with the infection is terminally ill or vegetative, clinicians may feel that the overall prognosis makes any intervention futile.

End of Life Choices

Difficult ethical dilemmasincluding the right to refuse, or to request the withdrawal of, life-sustaining treatmentfreq uently occur at the end of life. Emotional debates about physician-assisted suicide and assisted suicide in general reflect concerns that health care institutions and professionals do not always adequately manage death and dying. Oregon voters approved a "Death with Dignity" law that empowers physicians to prescribe lethal doses of medication to terminally ill patients. Eleven other states (California, Colorado, Connecticut,

Maryland, Massachusetts, Michigan, Nebraska, New Hampshire, New Mexico, Washington, and Wisconsin) are considering physician-assisted suicide bills. The Oregon law is under legal review, but even if the law is upheld, is it ethical? If pain were managed better, perhaps chronically and terminally ill individuals contemplating suicide to escape a painful death and/or to avoid becoming a burden on their families, might recognize and consider alternatives.

Clinicians have improved their pain management abilities. Some physicians remain concerned that if they provide enough analgesics, such as morphine in a terminally ill cancer patient, they will expedite the patient's demise.

From an ethical perspective, the intent of the intervention is of primary importance. A clinician prescribing morphine for the relief of pain is not doing so with the intent to kill but rather to provide comfort. Interestingly, if patients are allowed to self-administer morphine, they often use less, since the anxiety associated with anticipating unrelieved pain is eliminated.

A properly designated surrogate decision maker should be able to consent to the withdrawal or withholding of life-sustaining treatment for an incapacitated adult. Surrogates and clinicians need to cooperate to form a substituted judgment or to determine what is in the patient's best interest. That standard to be applied is determined by the state's law and the information provided by the patient in an advance directive and in prior statements.

Options available and the process to be followed in regard to end of life decision making differs among the states because of a U.S. Supreme Court decision. That ruling allowed individual states to determine what constitutes "clear and convincing evidence" of a patient's wishes. In addition, the court recognized artificially administered food and fluids as treatment subject to withdrawal under certain circumstances. That position on the withdrawal and withholding of nutrition and hydration was supported by the AMA.

Scott Horn suffered a stroke and had surgery. After surgery, he was unable to speak or move his limbs and was fed through a gastric tube. His father and sister asked that the feeding tube be removed. A neurologist found Horn to be in a persistent vegetative state, and the hospital disconnected life support. His ex-wife interpreted Horn's eye blinks as signals that he didn't agree with removing life support. Horn's ex-wife sued for $10 million for trauma and fear experienced by Horn. A jury ruled that the hospital and the doctors were not negligent.

Nancy Cruzan, a woman in her twenties, existed for a number of years in a persistent vegetative state. Her parents petitioned the court to allow the removal of a feeding tube from their daughter. In an attempt at substituted judgment, they based their request on what they believed Nancy would have wanted. In the only right to die case heard by the Supreme Court, the Court upheld the right of the state to determine, as narrowly or as widely as it chooses, what constitutes "clear and convincing evidence" of a patient's wishes. The parents' request was denied.

The Cruzan decision allowed Missouri to maintain the most conservative standard in the United States regarding the withdrawal or withholding of life-sustaining treatment. New York is the next most conservative state.

End of life decisions include choices about the management of pain, resuscitation, and the aggressiveness of interventions. While the treatment plan for a terminally ill patient may be appropriately nonaggressive, each decision must be treated and documented separately. It may be appropriate to discuss a do not resuscitate (DNR) order with the patient or the designated surrogate while the patient is a candidate for palliative surgery or treatment in an intensive care unit. In no case should the patient be denied nursing and basic supportive care by the clinicians on the caring team. In contrast, the Baby K court ruling held that respiratory support for an anencephalic infant was "stabilizing care" within the meaning of federal law prohibiting patient "dumping." If such treatment was requested, the law did not allow an exception for comatose patients or medical conditions that could ultimately result in death.

Since no national end of life standard exists, risk managers must be familiar with the law related to end of life decision making in their particular state. For example, New York and Georgia have specific laws regarding DNR orders. Within the parameters prescribed by law, dying patients and their families should be treated humanely and with dignity. Communication and documentation is vitally important at this time.

Research on Human Subjects

Eventually, new treatments have to be tested on humans, and these research subjects could be harmed as a result of the experimental therapy. In some cases, investigators have abused participants in their zeal to discover a miracle treatment. To protect the design of a clinical research study, researchers may discuss whether or not to treat subjects or to continue the protocol. Institutional review boards (IRBs) were created to resolve these considerations before the research begins.

Abuses During Research Studies

Scientific organizations such as the Institute of Medicine and the National Academy of Science identify three types of research behavior that must be challenged: "questionable research practices, misconduct in science, and other misconduct." Leaders of these professional groups called for ethical standards to exceed legal mandates.

Whenever the subject of the abuse of human subjects by clinical researchers arises, the medical experiments of Nazi doctors during World War II come to mind. Retrospective investigation of the Nazi atrocities led to the Nuremberg Code and the Declaration of Helsinki, which endeavored to establish high moral standards for the conduct of research on human subjects. Although the abuses of Nazi Germany were outrageous to the extreme, other cases of obvious abuses of human subjects have occurred closer to home.

In the Tuskegee syphilis study, conducted by the U.S. Public Health Service from 1932 to 1972, research subjects were poor black share-croppers in Macon County, Alabama: 399 men in the late stages of syphilis and 201 men who served as controls. For forty years, these men were studied, initially to observe the course of undertreated syphilis, and later of untreated syphilis, before and after the discovery of penicillin. This study was well known among physicians locally and was the subject of publications in major national professional journals during those years. Public outrage erupted in 1972 when an Associated Press reporter broke the story to the general public, using information from a whistle-blower who was a former public health worker. Subsequently, the Tuskegee study stimulated emotional public discourse and increased the scrutiny of clinical research involving human subjects in the United States. In the era of AIDS and HIV disease, the Tuskegee study continues to have a legacy. Many individuals from minority communities are suspicious of clinical trials, with good reason.

Both the Willowbrook and the Tuskegee studies were catalysts for reform in research on human subjects in the United States. A reform measure established the National Commission for the Protection of Human Subjects in the 1970s. This commission produced several volumes of guidelines, including The Belmont Report. Another result of reform was the establishment of the Office for Protection from Research Risks at the National Institutes of Health.

Additional examples of abuse of human subjects in the United States were exposed by Henry Beecher in a landmark article in the New England Journal of Medicine in 1966. Many of these studies had a high ratio of harm to benefit and were conducted without fully informed consent.

The discovery and study of possible abuses of human subjects continue, as evidenced by the current deliberations of the White House Advisory Committee on Human Radiation Experiments concentrating on post-World War II abuses related to radiation exposure.

Clinical Trials Versus Treatment

Participation in clinical trials must be voluntary and lack of participation must not compromise basic health care. It is an unfortunate reality that participants in clinical trials often receive increased attention from health care providers because of the research design and the data collection methods. Blurring of distinctions between clinical research and treatment in the eyes of prospective participants is a particular consequence of the AIDS epidemic.

Early in the epidemic, people infected with HIV, and their advocates, were desperate for any ray of hope and any possible therapy. Since no accepted therapy was available, they demanded access to the few clinical trials showing any promise. This demand moved research goals from primarily protecting human subjects from harm to promoting maximum access to clinical treatment, while at the same time limiting the potential burden or harm and avoiding exposure to poorly designed research. These goals remain a significant challenge for IRBs.

Institutional Review Boards

A vital institutional safeguard for human subjects in clinical research is the institutional review board, or IRB. The first federal policy requiring review by an investigator's institutional colleagues was issued in 1966. Shortly thereafter, this policy was extended to cover all U.S. Public Health Service grants. In 1974, policies and guidelines were revised and issued as regulations by the Department of Health, Education and Welfare. These guidelines required the IRB to consist of at least five people, including community representation from individuals not employed by the institution conducting the research. An IRB had to review the proposed research for its "legal, professional, and community acceptability."

IRBs are active in all academic medical centers, community hospitals, and organizations involved with the conduct of medical research and clinical trials. With an interdisciplinary membership and representation from the community, the IRBs are responsible for reviewing proposals for research involving human subjects, including both invasive and noninvasive studies which may involve patients and/or staff. IRBs are responsible for reviewing the research methodology for soundness and informed consent procedures to make sure that they are clear, understandable, and inclusive. Importantly, the IRB must consider the relative balance of risks and possible benefits to research participants. Studies involving human subjects should not be unduly harmful, and involvement must be voluntary. Involvement in a clinical trial must not be a prerequisite for basic health care. In addition, the IRB is responsible for continuous monitoring as the study progresses and for investigating adverse reactions.

Ethics Committees

To assist in the resolution of complex ethical dilemmas, health care institutions have established ethics committees with roles, responsibilities, and authority explicitly delineated. In addition, organizations have examined the composition of these committees and the varied guidelines for selecting members. Furthermore, the relationship between risk managers and ethics committees had to be clarified.

Role, Responsibilities, and Authority

Most American hospitals have one or more ethics committees, and the number is likely to increase as accrediting agencies such as JCAHO require attention to patients' rights and ethical issues during their institutional surveys. Utilization and effectiveness of an ethics committee varies greatly and may depend on and reflect its membership. If the ethics committee members are all upper-level administrators, for example, staff members, patients, and families of patients may be reluctant to ask the committee for assistance.

The precursors of hospital ethics committees were the dialysis committees in the 1960s, as well as the committees on abortion and sterilization that existed for decades in Catholic hospitals. When the Karen Ann Quinlan 1976 court decision61 mentioned the use of the hospital's ethics committee, most hospitals did not have one. Ms.

Quinlan happened to be a patient in a Catholic hospital in New Jersey that had an ethics committee to consider issues of abortion and sterilization.

As the field of bioethics has grown, the use of ethics committees to consider complex cases has become a stronger recommendation. Federal government recommendations appeared in the Baby Doe regulations, and infant care review committees in neonatology have become more common. Ethics committees vary in who they report to: hospital administration, the board of trustees, the medical board, or a specific clinical department.

Usually, ethics committees have three roles in health care institutions: education, policy development, and consultation. Ethics committees spend considerable time educating themselves, their hospital staff, patients, and the broader community served by the institution. This education includes knowledge of basic ethical principles, institutional policy relating to ethical and legal issues, and a basic understanding of the law as it applies to health-related issues in the particular geographical location.

Policy development related to ethical and/or legal issues also concerns ethics committees. For example, the committee might develop a specific policy to implement the federal Patient Self-Determination Act or a state Do Not Resuscitate law.

Many ethics committees assume a consultation role in difficult cases. Usually, the bylaws of ethics committees allow a case to be brought to the committee by a patient, the patient's family, the patient's physician or nurse, or anyone involved with the care of a patient. Often, the dilemma is resolved by simply gathering together all the involved individuals, including the patient or surrogate, and providing an objective, neutral committee or subcommittee to hear the concerns and to facilitate communication. Sometimes the best option for the patient is pinpointed; sometimes the least bad option is identified. This type of group deliberation may provide some comfort, especially if decisions are being made by a surrogate. However, the ethics committee's recommendations are advisory, not binding. In some situations, the institution's administration is in the position of deciding whether to implement the committee's recommendations. Clinicians may decide that the recommendations violate their personal values, based on a conscience objection, and may request that another clinician be assigned to the care of the patient.

Composition of the Ethics Committee

There is no single model for an ethics committee. Committees can include physicians, nurses, social workers, allied health care professionals, and at least one community member who is not an employee and can view things objectively from the perspective of patients and their families. Some committees include representatives of the clergy, the hospital attorney, the hospital risk manager, and administrative personnel. In any specific case discussion, appropriate individuals with expertise not represented on the committee can be brought in as necessary. Clinical departments may choose to have their own ethics committees, in addition to a hospitalwide ethics committee. Departmental committees are most common in departments of nursing, but they may also be found in medicine, pediatrics, and obstetrics/gynecology. One of the most important and unique aspects of an ethics committee is its interdisciplinary nature. On the other hand, departments or professionals may feel more comfortable addressing issues within their own discipline, because they feel the problems are unique to their profession or department. This is a particularly common rationale for the existence of nursing ethics committees. Although these feelings are significant, there must be a communication link between departmental committees and the overall institutional ethics committee, since issues may overlap. In planning educational programs, it makes sense to pool resources and to plan complementary programs.

Relationship to Risk Management

Hospital risk managers are members of ethics committees in many institutions. Some committees include the hospital risk manager as an ex officio member without voting privileges. Critics contend that sitting on a committee whose primary role is to protect the patient and serve as an advocate for patient's rights is a conflict of interest for the hospital risk manager, who is responsible for protecting the institution. Putting the voting issue aside, an active communication link between risk management and the ethics committee is very appropriate.

In cases brought before the ethics committee, there may be a need for the patient, patient's family, clinicians, and other members to understand the limits of the law and the hospital's perception of risk and liabilityareas of a risk manager's expertise. A clinician may need to know if the hospital will support controversial decisions. Patients or family may also need to understand the hospital administration's position on a deliberation. In addition, when a case is brought to the attention of risk management, coexisting ethical issues may be identified. Thus, ethics committees and risk managers must work together.

Ethics are not just Values

Although ethical behavior is not mandated by legislation, individuals do initiate lawsuits if they feel that health care providers made the wrong decisions. In the face of complicated and perplexing patient care dilemmas, no "right choice" may exist, and varied rationales can justify the deliberate decision. Within a cost containment milieu, health care providers encounter high risk liability potentials embedded in ethical considerations. Fixed payment reimbursement schemes may promote "quicker and sicker" institutional discharges because money, not therapy principles, dictate early discharge.

An "OB express" may develop if insurers deny coverage when a mother stays in the hospital more than twenty-four hours after delivering her baby. These cost saving incentives can place health care professionals and institutions at risk when they violate professionally established ethical concerns about the patient-provider relationship. Risk managers work to protect their institutions from legal liability. There are many complex situations in the provision of health care in which the application of legal guidelines to the particular patient situation is not clear. Institutional policies and guidelines promoting ethical decision making are thus vitally important and necessary to render optimal patient care. A risk manager needs to be familiar with basic ethical principles, as well as the law applicable at all levels of government. In addition, extensive communication among health care providers, institutional representatives, patients, and/or surrogates fosters ethical decision making and reduces legal liability for institutions. An ethics program in a health care institution is certainly more than just values.

9

Assuring Safety and Security in Health Care Institutions

Ramifications of adverse safety and security incidents combine to create a serious threat to the financial well-being of any health care organization.

Prepared by the National Institute for Occupational Safety Hazards (NIOSH), 1 the list is a strong reminder of the potential dangers existing in a health care facility. Risk managers must be aware of and address these potential liabilities every day. Furthermore, employers are required to inform employees of all potential dangers under the Occupational Safety and Health Administrations (OSHA) right-to-know policy. Conspicuously, stress is absent from the hazard list, since stress is reported by workers in all areas and cannot be listed in a single location.

Stress was formally categorized as a job hazard only recently. In 1986, NIOSH identified the following clinical disorders resulting from job stress: affective disturbances such as anxiety, depression, and job dissatisfaction; maladaptive behavior or lifestyle patterns; and chemical dependencies or alcohol abuse. Furthermore, the most stressful job situations in any workplace occur in health care occupations: ranging from dealing with life-threatening injuries and illnesses to dealing with the demands of patients to dealing with the professional authority hierarchy. Isolation and depersonalization are not uncommon circumstances in large health care institutions with bureaucracies that frustrate employees. Employee burnout can result from an administrative failure to recognize the symptoms of workers who feel angry or powerless in such a demanding system.

As far back as 1977, NIOSH1 documented studies showing health care occupations among the job classifications with the highest rates for mental disorders. Additional research indicated that many health care providers had elevated proportional mortality ratios for suicide. A study of navy personnel emphasized that health care positions, such as hospital food service, should be considered among the high-stress occupations.

Infection Control

With an estimated one million accidental needle-stick injuries each year, health care workers are concerned about contracting AIDS or hepatitis from the blood of patients. This life-threatening employee safety anxiety is spurred by mass media stories about health care workers who allegedly contracted disease from blood-borne pathogens.

Risk of an HIV infection from an accidental puncture by a needle containing infected blood is only 0.3 percent. A research study in Italy found that needleless intravenous access, a standard procedure there, eliminated potential risks to health care workers; if adopted in the United States, this procedure would further reduce hazards for workers.

In contrast to the probability of becoming infected with HIV from a needle stick, the risk of contracting hepatitis B is far greater for the health care worker. Estimates indicate that each year twelve thousand health care workers will contract hepatitis B and 250 of them will die. Several measures are taken to minimize the risk of blood-borne pathogens. An increase in the use of laparoscopic surgery decreases blood exposure in the operating room.5 Moreover, since only one in four needle sticks happens during the drawing of blood, precautionary disposal and trash handling techniques should be emphasized.

Universal precautions are important not only against blood-borne pathogens, but also against airborne pathogens, especially tuberculosis (TB). Between 1985 and 1991, the incidence of TB more than doubled in some U.S. cities.

Universal Precautions

Universal precautions effectively prevent contamination from all blood-borne pathogens, including HIV and hepatitis. Facilities should adopt universal precautions to reassure employees and to reduce the spread of infections. Importantly, the OSHA regulations concerning blood-borne pathogens require the implementation of a precautions program, put the responsibility for compliance on the facility, and impose heavy fines for failure to comply. In addition, hepatitis B vaccinations are required for all workers with the potential for on-the-job exposure. If a worker is exposed, there is a mandatory investigation of all exposures.

The adoption and use of universal precautions procedures is usually a formal policy and protocol for a health care facility. The precautions are:

1. Wear gloves to prevent the exposure of skin and mucous membranes to potentially infectious materials, including blood.
2. Remove and discard gloves immediately after finishing a procedure; avoid touching anything another person might touch without gloves.
3. Make point-of-use disposal units widely available to prevent sharps injuries.
4. Use gowns and aprons to prevent the anticipated soiling of clothing by blood or body fluids.
5. Wash hands before and after any contact with patients.
6. Use goggles and masks in procedures involving splashes or droplets.

Common sense should make these safety measures second nature for workers. Yet, nosocomial infection is still a leading cause of morbidity and mortality throughout the world. The risk of transmission of pathogens from patient to patient via the hands of health care workers increases as invasive procedures and devices become more common.

In 1847, Ignaz Semmelweiss, a physician in Vienna, demonstrated that antibacterial methods for cleaning hands decreased infection and mortality in hospital wards. Although hand washing is the simplest and most effective prevention strategy, studies find that physicians, nurses, and ancillary workers do not always wash their hands between patient encounters.

Infectious Waste Management Plan

Each health care organization, whether a hospital, ambulatory surgery center, or nursing home, should prepare an infectious waste management plan that:

- Defines and designates those wastes to be considered and handled as infectious material.
- Segregates infectious waste from noninfectious waste.
- Establishes packaging standards for waste disposal.
- Sets storage guidelines.
- Specifies disposal methods.
- Details contingency measures for emergency situations.
- Arranges for staff education.

Infectious wastes originate from various sources: from patients diagnosed with communicable diseases; from laboratory cultures and biologicals; from blood products; from disposables used in treatment in dialysis units; and from sharps and wastes from surgery and autopsies such as dressings, sponges, drapes, tubes, and rubber gloves.

To prevent contamination, infectious wastes should be discarded in easily identifiable containers and plastic bags, usually red or orange colored. These containers should be able to endure rough handling, lengthy storage, bumpy transportation, and varied treatment prior to ultimate disposal.

Training in universal precautions as well as in infectious waste management are vital elements in a risk prevention program to protect staff, professionals, patients, and visitors from contamination.

Emergency Situations

Advance planning for frequent or occasional emergency situations prevents individual or group injury, reduces the spread of contaminants to other people or geographic areas, and limits disability. Appropriate policies and procedures should be enacted and periodically reviewed by the committees that analyze incident reports and the results of concurrent investigations of each emergency.

Each emergency incident, whether fire, spillage, chemical, radiological, or biological, can be handled in a distinct manner with a quick application of absorbent material, use of emergency showers, and isolation of the contaminated areas.

Fire Prevention

Fire prevention and disaster plans are critical to the safety of personnel and to liability loss reduction efforts. A meaningful and efficient way to improve safety precautions is to learn from the mistakes of others, particularly when the adverse event is a similar occurrence.

However, many organizations today still engage in the same dangerous patterns of blocked exits, inadequate fire detection, and limited fire suppression systems. These deficiencies create an environment of fear and panic when a fire endangers life and limb. Everybody in the health care organization must be involved with the fire control plan, which should include specific policies and procedures to be followed, the assignment of duties to specified personnel, and periodic drills on all shifts.

An understanding of prevention, the use of fire fighting equipment, evacuation procedures, and control and containment techniques helps minimize the extension of fires; limit staff, patient, and visitor injury; restrict property damage; and decrease income loss and liability. Basic fire prevention steps are represented by the acronym RACE:

- Rescue and remove anyone in immediate danger.
- Alarm everyone by activating the nearest fire alarm box.
- Confine and contain the fire and smoke by closing all doors and windows.
- Extinguish the fire with portable extinguishers, wet sheets, or blankets.

Employees of the facility's management and administrative departments usually are members of the fire safety committees: the fire control team, or fire brigade; the rescue operations team; or the utilities repair team. The duties of these committees are:

Teams are flexible in the functions they perform and may be dispatched to execute other significant duties. Primarily, each team protects life and property and extinguishes fires, where possible. Community fire control assistance must also be invoked from the local fire department and is usually directly contacted through the facility's alarm systems.

Indoor Air Pollution

Physical plants can affect the health of patients, visitors, and staff. Depending on the extent of services offered in a health care facility, indoor air pollution through contamination by biological or chemical pollutants can be a potential catastrophe. The importance of an inflow of outside air to avoid hazards must be recognized. A lack or blockage of air can produce a variety of ill effects on a building's occupants.

Air quality deficiencies are often traced to inadequate ventilation resulting from the improper use and maintenance of heating, ventilation, and air conditioning systems. Biological contamination quickly arises when excessive moisture collects in a ventilation system and provides the ideal growth conditions for mold and mildew. In addition, chemical contaminants from building materials may seep into the facility's system, and it is not always easy to pinpoint the source of the problems. When no cause seems to be readily identifiable, simple air testing often supplies the answer. For maintenance of optimal air quality, the American Society of Heating, Refrigeration, and Air Conditioning Engineers recommends the following levels: temperature 76°F; relative humidity 40%; air circulation less than 45 feet/minute; and carbon monoxide levels usually 250 to 300 parts per million.16 These readings should be monitored at regular intervals to quickly identify any problems.

Technological suggestions for achieving clean air include:

1. High performance filters to remove air-borne particles.
2. Adsorbent beds for the removal of specific gaseous particles.
3. Ultraviolet light to kill biological contaminants.
4. Electric air cleaners and ion generators whose electric charges are capable of removing airborne particles.

In operating rooms, employees may be harmed by exposure to nitrous oxide (N_2O). Risks include "decreased mental performance, hearing and visual ability, and manual dexterity, as well as reduced fertility, spontaneous abortion and possible neurological, renal and liver disease." Scavenging systems to vent unused and exhaled gas may create a false sense of security. Control measures to reduce leakage of N_2O from the anesthesia delivery system, training of personnel in appropriate engineering maintenance procedures, protective gear, and monitoring of ventilation and concentrations of gas are advised and explained in the guidelines of the National Institute for Occupational Health and Safety.

"Recreational use" of N2O is extremely dangerous, but the gas has been subject to abuse because of its psychogenic effects. Numbness, loss of balance, and damage to the spinal cord are also attributed to abuse of this gas. Attention to access, storage, and daily accounting for usage will help deter pilferage and misuse.

In an effort to improve air quality and safety, regulatory standards are being imposed on hospital incinerators where medical waste has traditionally been burned. Emission regulations aim to enhance clean air for the community and to reduce the spread of pathogens and toxic smokestack emissions. Since compliance with the Environmental Protection Agency's mandates, as well as with state and local laws, is quite expensive, some facilities are hauling the waste to regional incinerators, if available, to avoid being fined.

EMPLOYEE HEALTH INTERVENTION STRATEGIES

With the American population participating in a variety of wellness activities, it makes solid business sense for health care organizations to offer those programs on the job. Investigations conclude that the dollar investment is returned manyfold in the form of lower absenteeism and increased productivity.

Health Promotion

In addition to the obvious commitment to patient welfare, a health care facility needs to accept responsibility for its workers. To be considered are not only the legal aspects of occupational hazards and safety, but also the financial stake of maintaining a happy, healthy staff. A 1993 survey of 1,034 employers reported that 76 percent adopted a health initiative or early intervention strategy to promote healthier employee living. Approximately 80 percent included training in their health promotion activities covering risk factors from back care to fitness to tobacco use and chemical dependency. OSHA proposed an ergonomics rule to identify certain "signal" risk factors in the workplace, such as repetitive motions, awkward work posture, and forceful manual handling. This rule could cost businesses $4.4 billion a year, but within five to seven years, it is expected that this expenditure will return $14 billion in savings.

PREPLACEMENT PHYSICALS AND CONTINUOUS MONITORING OF EMPLOYEE HEALTH

Guidelines for the evaluation of an effective health care facility's occupational health and safety program have been published by NIOSH. This program begins with a preplacement physical examination and an occupational history for all new employees. There are periodic health appraisals for workers exposed to a hazardous environment, returning from an absence due to illness or injury, transferring to another department, or retiring. Medical examinations are specified, and confidential records need to be maintained in the health unit. In addition to the job orientation, health, safety, and environmental information, selective immunizations should be provided to all personnel on a continuing basis. Information should deal with safe work habits and the use of the occupational health unit for reporting injuries and illnesses.

Health care facilities need to provide twenty-four-hour medical, psychiatric, or consultative services for staff with counseling programs to handle general problems ranging from substance abuse to HIV infection.

Workers' Compensation

Avoidable occupational exposures to hazards forced employers to pay $21.6 billion in direct workers' compensation expenses in 1993.25 Exposure to body fluids can result in a direct cost to the hospital of anywhere from $200 for exposure to hepatitis to more than $100,000 for exposure to the HIV virus. Back injuries account for approximately 31 percent of all employee injuries. In 1993, about 50 percent of employee back injuries in health care workers occurred during patient assist procedures. A survey of seventy-five U.S.

Fortune 1000 companies and forty-five selected Canadian companies analyzed disability cost trends, and 53 percent reported rising cost levels. A majority of nonoccupational disability costs were attributed to (1) mental or nervous disorders and chemical dependency; (2) cardiovascular problems such as heart disease, stroke, and circulatory problems; and (3) back injuries and other musculoskeletal impairments.

Employee stress, an aging workforce, and adverse economic conditions were most frequently named as contributing factors to these conditions. Moreover, depression is fast becoming more prevalent on the job. Data from the National Institute of Mental Health suggest that eleven million Americans are clinically depressed at any particular time.

Of the companies surveyed, a majority have already or are in the process of establishing disability management procedures, and 52 percent have instituted changes in their disability benefit plans. A common feature in the disability management plans is a wellness promotion program and a focus on controlling health risks. There was a trend toward techniques to reduce the number of claims and to ensure that employees receive appropriate care and rehabilitation services. These practices enable a health care organization to safeguard the welfare of its workforce and to eliminate unnecessary expenditures linked to disability.

Emergency Preparedness and Disaster Planning

After the April 19, 1995, bombing of the federal office building in Oklahoma City, the local medical community proved it could withstand the challenge presented by the worst domestic disaster in U.S. history (more than 160 people were killed). Physicians and nurses rushed to help the victims minutes after the blast. That incident illustrates that a health care facility needs to be prepared for the chaos of an outside disaster, as well as for any catastrophe arising within its doors. Assuming that injured people are transported to the nearest treatment facilities, any event resulting in a large number of casualties in a single facility's vicinity can be considered a disaster.29 Primarily, a facility needs to be prepared to handle any situation within its geographic range to prevent additional harm to the community and to minimize the loss and suffering of victims.

Ultimately, the nature, scope, and location of the disaster determine a health care facility's role in treatment, since these factors determine the response and plan of action. A facility must be prepared for a sudden influx not only of patients, but also of visitors and mass media representatives. Since these demanding scenarios tax the entire institution, all departments should restrict third-party visits until after the event. Having areas that are designated for members of the media helps avoid chaos and prohibits unwanted persons in treatment rooms. These measures alleviate excessive strain on a security team occupied with hazards from traffic control, freeing up elevators, and restoring telephone lines. Periodic disaster drills using simulated patients, visitors, and media provide practice, generate reports for safety committee review, and satisfy government regulation authorities. Exhibit 8-2 illustrates the scope of internal and external disasters.

Safe Environment

Safety is one area where even a health care business continuously accommodates the public's expectations for corporate responsibility. Health care facilities need to view themselves as equivalent to major industrial sites or plants when it comes to safety considerations. Unfortunately, "major industrial accidents are just as likely to occur today as they were ten years ago." 30 An effective safety program is concerned with the health and well-being of all employees, professional staff, patients, and visitors. Developing a successful safety program means:

1. Designing programs to cover all potential hazards and to address regulatory requirements.
2. Assigning roles and responsibilities to all staff members.
3. Implementing management processes to develop and maintain policy, procedures, and standards.
4. Being willing to provide appropriate resources such as specialists for advice, specialized equipment, a well-trained workforce, and documentation on proper protocol.

In the event of an unfortunate accident, the adverse incident should be investigated and reported to ensure that the injured are properly cared for and restored to full health.

Facility Safety Plan

With the rapidly rising cost of rendering health care, the public focuses its attention on all aspects of the care delivery system. Generally, facility safety and security planning can be viewed as lowering the cost of health care. It should not be difficult for management to decide between increased expenditures to improve safety now or tragic deaths and possible criminal charges later.

Risk prevention measures to reduce these liability trends can improve a facility's fiscal standing. Traditionally, safety teams consisting of members from the clinical, ancillary, and administrative departments have addressed risk issues, focusing on improved education and convenience for staff in all risk areas. A simple facilitywide approach serves as the primary intervention strategy to reduce the rising operational costs for a health care facility. Comprehensive facilitywide safety programs should be developed, implemented, monitored, and supported by the administration. The main purpose of the safety program is to reduce losses from occupation-related injuries and illnesses, as well as from harm or property damage affecting patients, visitors, and other professional staff.

Multidisciplinary committee membership should include representation from administration, professional staff, and faculty departments. Additional members to include are the risk manager, quality assessment director, and hospital engineer. A facility safety officer should chair the committee and provide leadership for the organization's safety plan. Many large institutions have subcommittees with specialists and technical staff that are concerned with environmental safety, radiation control, and the health of patients and employees.

Policies and procedures should be developed with the cooperation of the safety committee and the various institutional departments. Essential components in creating the facility safety plan must conform to mandatory government regulations, to voluntary JCAHO standards on life safety, to the standards of other accrediting bodies, to advisories of the National Council on Radiation Protection, and to the National Fire Protection Association's Life Safety Code®.

Reports to the administration and board of trustees should indicate trends and areas of concern to address incidents, infection control, and life safety programs. Full commitment by management is the first step toward successful implementation; the message and example will quickly filter down to every individual. Managers must go beyond legal requirements or appearance concerns. New OSHA rules passed in 1995 can levy fines up to $70,000 per citation. However, even without the threat of OSHA violations, "It's better to spend money... on preventing injuries than paying for the injuries themselves."

Security and Health Care Organizations

Concomitant with the increasing incidence of violent crime and surging litigation costs, a new health care environment is emerging.39 Despite the dangers, the risk manager is constantly confronted with balancing frugality against the option of even tighter security. How can requirements of the health care facilities be met without compromising the needs of the individuals directly affected? Security plans involve viewing the facility security force as a profit-preserving center with an impact on every department. Adequate security measures can directly affect the facility's fiscal health by protecting existing assets and reducing future losses. Security departments must provide the following services: protection of life and property; prevention and detection of crime; apprehension of offenders; assistance to those who use the facility; and the perception of a safe environment, including visible functions such as keeping the peace, directing and arresting criminals, controlling facility access, directing vehicle traffic, responding to fire alarms, conducting criminal investigations, and maintaining a liaison with local law enforcement agencies.

Violence on the Job

Considering violent and abusive behavior of patients, visitors, or staff to be "part of the job" is no longer acceptable, nor is it safe, as facilities find themselves confronted with more and more dangerous situations every day.

Although not on the occupational hazard list, violence is a significant concern for health care workers and risk managers alike., 41 In an American Management Association survey, about 52 percent of human resources managers reported at least one violent incident involving their companies since 1990. Of the five hundred private company managers questioned, more than 30 percent reported multiple occurrences. According to the Bureau of Labor Statistics, 1,063 (17%) of the 6,271 fatal occupational injuries in 1993 were the result of homicides. While health care providers were not among the occupations with the greatest incidence of homicides, they are regarded as a group at an ever-increasing risk for work-related injuries.

As official standards and requirements for policy and legislation are developed to combat this disturbing trend, the importance of the OSHA terminology is apparent. OSHA defines "occupational injury" as: ... an injury which results in death, lost work days, loss of consciousness, restriction of work or motion, termination of employment, transfer to another job, or medical treatment after first aid.

Risk factors detailed in a NIOSH alert on security included: an exchange of money with the public; working alone; late night or early morning hours; valuable property on the premises; and especially community settings in high crime areas. These risk factors apply particularly to health care institutions that are open twenty-four hours a day, have employees working alone, have valuable property on the premises, and have locations in dense population settings.

This survey is considered to be the best indicator of health care crime available. On their own, the number of incidents and the amount of money in personal and corporate losses are alarming. Of all the possible victims in these hospitals, employees are most affected, specifically in their own work area. Crime is all around the institution and may be committed by fellow employees. Viewed in the context that the 270 U.S. hospitals in this survey represented only 3 percent of the total number of hospitals in the country, simple statistical projections reveal the epic proportions of this problem.

Vulnerability to Violence

A telephone survey of nurse managers in Philadelphia provided an eye-opening realization of the aftereffects of the increasing number of violent incidents. Every respondent expressed concern for staff safety and their own private property. Concerns pinpointed the need for an "imposing presence" in the emergency department (ER), more security in the parking lots, and a more aggressive approach to concealed weapons brought into the ER.

Among the causes of violence mentioned by the nurse managers were long waits, overcrowded waiting rooms, previous problems in an emergency department, the perception of being ignored, and a lack of social service resources that have the potential for remedy. A security expert described the past sanctity of hospitals as "like churchesnot even the bad guys would bother them. But the increase in violence throughout society is spilling over into health care. Criminals have finally figured out that hospitals are good and relatively easy pickings." Hospital policies such as the open door for visitors aim to project the image that the facility is friendly and homelike. This policy translates into freer access for the public, including criminals, to blend easily into the environment. Current reports focus on workplace-related violence as an occupational hazard, especially in parking areas, emergency departments, and psychiatric services.

Parking Areas are High Risk

Security concerns need to include institutional areas such as parking lots, garages, the surrounding grounds, and public streets. Crime reports indicate that a substantial amount of crime associated with health care facilities occurs in parking and adjacent areas. In the IAHSS crime survey report, the volume of crime in parking areas illustrates the risks. Administration must consider these locations to be a wing or section of the facility and address their unique security

demands. Grant Medical Center (Columbus, Ohio) employed technology to monitor their four parking lots and three multistory garages. Using the computer database, security can retrieve employee photos on a video screen for comparison to visual images being monitored on any one of the fifty-five closed circuit television sets installed on the grounds. With the help of panic buttons and intercoms for the garages and parking lots, the facility's security forces can determine the source and extent of any problem that may arise. Children's National Medical Center (Washington, D.C.) went even further in its efforts to fight crime: to bolster the efforts of regular security patrols, pan and tilt cameras and passive infrared motion detectors were installed in the parking structures and in sensitive hospital locations.

Approaches to Violence

Naturally, emergency rooms are the first to encounter the spillover from any increased violence on the streets. With more than half of the reported violent incidents taking place in the ER, studies estimated that as many as 10 percent of all patients seen there could be classified as violent.

In a review of violence in forty-seven pediatric emergency departments, more than 75 percent reported one or more verbal threats per week and significantly more in ERs with longer waiting periods. Physical attacks on staff were cited in 75 percent of these settings, and 25 percent noted actual injury.

Waiting time is a primary instigator of violent acts. Frequently, certain behavior while waiting is a telltale sign warning of a violent patient. Clues include how the patient was injured, hints of agitation or anger, apparent stress, and circumstances involving family and friends. Medical residents in emergency medicine in thirteen programs in California were "worried about their own safety" (62%) and believed that their hospital program did not provide adequate safety (50%). In addition, these respondents were overwhelmingly in favor of some form of gun control.

Another study concluded that more than 20 percent of violent episodes in hospitals were instigated by nonpatients. Nonpatients should be kept out of the treatment area. Moreover, if they appear disruptive, they should be asked to leave and/or be escorted out of the waiting area. Periodically, staff can interact with family and friends in the waiting area to update them and to answer nonmedical questions.

The number of weapons confiscated from patients has grown as more and more people have begun carrying weapons to protect themselves. "Few people intend to use weapons when they seek medical treatment at emergency departments, but patients and visitors in the ED are often in a highly volatile emotional state."

Although weapon screening is an approach toward the potentially violent patient, it is not always the most effective. A five-year study at a forensic hospital revealed that most violent incidents relied on weapons of opportunity available at the attack site. Staff members were frequently the targets of furniture-wielding assailants. Besides furniture, objects commonly used as weapons included writing instruments and eating utensils. Providers need to survey their environments to eliminate as many unnecessary items as possible. To make security and safety procedures unique and applicable to the facility, there has to be an individualized response to the situation.

In addition to containing the attacker, hospital security had to evacuate the bottom two floors of the building, control outside traffic, set up a liaison with the Los Angeles Police Department, and coordinate intelligence at the operations command post. Following the shootings, fear was an ongoing problem in the security force as well as among the ER staff. Reverberations of the tragedy spread throughout the southern California hospital community as facilities became conscious of their own vulnerability.

Workers rallied to support the California OSHA legislation to combat violence in health care facilities through mandated enforcement of guidelines for a safer working environment. Controls recommended for the emergency department included:

- Alarm systems or panic buttons installed at nurses' stations, triage stations, registration areas, hallways, and lounge areas with twenty-four-hour monitoring and a telephone link to the local police department.
- Metal detection systems installed at all ER entrances.

- Seclusion or security rooms designated for confused or aggressive patients.
- Bullet resistant glass for protection in triage, admitting, or other reception areas.
- Strictly enforced limited access to ER areas enforced by key or code locks.
- Closed circuit television monitors to survey concealed areas.
- Recommended "work practices and administrative controls" were also included in the legislation.

In a national telephone survey of 250 hospitals with emergency departments, security measures differed depending on hospital size, ED census, suburban and urban locations, and teaching status. Generally, on-site security presence increases with hospital size and high census, as does the availability of closed circuit television surveillance, alarm buttons, and detection rooms. Smaller rural facilities are more likely to lock the ED doors at night.

Along with the California OSHA legislation, the federal Centers for Disease Control and Prevention joined the fight against violence by funding studies to examine the circumstances surrounding deaths and injuries from shootings. Study findings may assist in the development of prevention programs against gun violence.

Intervening with Violent Patients

Effective communication strategies facilitate the defusing of a potentially explosive confrontation with violent patients. Calling a patient by name and explaining the reason for a delay or other problems are considerate steps and demonstrate that the facility respects and cares about its patients. While patients have a right to treatment, however, health care workers have a legal right to a safe workplace.

Reasonable force can be used against patients if necessary to prevent harm or injury to themselves or to others.

The State University of New York Health Science Center at Brooklyn (New York) 60 uses a team approach toward agitated or violent patients in need of control for their own safety or the safety of others. Psychiatric nursing staff and public safety department staff meet and jointly train in appropriate methods of restraint of patients, when necessary, in the psychiatric unit. Policies and procedures have evolved concerning the administrative control of each situation, the physical control of the patient, and the roles of the nurse and safety officer. The staff agreed on prescribed methods of restraint, as well as the team leadership at each stage: medication, protective devices, and physical control. Clues drawn from many sources identify specific populations as violence predictors:

- Adolescent males
- System abusers
- Homeless persons
- Individuals with dementia
- Members of gangs (indicated by tattoos, etc.)
- Individuals traumatized by a recent conflict
- Previously violent individuals

OSHA recommends several educational resources that employers can integrate into their violence prevention programs. One example is the video training program offered by the National Crisis Prevention Institute (Wisconsin). This self-teaching program allows employers to practice safe strategies for deescalating potentially violent situations.

In the event of a violent outburst, facilities need to be concerned with taking the proper course of action. Mount Sinai Hospital (New York) offers a model for violence preparedness. As early as 1982, the hospital developed a "disruptive patient task force" that may still be considered innovative in comparison to the lack of protocol and training in many health care facilities today. An interdisciplinary task force organized protocol, policy, and procedures for managing disruptive incidents. An integral part of the plan includes a crisis report filled out for each situation, analyzed by a reviewing committee, and further utilized to identify trends or patterns of violent incidents that need attention.

Violent and/or aggressive patients are separately flagged in a "Log of Disruptive Patients." Logs are distributed monthly to security, emergency department admitting, outpatient admitting, and inpatient admitting. Patients entered into these logs are sent a letter, approved by the hospital's legal department, stating that any future ER visit will require supervision. To respond to a violent situation, the Mt. Sinai task force established a twenty-four-hour crisis team that can be called. Responding to buzzer panic alarms installed in locations such as the emergency department triage desk, the nursing stations, and the trauma room, the crisis team acts according to a specific protocol.

In addition to these intervention techniques, the task force implemented an assertive six-step education program customized to meet the needs of individual departments:

1. Recognition: Train staff not to ignore what they see and hear.
2. Alert: Train staff to know who their resources are and how to alert them.
3. Preparedness: Determine what happened, review incidents, and develop protocols and policies that involve staff.
4. Design: Strive to balance aesthetics with functionality when considering new construction or renovation.
5. Education: Determine training needs and how to accomplish them internally or with external specialists.
6. Enforcement: Hold all people to the same standards of accountability for their actions.

PROTECTING PATIENT VALUABLES

Patients are usually admonished to leave valuable personal items of jewelry, clothing, and electronic devices such as radios, cassettes, and CD players at home. Despite the warning, many patients bring valuables into the hospital or other facility when admitted. Usually, the loss of patient valuables is blamed on aides and housekeeping staff. Although the dollar value for replacement is usually comparatively small, the inconvenience, sentimental value, and fears generated are high. Reports of such losses to security and risk management personnel result in an investigation, but the stolen items are rarely recovered. Analyzing the data on such incidents to identify trends in location in the facility and shift may help uncover perpetrators. Payments on these claims are within the realm of "petty cash." In these cases facilities may choose not to invoke their insurance carriers and have options of settling or ignoring these claims.

Documentation of all items belonging to a patient should be detailed, using objective language to describe jewelry, money, dentures, eyeglasses or contacts, hearing aids, prostheses, and clothing. Receipts for valuables to be stored in the institution's safe should be noted on the medical chart, as well as in conversations concerning potentially unprotected items to be kept in the room.

Patients should be involved in security measures to create a true team effort with a win-win outcome. Encouraging patients to take steps to protect themselves is a preventive measure that benefits both provider and patient. Upon admission, all patients should be given tips and helpful advice.

Patients who wish to protect their valuables should follow these guidelines:

1. Leave valuables and credit cards at home. Anything important should be kept in the hospital safe with a detailed receipt issued to the patient.
2. Make sure any staff in your room is wearing photo identification.
3. Leave your room only if a trusted person is present, if possible.
4. Do not trust other people with valuables or children.
5. Do not get involved in any incidents, particularly in the ER.
6. Make arrangements to have a relative or friend with you in the recovery room after surgery.

7. Use the hospital patients' rights advocate staff to address any concerns or needs.
8. Know and exercise your rights as a patient.

Criminal Behavior

As hospitals and other health care facilities improve their image by making visiting hours and access less restrictive, more criminal miscreants from the local community enter the premises for unauthorized and unwanted activities.

Statistics from the National Traumatic Occupational Fatalities Surveillance System revealed that homicides accounted for 20.3 percent of the deaths sustained by health care workers from 1980 through 1990. Of the 106 deaths reported, the greatest number of homicides were among pharmacists (27) followed by physicians (26), registered nurses (18), nurses aides (17), and other health care workers (18). Firearms, as weapons, contributed to 78 (73.6%) of the health care worker homicides as compared to about 60 percent for all homicides in the United States. Pharmacists in community pharmacies are at greatest risk, because of the availability of controlled substances as well as of cash. There is an ever present danger from desperate illicit drug and substance abusers needing both.

It is not always easy to identify people who have unauthorized weapons or who will use knives or instruments for evil purposes. However, every time a weapon is confiscated, an incident report should be filed with the risk manager. This process allows the administration to analyze developing trends before deciding on a risk intervention strategy. Although a reduction in the number of weapons on the premises is a prudent first step, efforts need to be directed toward eliminating all types of confrontation, with or without weapons.

Employee Criminality

Criminal acts in health care facilities are not always perpetrated by outsiders. There is a danger in overlooking another major source of crime in health care facilities: employees. Police reports indicate that thefts by employees occur in 76 percent of hospitals nationwide, by far the most common crime by an insider. Budget considerations may curtail an adequate background check as facilities increasingly depend on temporary employment agencies for employees. "The turnover rate of hospital employees is now the highest it's ever been. Any attempt to check the backgrounds of such a transient population is basically very difficult. People cross state and country borders and even change their names." Addicts may even apply for hospital jobs to gain easier access to drugs. American Hospital Association reports indicate that nine out of ten hospital workers who abuse drugs steal them from the hospital where they work.

As a risk, employee theft and embezzlement at health care facilities are often overlooked. Prime targets for theft, such as pharmacies or patient rooms, necessitate procedures to prevent criminal actions and to protect individuals.

Criminals are becoming more creative and innovative. Techniques have evolved far beyond the simple stealing of wallets or petty cash. Employers need to be on the alert for forged checks, padded payrolls, the creation of fictitious employees, and varied unique diversions of funds. Reference checks, verification of school attendance, and proof of degrees received help ascertain an applicant's trustworthiness. An operating system of checks and balances needs to be in place to safeguard a facility's assets and to safeguard the financial well-being of a company or institution. Tactics that reduce the opportunity for fraud also ensure the rapid discovery of foul play.

- Some actions designed to reduce employee theft include:
- Limiting check writing authority.
- Requiring dual signatures on all financial transactions.
- Having employees check each other's work.
- Limiting access to bank accounts.
- Using an outside auditor or accountant for periodic reviews.
- Obtaining a fidelity bond for employees.

- Establishing and maintaining internal controls.
- Accounting for daily cash differences.
- Setting a good example (e.g., not using the company's cash to buy lunch).

Quick, decisive action is imperative when a theft occurs. Investigations should be prompt and thorough, with appropriate attention to due process. Relevant law enforcement agencies and insurers need to be informed of the circumstances, and remedies need to be instituted to prevent similar circumstances in the future.

Violent acts by employees unfortunately threaten health care staff and facilities and all work environments. Violence in the workplace is increasing, with incidents, in decreasing order, such as verbal abuse, vandalism, physical fights, stabbings, and shootings. Blamed for this increase in incidents is stress, along with corporate downsizing, alcohol and drug abuse, and the availability of firearms. Damaging acts of violence by employees occur every day and cost businesses an estimated $75 billion each year. Defusing the anger and aggression rather than trying to confront the violence directly is the most challenging task.

Varied criminal acts by employees include accepting gifts and gratuities for services; purchasing cigarettes, alcohol, or contraband; gambling; and running prostitution rings.

Property Control

Apart from petty theft of small personal items such as radios or jewelry, grand larceny in the form of pilfering of hospital supplies and stealing of major equipment may occur. Appropriate inventory controls are required for monitoring the use of consumable supplies, whether bandages or food. Protection of these items from unauthorized removal can be aided by locking of storage areas and delegation of personnel for access and accountability. Drugs, biologicals, chemicals, instruments, disposables, and housekeeping and food supplies are all replenishables that may be attractive for personal use or sale by those with criminal intent or inclined to a little "white collar" crime. The use of stickers or tags on equipment owned by the hospital or facility can help identify items moved within the facility or being taken out of the facility. All large bags, boxes, or equipment moving in or out at doors or loading docks should be scanned to prevent theft of or damage to these items. Prompt distribution of all receivables is a major key to property loss control. If small packages containing highly valuable items, such as computers or technical instruments, are received, they should be delivered to the departmental addressee on the same day, if possible. Otherwise, storage in a secure area is imperative. Certainly, loading docks and storage areas, when not in use, should be specially secured to deter intruders and prevent losses.

Securing Information Systems

Health information systems can be protected with various levels of security approaches, depending on the systems in place and the anticipated breaches of security to be prevented. Destroying data, modifying data, and rendering the system inoperable may be attributed to a virus brought into the system by infected diskette or downloaded programs; that possibility requires continuous attention. Problems can arise from theft of computer programs or unauthorized use of the computer networks by employees for their own personal business or by disaffected employees seeking to sabotage the system.

The arrival of the computer Internet and its widespread accessibility through generic local area networks (LANs) have exacerbated the complexity of keeping data secure from unwarranted intrusion. Smaller health care organizations and facilities depend on discrete systems for specific functions, such as accounting or personnel or patient care data, with only a few designated people having access and limited ability for computer program interaction. Large institutions no longer use these stand-alone systems and are now models of system interconnectedness via computer networks for all types of data concurrently entered and retrieved for management and patient care purposes.

- Data in such systems can be classified into several categories:
- Administration systems: executive information systems, personnel, budget, purchasing, accounts payable, property control.
- Patient management data: demographics, admission/ discharge/transfer (ADT) information.
- Clinical data: medical records, notes, physician orders, laboratory tests and results, treatments.
- Ancillary: pharmacy, radiology, ECG.
- Facilities operation data: engineering systems, utilities.

In and of themselves, these information systems are large databases, but as part of a network, the interconnectedness complicates security measures.

Patient accounts data systems depend on the ADT information as well as on the clinical data for billing and charges, for laboratory tests, for pharmaceuticals, for treatments, for imaging tests, and for operating room use. Similarly, clinical data systems activate and interconnect physicians' orders with laboratory testing and results, orders for medication with pharmacy distribution to the patient care floors, and therapeutic nutrition orders with appropriate dietary response, even to the point of dietary orders of supplies of fruits and vegetables.

Many discrete systems are used for diagnostic and treatment purposes, for research, for physiological monitoring systems used in intensive care units, cardiac care units, the operating rooms, and some treatment step-down units. These systems have on-line real-time capacity for immediate medical care use or trending for patient care. Additionally, other workstations can use clinical data or information from libraries and learning centers.

Unlawful intrusion of computer networks is facilitated by the Internet and by telephone dial-in capabilities of people external to the organization or facility. Data diversion may be used to perpetrate credit card fraud on personnel or patients. Confidential records may be sought in order to modify data, to destroy medical records, or to enter spurious information. Theft of software programs installed on computer terminals attached to the network, by employees or others, for use external to the facility is another potential risk.

Several counteractive strategies need to be in place to secure the protection of information:

- Physical security: physical access limitations; locked areas to prevent theft of computer hardware, software, and supplies; workstations in secure areas on the premises.
- ID and password protection at different levels: restricted access to specified levels of network; restriction of application level for uses of specific programs and/or systems; restricted access to classes of records (i.e., personnel or patient) and to fields (i.e., name but not social security number); protection of individual user passwords with frequent changes in passwords.
- Dial-back systems: confirmation of authorization when there is an internal or external dial-in capacity.
- Virus screening programs: utilization on a recurring basis; no disks or programs to be utilized without automated virus scanning protection.
- Storage of data in encrypted form: unauthorized retrieval will yield incomprehensible results.
- Storage of data on removable disks: encouragement of researchers and students to protect their own data by transferring and storing data on "removable disks"; storage of data away from the hard disk at the workstation or the network itself.
- Audit trails: incorporation of audit trails in all data systems to document every transaction, including unauthorized use.

Advanced computer technology to assist administration and patient care givers requires sophisticated countermeasures to reduce unauthorized and criminal access to the use of files for purposes not originally intended. Risk managers will need to rely on the health information specialists to recommend, develop, and implement specific security measures for the facility's data systems. Reporting of incidents and occurrences relative to these information systems and investigations will require cooperation among risk managers, health information specialists, security personnel, and administrators to analyze trends and to prevent future incursions.

Proactive Security Departments

According to one definition, the role of health care security "is and always will be the protection of people and property, with a secondary role to provide other specifically defined services to the hospital community." Although maintaining the status quo is no longer acceptable, security must stress the dynamic process that is required to allow employees, patients, and visitors to pursue their normal daily activities in a secure manner without creating an armed camp. Security staff members have access capabilities to allow professionals entry to the pharmacy, laboratory, and radiology in otherwise off-hours. They also respond to major emergencies and both internal and external disasters. In special circumstances, facilities expect cooperation of security staff at sites of cardiac arrest or organ or infant transport. Incident reports are maintained in the security department along with investigation results, and they are reported periodically to the safety committee that also includes a representative of risk management.

With a multitude of decisions to be made regarding security, a facility's director of security82 is a critical asset in the operations. A security director can rapidly become the trusted colleague of a facility risk manager. A security force protects life and property, detects potential criminals, and prevents crime. When viewed as a proactive police, fire, and safety operation, security force increases in importance dramatically. "Security can no longer be considered a nonrevenue producing part of the company." A facility simply cannot afford to underbudget or understaff this vital department.

Security directors should participate in selecting security staff to meet the agreed-upon managerial expectations. Initially, the administration's objective is to establish a quality security team that will work well and complement the director. In New York State, all security guards are required to have background checks and eight hours of preemployment training prior to being granted registration under the provisions of the Security Guard Act of 1992. Individual identification numbers are provided for each security guard independent of their location of employment, health care institution, or other circumstances. Employers must provide sixteen to forty hours of training each year for employees to continue their active registration. Facilities have a legal responsibility to protect their patients, their visitors, and their workers. Risk managers need to plan how to handle the possible litigation stemming from a violent patient or family member.

Administration must be concerned with injuries sustained by individuals being restrained, by innocent bystanders unable to escape, and by employees directly in danger. This legal liability demands that security personnel be properly educated and trained. Presbyterian Health Service Corporation's security department requires one year of college, with a law enforcement or security major. One year of college may not seem like a demanding regulation, but it exceeds that of many local police departments. Certification from the International Association of Healthcare Security and Safety is valuable for its emphasis on a wide range of factors, from getting along with staff to restraining patients. Public image has to be considered in the context of an antagonist's perceptions of the facility. In a chaotic ER setting, visible armed police or security can be interpreted as an encouraging symbol of authority.

Security guards pose special risks for organizations, since their mere presence complicates insurance arrangements for a facility. Spurred by widely publicized incidents such as the kidnapping and murder of an Exxon executive, legislators have aimed to formalize minimum standards for the training and licensing of security staff. In 1993, the state of Washington passed a law delineating the authority to license and to regulate private detectives and security guards. New York passed a law setting minimum standards for registration, training, and liability insurance coverage for proprietary and contract guards. These laws and similar legislation have become necessary to push back the rising tide of litigation by outlining reasonable and proper liabilities. Insurers, lawyers, and risk managers alike agree that an essential step in prevention is a thorough background check of applicants for security positions. A 1979 Illinois court set a precedent in ruling against a detective agency: "The employer knew, or should have known (the guard) was unfit for the position sought to be filled."

Consultants advise dealing directly with private security firms, since they are professionals, and elements of the risk and responsibility can thus be transferred and shared. After security guards are hired, they should understand the policies and procedures and the duties expected of a guard in a health care facility. This safeguard reduces the employer's probability of being found negligent in a court.

To screen potential security personnel, employers should:

1. Inform the applicant that a background check will be made, and have the applicant sign a waiver.
2. Take special care with the application form regarding the difference in listing criminal convictions versus arrests.
3. Have the applicant obtain and provide any special information from previous employers.
4. Demand references and check them thoroughly, verifying previous employers.
5. Ask former employers for evaluations on performance; request specific examples on judgment or honesty.
6. Check the validity of all licenses.
7. Start a file on the applicant, documenting calls, references, and checks.
8. Wait until after hiring to administer personality tests; instead focus on background checks.

Cost containment and budget crunching force security staff to accept increased responsibilities and workloads. With security guards forced to double as couriers, record keepers, and bus drivers, the surveillance capabilities and response times will be reduced. However, a team-building approach can develop a unified security force, even in the wake of budget cuts. Proper utilization of manpower is crucial. The creation of an environment filled with enthusiasm and positive feedback strengthens the workforce. As the staff sees visible signs that attention is being paid to their security needs, they are more likely to participate willingly, and tighter security can improve staff productivity and quality of service.

Technology Enhanced Security

In the wake of the security violence risks facing health care facilities, new innovations and improved security systems are in demand. Institutions have turned to technology to confront their concerns for the security and safety of patients and staff. William Beaumont Hospital (Royal Oak, Michigan) serves as a model for security measures. Alarmed about patient surveillance, infant abduction, violence, pharmaceutical control, and the easy access to the facility by strangers, administrators sought an integrated system to meet all these needs. They selected a fully automated system that incorporates card access, closed circuit television (CCTV), door monitoring, and alarm systems.

In conjunction with CCTV or separately, photo identification badges and access control are two security interventions that go hand in hand. This control enables the monitoring of staff and their movement about the facility and documents the time and date of personnel locations. Electronic tagging of identification bracelets warns of abductions from the nursery or the wandering of the elderly. Antennas with frequency codes can be installed at all exits to emit audio and visual signals to a monitoring station for immediate response if the matching frequencies are detected.

Technology helped Michael Reese Hospital (Chicago, Illinois) administrators to improve security via the BadgePro Video Imaging System. This system creates computer-generated identification cards for employees from a video-recorded display instead of using cut-and-paste laminated cards. These new ID cards can provide access control along with identification. This feature regulates everything from time cards, to building access, to obtaining surgical scrubs, and to entering employee parking areas. A termination date encoded into a magnetic strip limits the access and privileges of temporary workers.

At Bethesda Memorial Hospital in southern Florida, newborn babies wear electronic antitheft devices developed by Innovative Control Systems (Waukesha, Wisconsin). Several cases of infants abducted from hospitals in the region caused many hospitals in southern Florida to install security systems to safeguard infants.

Additional Security Measures

In addition to increased armed security forces, canine teams may patrol and fences may surround the facility grounds.87 Stamford (Connecticut) Hospital opted to add a canine patrol to its security measures. Dogs cost approximately $6,500 each and receive two hundred hours of training before patrolling the hospital grounds during swing and night shifts. In addition to police dogs, gentler breeds can patrol inside the facility without intimidating the patients.89 At Loma Linda Medical Center (California), the canine teams have been a success since their introduction in 1985. Popular with the patients and employees, one dog even stays in the ER at night to add a pacifying effect. Nobody has ever been bitten accidentally. A combination of improved lighting and dog patrols has reduced the hospital's crime rate by 80 percent.

Personal and property crimes are frequent problems because many health care personnel work evening and night shifts at facilities in high-crime areas. However, crime occurs in all locations, from inner-city to rural, and risk managers should not be lulled into inactivity by their tranquil location. Protecting workers from assault in and around health care facili to its security measures. Dogs cost approximately $6,500 each and receive two hundred hours of training before patrolling the hospital grounds during swing and night shifts. In addition to police dogs, gentler breeds can patrol inside the facility without intimidating the patients. At Loma Linda Medical Center (California), the canine teams have been a success since their introduction in 1985. Popular with the patients and employees, one dog even stays in the ER at night to add a pacifying effect. Nobody has ever been bitten accidentally. A combination of improved lighting and dog patrols has reduced the hospital's crime rate by 80 percent.

Personal and property crimes are frequent problems because many health care personnel work evening and night shifts at facilities in high-crime areas. However, crime occurs in all locations, from inner-city to rural, and risk managers should not be lulled into inactivity by their tranquil location. Protecting workers from assault in and around health care facileties is a growing problem. Some suggestions for making health care facilities safer include:

- During shift changes, encourage car and van pools and provide security escorts and shuttle services.
- Improve visibility with increased lighting, stairwell and elevator mirrors, and other physical changes.
- Post escape and evacuation routes.
- Install locks on all outside doors to prevent unwanted entrance to, not exit from, the building.

Safety and Security in Ounces and Pounds

Paraphrasing an old proverb, "An ounce of prevention is better than a pound of cure." Safety and security activities in a health care facility need to focus on the same concept. To achieve their goals, risk managers must make the safety and security programs an integral part of operations, as well as a sound financial investment for the future. Safety and security activities have been practiced throughout industry for many years, and innumerable ideas are waiting to be adapted for health care organizations. Risk managers are supported by major legislation and OSHA regulations to help provide a safe health care environment. Surveillance and monitoring of potential risks are bolstered by rapid advances in security technology and cooperative team approaches to prevent incidents of unsafe practices, and to react appropriately to incursions on security of people and property. There is no doubt that a prudent safety and security risk management program reduces the potential for liability, while delivering cost savings.

10

A Primer on Medical Malpractice

Medical malpractice is controversial and sometimes complex; it affects all health care providers, patients, physicians, lawyers, institutions, and insurers. Numerous investigative reports, by the U.S. General Accounting Office (GAO), about medical malpractice related to Medicare, Medicaid, the Veterans Administration and fraud in the provision of health care services demonstrate the national concern with medical malpractice.

A Science of Mistakes

A Harvard Medical Practice Study in 1984 reviewed more than thirty thousand medical records from fifty-one New York State hospitals and found that adverse events and negligence occurred in 3.7 percent of hospitalizations; 2.6 percent of these instances caused permanent disability, and 13.6 percent resulted in death.

This Harvard study echoed the findings of the only other large-scale estimation of the incidence of iatrogenic injury and substandard care, the California Medical Association's Medical Insurance Feasibility Study. In 1977, California researchers reported an adverse event rate of 4.6 percent and a negligence rate of 0.8 percent.

Devastatingly, the third Harvard report in the series (Localio, 1991) declared: "Medical-malpractice litigation infrequently compensates patients injured by medical negligence and rarely identifies, and holds providers accountable for substandard care."

Brennan found that certain types of hospitals have significantly higher rates of injuries, because of substandard care. Furthermore, Leape's analysis4 indicated that 67 percent of the adverse events were caused by nonphysician errors, not physician negligence, and he concluded:

Physicians and nurses need to accept the notion that error is an inevitable accompaniment of the human condition, even amongst conscientious professionals with high standards. Errors must be accepted as evidence of system flaws not character flaws.

In a comment related to Leape's article, Blumenthal applied total quality management and opted to redirect medical errors into "medical treasures" because the flaws were exposed and corrected.

Administrative orders dictated that any time surgery involved an organ or limb that comes in pairs, staff would write "NO" with a black magic marker on the organ or limb that should be left alone.

A Lancet editorial offered advice in a similar vein. What practical lesson does this "science of mistakes" have for providers? To diminish errors, attention should be paid to alterable features outside of the system. Health care providers should attempt to learn as much as they can about people, about how illnesses affect them, and about which treatments work best. "Success in bringing patients to health or relief requires the broadest possible knowledge of anything relevant to the illness."

In a unique theoretical approach, Senders concluded that "there are few or no `medical errors'; there are many errors that occur in medical settings." An error differs from an accident in that the error is a behavioral matter while the accident is an unplanned event. Behavioral errors can involve a misperception, a mistake, a slip, an omission, a commission, an insertion, a repetition, or a substitution, and they may be endogenous or exogenous. Advocating "failure mode analysis," Senders advised evaluation of all incorrect actions and prevention interception. In essence, the technique demands identification of the modes of error in medical settings; prediction of the expressions of those errors; use of training and design to improve self-detection; and the interdiction of their transformation into accidents.

An error, advertent or inadvertent, is one thing, but it has happened that district attorneys have escalated medical mistakes from malpractice into criminal charges.

MEDICAL MALPRACTICE LAWIN BRIEF

Negligence is a civil, as distinct from criminal, wrong and is part of the law of torts. Within the field of negligence, the term "malpractice" refers to negligence as it applies to professionals such as physicians, dentists, nurses, technicians, attorneys, and accountants. "Medical malpractice" relates to professionals within the health care industry, to organizations that provide health care, or to the institutions in which health professionals practice, such as hospitals. An examination of the general principles of negligence provides the foundation for an understanding of medical malpractice.

Negligence

Usually, negligence is defined as the failure to exercise ordinary care. But ordinary to whom? If the law set the measuring standard too high, the day-to-day conduct of most of us would, by definition, be negligent. Consequently, lawsuits would involve standards of conduct that only a small fraction of the population could ever achieve. Defendants would be held to standards that they could not possibly attain. On the other hand, setting the measuring standard too low creates a situation in which the vast majority of injuries caused by "negligence" would go uncompensated, since the conduct would not have fallen below the legal standard. Therefore, the law sets the standard by which it judges the conduct of each of us by "reasonable" person criteria. By legal definition, negligence is a failure to exercise that degree of care which a reasonably prudent person would have exercised under the same circumstances.

Does that mean that every time someone fails to exercise ordinary care, a legal cause of action for negligence is created? An answer to the puzzlement lies in the quintessential explanation of negligence in a famous 1928 decision of U.S. Supreme Court Judge Benjamin Cardozo. Although the New York Court of Appeals recognized that the actions of the LIRR's employees pushing the man may have been negligent, it concluded that that was not enough upon which to base liability.

Negligence is not actionable unless it involves the invasion of a legally protected interest, the violation of a right. Proof of negligence in the air, so to speak, will not do.... In every instance, before negligence can be predicated on a given act, background of the act must be sought and owed a duty to the individual complaining, the observance of which would have averted or avoided the injury.... Negligence is not a tort unless it results in the commission of a wrong, and the commission of a wrong imports the violation of a right,... (H)e must show that the act as to him had possibilities of danger so many and apparent as to entitle him to be protected against doing it though the harm was unintended.

In essence, negligence is founded on the relationship between the actor and the victim. That relationship must be recognized by society as establishing a legal duty between the two. This requirement that a duty exist between actor and victim may produce contrary resolutions of similar factual patterns. A person can commit a single act that inflicts identical injuries on two different victims, but negligence law may bar recovery by one of the victims, while allowing recovery by the other.

In and of itself, the existence of a duty is only the condition precedent to negligence. Specifically, negligence can occur only when there is a failure, or breach, by the professional to abide by the applicable standard of conduct established by that duty. Despite the existence of the requisite relationship between the health care provider and the victim, not every injury caused by the provider's conduct will be the result of negligence. If a patient dies from a heart attack during an operation, death may not be attributable to the surgeon's conduct; death may have resulted from the normal risks of the operation and/or from circumstances beyond the control of the surgeon. For the law to recognize the professional's culpability, the challenged conduct must have caused the injury or at least have been a causal link in a chain of events.

Four requirements define an act as one of negligence:

- A legally recognized relationship exists between the parties.
- The health care worker has a duty of care to the patient.
- The health care worker breached the duty of care by failing to conform to the required standards of care.
- The breach of duty was the direct cause of harm, resulting in compensable damages for the negligent actions.

Generally, damages are measured by a comparison of the condition of the victim before and after the injury. If the victim is a wage earner, lost wages will be a factor, as will medical expenses and the victim's pain and suffering. Those who earn high wages will be compensated more than the poor. Younger victims are worth more than the elderly. A slow, lingering, painful death is more valuable than an instantaneous one.

This woman may have been scared, perhaps trembling with increased anxiety, but she suffered no compensable physical harm or damages.

Medical Malpractice

Within the context of medical care, negligence is the improper treatment or neglect of a patient. To constitute medical malpractice, the commission or omission of an action causing the injury must arise from the exercising of professional medical judgment. Failure of a nurse to properly maintain an intravenous tube constitutes professional malpractice, whereas failure to properly supervise the patient in the bathroom is ordinary negligence. Liability for malpractice may be imposed on individual providers of medical treatment or services, such as physicians, surgeons, dentists, nurses, therapists, and technicians, as well as on the facilities where services are rendered. A clear explanation of medical malpractice emerges from a ruling in an 1898 lawsuit: A physician and surgeon, by taking charge of a case, impliedly represents that he possesses, and the law places upon him the duty of possessing, that reasonable degree of learning and skill that is ordinarily possessed by physicians and surgeons in the locality where he practices, and which is ordinarily regarded by those conversant with the employment as necessary to qualify him to engage in the business of practicing medicine and surgery. Upon consenting to treat a patient, it becomes his duty to use reasonable care and diligence in the exercise of his skill and the application of his learning to accomplish the purpose for which he was employed. He is under the further obligation to use his best judgment in exercising his skill and applying his knowledge. The law holds him liable for an injury to his patient resulting from want of the exercise of knowledge and skill, or the omission to exercise reasonable care, or the failure to use his best judgment. The rule in relation to learning and skill does not require the surgeon to possess that extraordinary learning and skill which belong only to a few men of rare endowments, but such as is possessed by the average member of the medical profession in good standing.

Physician-Patient Relationship

Liability for medical malpractice is predicated on the establishment of a relationship between physician and patient. Legally, a relationship is created when there is treatment, expectation of treatment, or diagnosis for the purpose of treatment. This relationship may by established by express or implied agreement.

A patient may verbally agree to treatment or may do so without actually saying the words. Usually, the patient goes to the physician, a relevant interaction occurs between the parties, and there is agreement that the diagnosis, treatment, and consultation will ensure compensation. Yet, the physician-patient relationship and agreement is similarly established by the treatment of an unconscious patient brought into an emergency room.

In the context of this relationship, the physician may thought to be hired for only a specific limited purposeto perform a preschool or camp physical examination, for example. Because of the limited nature and scope of such a physician-patient relationship, there is no duty on the physician to give specialized advice or treat the patient for a previously undiagnosed condition.

Duty to Perform Professionally

Medical practice deals with medical science and skills that are outside the knowledge of the ordinary or average person. Thus, the standard by which conduct is measured must be altered to accommodate the specialized area of medicine. Physicians must possess the skills and knowledge that reasonably competent physicians possess, a standard comparable to the one that applies to lay people, who are legally bound to act as reasonably prudent individuals. A legal duty is imposed on physicians to use ordinary and reasonable care in the exercise of such skill and knowledge, tempered with a duty to use their best judgment.

Establishing the "reasonably competent" physician as the standard by which to measure the conduct of doctors may seem unusual. However, a comparison with the law of ordinary negligence demonstrates the wisdom of the standard. If all physicians were required to possess the skill and knowledge possessed by "excellent" doctors, 85 percent of the physicians would fail the test. On the other hand, if the standard were the skill and knowledge of the "fair" doctor, society would be condoning treatment and conduct that produces injuries for which there would be no compensation.

Since medicine is an inexact science, the mere possession of the requisite skill and knowledge is not enough. Through the law, society imposes a duty on physicians to always use their best judgment. There is no liability when physicians make an error in judgment, provided they have not deviated from accepted medical practice.

At times, the line of demarcation between malpractice and an error in judgment is difficult to ascertain. Moreover, the duties to use "best judgment" and to follow "accepted medical practice" often conflict with each other. If a patient can demonstrate that the decision to follow accepted medical practice was a violation of the duty to exercise best judgment, the physician may have been guilty of malpractice. Traditional doctrine states that a physician should be held only to that degree of skill and knowledge possessed by the same reasonably competent physicians of the specific area of practice. Several courts have expanded the original restrictive definition to require that physicians must keep up with advances in their respective field, in addition to conforming to community standards. Moreover, the notion of community or locality against which conduct will be measured is not fixed, but may fluctuate according to the nature of the particular part of the country involved. If physicians practice as specialists, they are held to the standard of the skill and knowledge possessed by reasonably competent similar specialists. This level of skill and knowledge is greater than that possessed by general practitioners.

Sources of Professional Standards

Although it is understood that health care professionals will be judged by standards of behavior, no universal statement of professional standards applies to every possible provider in all possible situations. In addition to the opinions of experts and the actual practices of health care providers, there are several sources of professional standards:

- Government statutes and regulations on licensure, certification, and professional conduct.
- Standards developed by professional societies and credentialing agencies.
- Voluntary accrediting agency standards such as techniques to minimize risks of infection, or staffing norms for intensive care.
- Administrative policies and rules of a hospital or other institution.

Additional Theories of Liability

Several other theories of liability are common, and risk managers should be aware of legal actions related to these theories of informed consent, strict liability, res ipsa loquitur, and vicarious liability.

Informed Consent

Court decisions affirm that a patient has the right "to determine the course of his own medical treatment" and to "decline medical treatment." A physician has a duty to explain to the patient the diagnosis, the prognosis, the proposed treatment, the treatment alternatives, and the risks and benefits of each. These are the legal elements of informed consent.

In a lawsuit claiming lack of informed consent, the plaintiff has the burden of proving that the defendant failed to disclose material risks that would have been disclosed by a reasonable physician under similar circumstances. That the treatment was medically sound is no defense. A patient still has the right to decide whether or not to consent to the treatment.

Strict Liability

Under normal theories of malpractice and negligence, professionals are liable if their conduct is "at fault." In the doctrine of strict liability, however, liability is assessed irrespective of fault in certain limited areas.

This doctrine has its greatest impact on the sale of products. A manufacturer of a product sold on the open market ordinarily is strictly liable for any injuries caused by a defect in the item, without regard to questions of improper or negligent conduct. Since the manufacturer is in the best position to control the product and to ensure its safety, the risk of loss is viewed as another cost of doing business. Strict liability may be applicable in connection with the ingestion of pharmaceuticals, radiological diagnostic services, and the utilization of medical devices. This doctrine of strict liability has not been widely applied with respect to the mere rendition of medical services.

Res Ipsa Loquitur

Res ipsa loquitur means "the thing speaks for itself." Courts relying on this doctrine require a plaintiff to demonstrate the following four elements:

- The injury would not ordinarily occur in the absence of negligence.
- The injury was caused by the actions or instrumentality within the exclusive control of the defendant.
- The injury is not due to any action on the part of the plaintiff.
- The evidence surrounding the circumstances relating to or concerning the injury is mostly within the control of the defendant.

Vicarious Liability

In medical malpractice, the doctrine of holding one person liable for the acts of another depends on the theories of agency and control. Courts have held that where two physicians jointly participate in the diagnosis and treatment of a patient, each is liable for the other's negligent treatment. As opposed to the rule with respect to a partnership, membership in a professional corporation does not in itself make one physician shareholder vicariously liable for the malpractice of another physician shareholder. In the absence of supervision or control, the referral of a patient from one physician to another does not make the referring physician liable for the malpractice of the other physician.

Hospital Liability for Medical Malpractice

A court ruling summarizes the legal responsibility of the hospital:

Present day hospitals... do far more than furnish facilities of treatment. They regularly employ on salary basis a large staff of physicians, nurses and interns, as well as administrative and manual workers, and they charge patients for medical care and treatment.... Certainly, the person who avails himself of "hospital facilities" expects that the hospital will attempt to cure him, not that its nurses or other employees will act on their own responsibility.... Hospitals should, in short, shoulder the responsibility borne by everyone else. There is no reason to continue their exemption from the universal rule of respondeat superior.

Hospital liability is based on two theories: (1) respondeat superior and (2) ostensible agency, or agency by estoppel. An institution may be responsible for the conduct of the physicians who practice there, as well as for its own actions. However, a hospital is an artificial entity, usually assuming a corporate form. As a corporation, a hospital cannot act except through its employees or other agents. Given this situation, the law adopts the practical approach that the employer is in the best position to control its employees, and applies liability to the employer through the doctrine of respondeat superior. Vicarious liability of the employer means that employers are responsible for the negligent conduct of their employees when those employees are acting on behalf of the employer. At one time, the law exempted charitable organizations from vicarious liability, but modern legal theory has eliminated that immunity.

Respondeat superior is manifest in individual employees of the hospital, such as nurses, therapists, technicians, service personnel, and other administrative personnel. Even though the nonmedical staff may not provide professional services, the hospital is liable for their conduct by the ordinary rules of negligence. A complex problem arises when hospitals contract with third parties to provide medical and other professional services. In such situations, courts hold these individuals to be de facto employees. Consequently, the hospital is liable for their negligence just as if these professionals were employed by the institution. An alternate theory supporting hospital liability is that the hospital is "holding out" these professionals as if they were employees.

Although the courts have not been uniform in applying the doctrine of respondeat superior to these contracted services, they often identify specific indicators in determining liability: How much control does the hospital exert over the person? How does the hospital pay for the contracted services? Are the rendered services normally performed by an employee? Who owns the equipment used? What choices are available to the patients? This problem of contracted services may be examined from two perspectives: that of the patient and that of an objective observer. Plaintiffs who hold the hospital vicariously liable for the malpractice of its independent contractors rely on support from both perspectives. Through an examination of the factors appurtenant to the contractual relationship, the plaintiff may attempt to prove that the physician was a de facto employee or agent of the hospital. Alternatively, the plaintiff may attempt to demonstrate reliance on the fact that the physician practiced at the hospital. Because of that reliance, the patient did nothing else to verify the credentials of the physician, assuming that the hospital must have verified credentials and specified privileges for any physician who practiced within the institution.

The ostensible agency, or agency by estoppel, theory has been extended to hold the state of New York liable for the malpractice of an independent surgeon. After commencement of the lawsuit, the state sought to avoid liability on the grounds that the physician was an independent contractor, not an employee, and thus the state could not be held vicariously liable for his negligence. Citing Mduba v. Benedictine Hospital, the appellate division affirmed the lower court denial of the state's motion. Initially, the plaintiff had been examined by a state employee who then had arranged for the surgical consultation; the consultation took place at the facility, the surgery was performed at the facility, and the surgeon was assisted by a facility nurse.

The applicability of the doctrine of ostensible agency or agency by estoppel] depends upon whether the plaintiff could have reasonably believed, based upon all of the surrounding circumstances, that the treating physician was provided by the defendant hospital or clinic or was otherwise acting on the defendant's behalf.

As applied to contracted services, the doctrine of vicarious liability has an immediate and direct applicability to the emergency room, where patients are usually "service patients," or patients of the hospital itself (as opposed to individuals who enter the hospital only after referral from a private attending physician). However, vicarious liability also applies to physician services rendered to patients who are placed in the hospital by their private physician.

Anesthesiology is another area of practice that is likely to invoke vicarious liability. Anesthesia services are indispensable to any surgery and, as in the case of emergency room services, are typically contracted by the hospital. One anesthesiology group may provide such services, with each physician within the group having certain distinct responsibilities depending on the time and nature of the surgical procedure. An appellate court sustained a verdict against a hospital based on the alleged negligence of an anesthesiologist, citing Mduba v. Benedictine Hospital, a case involving an emergency room physician.

Employing the objectivity test, the court held that a jury could, but was not required to, find the hospital vicariously liable on the basis of the degree of control exercised by the hospital over the anesthesiologist. Although the court commented that the patient was not aware of the independent status of the anesthesiology group and instead relied on the hospital, the ruling did not, as a matter of law, hold the hospital vicariously liable pursuant to the estoppel theory. In other words, the court felt that each case should be judged on its own particular facts.

Logically, the courts can apply the same analytic approach to cases involving radiologists and pathologists. Points of discussion can center on the institution's control, the patient's subjective belief, or the patient's reliance on the facility. Ultimately, the court will render a policy decision based on the fact that a patient may enter a hospital through the emergency room, where the patient has no option regarding the treating physicians. That patient places the utmost trust in the institution and in the medical professionals who work there, without regard to the niceties of the financial arrangements between the hospital and those physicians. As recognized by one court:

Having undertaken one of mankind's most critically important and delicate fields of endeavor, concomitantly therewith the hospital must assume the grave responsibility of pursuing this calling with appropriate care. The care and service dispensed through this high trust, however technical, complex and esoteric its character may be, must meet standards of responsibility commensurate with the undertaking to preserve and protect the health, and indeed, the very lives of those placed in the hospital's keeping.

Corporate Negligence

Usually, a hospital is not liable for the negligence of its attending staff or nonemployed physicians, since it is assumed that these physicians exercise their independent judgment. Reacting to the realities of practice, however, modern theories of malpractice have developed the doctrine of corporate negligence. Under this doctrine, hospitals are liable for failing to review the credentials of its non-employed attending physicians, or for failing to monitor the quality of care rendered by such physicians.

In part, the duty of a hospital to monitor the credentials and performance of physicians and other professionals practicing under its jurisdiction was established and recognized by statute and industry self-regulation.

Under the federal Health Care Quality Improvement Act, hospitals and other health care entities must review the credentials and malpractice history of all physicians having admitting privileges. In a like manner, state licensure agencies and the standards of the Joint Commission on Accreditation of Healthcare Organizations (JCAHO) detail the responsibility of hospitals to review the credentials of health care professionals.

Contributory Negligence

Given the existence of medical malpractice on the part of a treating physician or institution, the law requires a causal connection between the defendant's wrongful act and the plaintiff's injury. Where the condition of the patient may be severely impaired at the outset, the causal relationship between the injury and the alleged medical malpractice may be difficult to demonstrate. Frequently, plaintiffs are guilty of some act of negligence that may have contributed to their own injury. In some jurisdictions, a jury finding that the plaintiff's own negligent actions contributed to the injury completely bars any recovery against the defendant. However, most jurisdictions allocate the damages according to the proportionate responsibility of the parties, applying the doctrine of contributory negligence.

LIABILITY THEORIES APART FROM MEDICAL NEGLIGENCE

Additional liability theories in health care institutions may begin with unintentional medical negligence and proceed to intentional torts such as assault and battery, libel and slander, and invasion of privacy.

Intentional Tort or Conduct

Negligence is an unintentional tort because the actor does not intend to cause injury to the victim. In contrast, an intentional tort involves a specific action to cause harm, such as assault and battery. An intentional tort may take place when a physician performs a procedure contrary to the specific directions of the patient, or when a patient's confidential information is improperly released.

Assault and Battery

The words "assault" and "battery" are usually used together, and people perceive them as having the same meaning. However, battery is defined as the nonconsensual, unlawful or wrongful physical constraint or touching of one person by another. Assault is the perceived attempt at a battery. When a physician performs a medical procedure on a patient without consent, an action for assault and battery may be appropriate. "Any non-consensual touching of a patient's body, absent an emergency, is a battery and the theory is that an uninformed consent to surgery obtained from a patient lacking knowledge of the dangers inherent in the procedure is no consent at all."

Libel and Slander

A defamatory written or printed statement is referred to as libel; slander is the speaking of such words to a third party. To be actionable, the words claimed to be defamatory must be false. If a physician discloses patient information that is not true, a defamation suit may be possible if the other elements, such as duty and damages, are provable. However, the physician may be liable under some other theory, such as contract or negligence, for the nonconsensual disclosure of truthful patient information.

Invasion of Privacy

A related cause of legal action to defamation is based on the invasion of privacy of the patient. For example, if a plastic surgeon used photographs of a patient, without the patient's consent, to advertise specialty services or procedures, the patient could sue for damages based on invasion of privacy. Typically, this situation involves the publication of "before and after" photographs.

Types of Damages

Courts may award different forms of compensation in successful actions against physicians, hospitals, or other health care providers:

- Compensatory damage awards cover economic losses for past and future medical and supportive care, or past and future loss of earnings resulting from physical impairment.
- Awards for pain and suffering, mental anguish, and loss of consortium are real and discernible but cannot be measured in economic terms.
- Punitive damage awards in excess of usual compensatory damages reflect gross negligence or deliberate wrongful intent, and are rarely granted except in the most egregious situations. In effect, they serve as an example to deter future similar conduct.

Statutes of Limitation

Statutes of limitation specify the maximum period of time after the patient's injury during which a lawsuit may be commenced, not terminated. If the lawsuit is not filed before this period expires, it is untimely and will be dismissed. The statutory period in the vast majority of states is between one and three years, but the time varies by state.

For example, New York State's statutory period is two and a half years. With some exceptions, the statutory period is "tolled" (deferred) during the infancy of a minor patient, and starts to run only on the patient's eighteenth birthday.

THE MOST COMMON AND MOST EXPENSIVE MALPRACTICE ALLEGATIONS

In recent years, the most frequently cited allegations in malpractice suits and the most expensive claims to settle have remained fairly constant. The five most common malpractice allegations are:

1. Surgery/postoperative complications
2. Failure to diagnose cancer
3. Surgery/inadvertent act
4. Improper treatment (birth-related)
5. Failure to diagnose fracture or dislocation

The five most expensive settlements relate to:

1. Improper treatment (birth-related)
2. Failure to diagnose hemorrhage
3. Failure to diagnose myocardial infarction
4. Failure to diagnose infection
5. Failure to diagnose cancer

In financial terms, the average payment, the median award, the settlement award, and the median settlement all declined between 1988 and 1993 period, and these amounts have dropped significantly since 1993. Large payments, more than $3 million, also showed a percentage drop in these comparisons. In the period 1988 to 1993, 5 percent of settlements and 11 percent of jury awards exceeded $3 million. In 1994, these awards were 1 percent and 8 percent, respectively. About 50 percent of the sued hospitals and 33 percent of the sued physicians were assessed damages by juries in 1994.

After being stable for many years, the frequency and severity of dental malpractice claims appears to be on the increase in the 1990s. Financial awards are of a much lower magnitude than medical malpractice awards; the most expensive settlement was for $150,000 and involved orthodontics.

BREAST, COLON, AND LUNG CANCER RISK APPLICATIONS

Failure to diagnose breast cancer is still the main liability risk reported by the Data Sharing Project of the Physician Insurers

Association of America (PIAA). This database includes more than 125,000 malpractice claims filed since 1985 and represents the insurers of 60 percent of the nation's physicians. "Physical findings failed to impress the physician" was the most common reason (35%) for the delay in diagnosis; failure to follow-up was a close second (31%).36 Physicians named in breast cancer suits in 1995 included radiologists (24%), obstetricians (23%), family physicians (17%), and surgical specialists (14%). A detailed 1994 study of five hundred claims found that 60 percent of the plaintiffs were under fifty years of age and that the average settlement was $307,000. PIAA advises physicians to be more aggressive in their diagnosis, especially with younger women. Another PIAA study identified liability mistakes in breast, lung, and colon cancer.38 In all three cancers, "a serious deficiency" in taking histories from patients was a major problem.

Another major problem, likely to be exacerbated when costs are considered, was that physicians did not order diagnostic tests in enough "suspicious" cases. In breast and colon studies, the leading cause of lawsuits was the failure or delay in ordering a specific test. "Inadequate evaluation" followed by failure to respond to an abnormal chest X-ray was the leading cause in lung cancer suits. Failure to perform an endoscopic exam was the major reason for delay in diagnosis of colon cancer, followed closely by failure to perform a barium enema study.

Relative to breast cancer, the study suggested six cautions:

(1) perform more careful examinations;

(2) order additional studies;

(3) explore complete family histories;

(4) follow up after lumps are found, even if the mammogram is negative;

(5) stress the importance of monthly self-examinations, particularly for women older than forty; and

(6) emphasize the importance of an annual or biennial mammogram for women older than forty.

Physicians must remember that mammograms are screening devices, not diagnostic tools. Even a fine needle aspiration can miss the malignant tumor, and pathologists need considerable experience to interpret the aspirations. Regarding colon cancer, physicians were urged to be more aggressive in treating younger patients. While it is uncommon for individuals younger than forty to have colon cancer, the probability goes up after age forty-five. Key symptoms include bleeding, change in bowel habits, anemia, and weight loss. "Absolute indications for study include multiple polyposis, familial polyposis, ulcerative colitis, and villous adenoma. Failure to pursue a `remote complaint' is a serious problem." The study strongly advised physicians to review prior X-ray films when considering a diagnosis of lung cancer. Regarding follow-up, the study said: "The importance of communicating the results of radiographic exams to the treating physician cannot be over-emphasized."

Medication Errors

Between September 1, 1990, and December 31, 1994, 4,215 medication related physician malpractice payments were reported to the National Practitioner Data Bank. Although 50 percent of the payments were below $30,000, the mean payment was $124,998.39 In another study based on data from twenty-two physician-owned professional liability insurance companies, the average settlement per case was $120,722. Analysis of the claim payment data makes medication error the second most frequent and second most expensive claim against physicians. Internal medicine and family practice specialists accounted for 59.3 percent of all the claims and 45.8 percent of all the settlements. Significant injury, such as quadriplegia and brain damage, occurred in 42 percent of the medication errors. In 21 percent of the cases, the patient died, and the medication errors were a major contributing factor in death in 84.3 percent of the claims. Significantly, most of the claims involved more than one error.

Medication errors involve the interaction and communication between and among the physician, the nurse, and the pharmacist; each party potentially contributes different types of errors leading to liability. In most cases, these medication errors are preventable. Incorrect dosage is the most commonly reported medication error.

In combination, the fame of the newspaper columnist and the well-known good reputation of the treating institution brought considerable notoriety to the case described in Box 9-18. In addition to the disciplinary proceedings brought against physicians, nurses, and pharmacists, the inquiries instituted by the JCAHO uncovered other areas of deficiency needing correction to prevent further casualties. Responding to the resulting recommendations, the hospital committed $1.3 million to an education program concentrating on drug treatment protocols and appropriate medical record documentation. "Indecipherable prescriptions are causing dangerous and costly illness" according to an American Medical Association report. Cost involves liability payments as well as longer hospital stays, significant illness, or death. Nurses should not rewrite illegible physician prescriptions or orders, because they could misinterpret the name of the drug or the dosage while copying the prescription. Additionally, the nurse could be charged with practicing medicine without a license. Proper protocol requires the nurse to request clarification of all orders directly, to avoid misinterpretation and clinical hazards. To avoid liability relating to the prescribing of medications, physicians should refrain from ordering unfamiliar medications, or drugs for conditions not normally handled by their own specialty. Medical record documentation should list all of the patient's current prescriptions, enumerate all known medication and other allergies, and detail discussions with patients about their medications. Legible prescriptions and discussions with nurses and pharmacists are important aspects of patient care, especially in cases of unusual treatment protocols.

To protect themselves, nurses must acknowledge suspected medication errors, report them to their supervisors and the attending physician, file an incident report, and document the event in the medical record. All adverse reactions of the patient, and notification of the patient and family should also be documented.

Examining adverse drug events from a systems analysis of medication administration, investigators identified sixteen major deficiencies leading to medication errors:

1. Failure to disseminate knowledge about the medication

2. Failure to check the dosage and identity of the medication
3. Failure to provide the patient with information about the medication
4. Failure to accurately transcribe the medication order
5. Failure to prepare for an allergic reaction
6. Failure to track the medication order
7. Failure to communicate with all involved services
8. Incorrect use of devices
9. Lack of standardization of dosages and frequencies
10. Lack of standardization of drug distribution within a unit
11. Lack of standardization of procedures in general
12. Improper preparation of intravenous medications by nurses
13. Problems resulting from transfers or transitions of patients
14. Unresolved conflicts between providers of care
15. Problems with staffing and/or work assignments
16. Lack of feedback about adverse effects of medication errors

These failures of the health care system are directly linked to the most common medication errors ranked by frequency of claims.

Drug administration errors are traumatic events for nursing personnel. Their self-esteem and confidence are shaken, and depending on the severity of the disciplinary process, their practice activities may change significantly.49 The support of professional colleagues is very important, along with the appropriate measures to counteract any adverse consequences of the error. Prevention of further occurrences can be addressed through an understanding of the dynamics of the incident, in conjunction with education and discussions with all pertinent staff.

Causes of pharmacist liability are identified by the Pharmacists Mutual Insurance Company as mechanical or intellectual. Dispensing the wrong drug accounts for 54.9 percent of the claims. More than two-thirds of the claims are for mechanical dispensing errors which can be controlled by the institution of relevant policies and procedures, prescription evaluations, careful computer entry and product handling, labeling, and dispensing. In this complex arrangement, there are several opportunities for cross-checking the appropriateness of the prescribed medication, dosage, administration orders, compounding, and preparation of admixtures and solutions. If prescription legibility is the problem, direct communication with the physician and the nursing personnel who transcribe orders is essential for preventing medication errors.

In Schroeder v. Lester E. Cox Medical Center, Inc., the hospital pharmacy was directly involved in a lawsuit.

Risk management responsibilities with regard to medication error incidents focus on diligence in reporting, documentation, and interaction with the physician-nurse-pharmacist triad in order to implement strategies for the future prevention of untoward events. Policies and procedures need to be continually reviewed, and incidents should be reported to the pharmacy and therapeutics committees. A comprehensive approach to this issue, with an emphasis on trending and education, are known to be successful.

More than 50 percent of the medication error reports are from hospital pharmacists, 4.8 percent from physicians, and 2.3 percent from nurses. Causes of these incidents include unclear and confusing packaging or labeling, suspected subpotency, and contamination. Drug administration dosage forms included injectables (35.5%), tablets (23.0%), and solutions (10.9%). 52 These manufacturing and quality control problems in the pharmaceutical industry present clear opportunities for risk management activities to reduce liability in clinical situations.

In an effort to reduce the improper use of drugs, the Food and Drug Administration has proposed that pharmacists provide patients with easy-to-understand "Medication Guides." More than 50 percent of Americans receiving prescriptions get no written instructions before using powerful drugs. Many patients leave health care facilities with prescription drugs for follow-up therapy but without written instructions. This FDA proposal would supply written patient information on drugs considered to have "serious and significant" health risks.

Obstetricians Under Fire

Two emerging and continuing trends have serious repercussions for both obstetricians and the patients who utilize their services: (1) the aggressive and sometimes violent activities of the anti-abortion movement and (2) the flight from practice of skilled obstetricians because of perceived risks of litigation. One of the tactics employed by the anti-abortion movement is to institute malpractice suits against physicians who perform abortions. In the past ten years, the Arizona Right-to-Life organization filed nine such actions. Although none resulted in a verdict against the physician, these suits had a demoralizing effect. As one doctor, who has been the object of several such suits, declared: "Even if they lose, they win." Physicians become uninsurable by carriers and their reputations are smeared. In Texas, Life Dynamics, Inc., distributed pamphlets to women leaving abortion clinics listing reasons to initiate malpractice suits against their physicians.

Whereas previously many attorneys had refrained from instituting lawsuits involving abortions, lawyers have become increasingly active in pursuing actions on behalf of women injured during negligently performed abortions. In New York State, criminal charges were lodged against one doctor whose patient died during an abortion. Physicians and hospitals are increasingly unwilling to endure the controversy and costs associated with the abortion debate. Thus, more and more health care facilities are refusing to perform abortions. As a result, residents in obstetrics and gynecology will have fewer opportunities to develop the operative skills necessary to perform successful abortions, and this lack of experience will continue to pose risk problems. Rising costs of malpractice liability insurance coverage for obstetric services have caused many physicians to stop delivering babies. Several other related factors have contributed to this situation: increases in malpractice claims against obstetric providers; fear of being sued; consolidations and closures of hospital obstetric services; issues concerning payments and Medicaid; and the daily stress of providing obstetric and gynecological services. Studies indicate different problems in urban and rural areas. A California study of family practice physicians who discontinued obstetrics demonstrated that even a 25 percent reduction in insurance premium was an insufficient inducement to resume obstetric services. Clearly, other issues were more of a demotivating factor than merely the cost of malpractice insurance. A review by the Washington State Physicians Insurance Exchange and Association of physicians who had discontinued obstetric practice showed that these physicians were more likely to be older, to be sole practitioners in an urban setting, and to have a higher rate of new obstetric malpractice claims. "Apparently, being named as the target of an obstetrical malpractice claim plays a significant role in the decision of some obstetricians to discontinue obstetrical practice." In essence, obstetricians are being driven out of business because of the combination of the high risk in this specialty to both the mother and the baby and the relentless pursuit of attorneys.

RISK MANAGEMENT ISSUES IN PROFESSIONAL LIABILITY LITIGATION

Certain personal and professional characteristics may be associated with providers believed to be at high or low risk of vulnerability to malpractice claims. Applying factors relating to the quality of the structure, process, and outcome of patient care, statistical analysis revealed nine variables that predict high or low risk. High risk was associated with increased age, surgical specialty, emergency department coverage, increased days away from practice, and the feeling that the litigation climate was "unfair." Low risk factors were linked to scheduling enough time to talk with patients, answering patients' telephone calls directly, feeling "satisfied" with practice arrangements, and acknowledging greater emotional distress.

Are there common issues surrounding professional liability lawsuits? A survey of defense attorneys in Georgia by MAG Mutual Insurance Company identified six key areas where risk managers could make a difference:

Unrealistic Patient Expectations

About 88 percent of the lawyers stated that the patient and/or the family were surprised by the adverse outcome. Either they had unrealistic expectations, or they were not adequately educated regarding the course of treatment. All written material and conversations should be documented and updated in the medical record when revised material is distributed. Defense attorneys will then know exactly what the patient was given at the time of treatment.

No Response to Complaints

A failure by the physician to respond to the specific complaints that had instigated a patient's visit to the physician was cited by more than 80 percent of the attorneys. Health care professionals should maintain eye contact, not interrupt when the patient is talking, and observe a patient's body language. Physicians should document in the medical record that the patient's complaints were considered before a treatment was determined.

Illegible Medical Records

Nothing damages a case more than the hesitant, inarticulate efforts of physician witnesses to read their own illegible handwritten medical record notes. About 77 percent of the lawyers identified illegibility as a significant problem, and this situation seriously inhibits the defense of a lawsuit. Incidentally, the "dictated but not read" annotation is not acceptable and has proven detrimental to the defense.

INSUFFICIENT INFORMATION IN MEDICAL RECORDS

Not only must the information in medical records be legible, but the data should be significant and timely. Almost 70 percent of the lawyers claimed that information relative to medications, allergies, problems, telephone calls, and so on was missing from records and that the operative notes were written more than twenty-four hours after the procedure.

A telephone record for each patient can document advice or prescriptions ordered directly from the pharmacy. Juries tend not to believe a physician who has no telephone log.

No Follow-up on Abnormal Tests

In many cases, information from diagnostic tests is not conveyed to the patient in a timely manner. Attorneys indicated that 62 percent of the suits involved the failure to follow up on abnormal test results. A system must exist to ensure that diagnostic reports are received, reviewed by the physician, acted upon, and placed in the record. A log of all diagnostic tests should be checked daily and not filed until it has been reviewed and initialed, and action, if required, has been taken.

Professional Miscommunication

The opportunity for miscommunication is always present, and although miscommunication in itself may not be the proximal cause of a lawsuit, the misunderstanding may lead to errors prompting a legal action. About 58 percent of the attorneys stated that miscommunication had occurred in many of their cases. Some common communication errors that can be remedied include:

- Lack of explicit directions or protocols for nursing personnel regarding when to notify the physician of a change in a patient's condition.
- Inadequate communication of a patient's deteriorating condition from nursing personnel to the physician.
- Failure to communicate the degree of urgency to other health care personnel.
- Lack of verbal communication from consultants, radiologists, or pathologists identifying an abnormality.
- Reliance on the assumption that no response from the referral physician indicates that the patient's problem was resolved.

These key risk factors, which are involved in a significant number of lawsuits, can be modified through the practice of the specific risk management techniques already mentioned. Certainly, the techniques are not overly cumbersome and can decrease the likelihood of being involved in a legal action and/or increase the defensibility in court.

Bibliography

Berry, A., Jarvis, R.: *Business Accounting for Hospitality and Tourism*, London, Chapman and Hall, 1995.

Clark, Mona: *Interpersonal Skills for Hospitality Managers*, London, Chapman Hill, 1995.

Donald, M.: *Customer Service in the Hospitality and Tourism Industry*, Englewood Cliffs, Prentice Hall, 1994.

Eberts, Marjorie: *Careers in Travel, Tourism, and Hospitality*, Lincolnwood, VGM Career Horizons, 1997.

Hubert, B.: *A Host of Opportunities: An Introduction to Hospitality Management*, Chicago, Irwin, 1996.

John Bowen, and James Makens: *Marketing for Hospitality and Tourism*: New Jersey, Prentice-Hall, 1998.

Kotler, Philip: *Marketing for Hospitality and Tourism*: New Jersey, Prentice-Hall, 1998.

Michael, John: *Principles of Hospitality Law*, London, Cassell, 1999.

Nelson, Bob and Economy, Peter: *Managing for Dummies*, Foster City, IDG Books, 1996.

Robert, C.: *Cases in Hospitality Marketing and Management*, New York, John Wiley, 1997.

Rocco, M.: *An Introduction to Hospitality Today*, Orlando, Educational Institute, 1998.

Rosenzweig, J. E.: *Organisation and Management*, New York, McGraw Hill International, 1963.

Swarbrooke, J.: *Marketing Tourism, Hospitality and Leisure in Europe*, London, International Thomson Business Press, 1996.

Thomas, F. : *Introduction to the Hospitality Industry*, New York, Wiley, 1995.

Index

□□□